T0305229

Narcissism in the Workplace

NEW HORIZONS IN MANAGEMENT

Series Editor: Cary L. Cooper, CBE, *Distinguished Professor of Organizational Psychology and Health, Lancaster University, UK*

This important series makes a significant contribution to the development of management thought. This field has expanded dramatically in recent years and the series provides an invaluable forum for the publication of high quality work in management science, human resource management, organizational behaviour, marketing, management information systems, operations management, business ethics, strategic management and international management.

The main emphasis of the series is on the development and application of new original ideas. International in its approach, it will include some of the best theoretical and empirical work from both well-established researchers and the new generation of scholars.

Titles in the series include:

Narcissism in the Workplace

Research, Opinion and Practice

Andrew J. DuBrin

Rochester Institute of Technology, USA

NEW HORIZONS IN MANAGEMENT

Edward Elgar
Cheltenham, UK • Northampton, MA, USA

Published by
Edward Elgar Publishing Limited
The Lypiatts
15 Lansdown Road
Cheltenham
Glos GL50 2JA
UK

Edward Elgar Publishing, Inc.
William Pratt House
9 Dewey Court
Northampton
Massachusetts 01060
USA

A catalogue record for this book
is available from the British Library

Library of Congress Control Number: 2011936422

ISBN 978 1 78100 135 6

Typeset by Sparks, Gloucestershire, UK – www.sparkspublishing.com
Printed and bound by MPG Books Group, UK

Contents

Preface

It is widely acknowledged that having a positive self-attitude, being self-confident, and having high self-esteem are worthwhile attributes in both work and personal life. To the chagrin of others, some people take these positive attributes to the extreme and become self-absorbed, self-adoring, self-centered, and show little empathy for the problems and concerns of others. In brief, they are narcissists.

A healthy dose of narcissism can facilitate career success, because reasonable concern with the self helps a person think of achieving important goals and being admired as a leader. The moderately narcissistic person often appears to be self-confident and charismatic. Yet extreme narcissism can hamper success because the narcissist irritates and alienates others in the workplace as well as in personal life. It is natural for work associates to want others to show some concern for them rather being totally self-preoccupied.

PURPOSE AND GOALS OF THE BOOK

The purpose of *Narcissism in the Workplace: Research, Opinion, and Practice* is to describe both the positive and negative features of narcissism, and also present strategies and tactics for dealing constructively with narcissistic traits and behaviors in oneself and others. Ideally, this book would serve as a workplace guide to capitalizing on the positive aspects of narcissism, and minimizing its potential negative effects.

Another key purpose of this book is to present information about narcissism in the workplace that is based on empirical research when possible, as well as opinion derived from systematic observation. Our aim is to take an objective look at the positive and negative aspects of narcissism within members of the workforce. In contrast, considerable writing about narcissism is simply a rant about the self-centeredness, lack of consideration, and low empathy of narcissists. Our emphasis with respect to the negative features of narcissism is to present coping tactics and strategies rather than simply condemning workers with strong narcissistic tendencies.

To help illustrate the presence of workplace narcissism, we present many examples and case histories of people whose activities are presented in the media, such as Donald Trump and Martha Stewart. Our labeling of these public figures as having narcissistic tendencies is based on their characteristics as reported in the media and occasionally by bloggers. In no instance do we pretend to have diagnosed the public figure based on a personal interview.

As a consequence of the purposes and goals of this book, it has several potential audiences. First among these are organizational professionals and managers curious about narcissism and its impact on work relationships and career advancement. Included in this group are people who are interested in learning more about factually based information on the subject of narcissism as this subject grows in interest. Second are students in such subjects as organizational behavior, organizational psychology, human relations, and leadership who would like in-depth knowledge about narcissism – a topic probably given no more than a passing reference in the subject fields just mentioned.

Third, scholars in the field of narcissism, self-esteem and leadership might find the integration of research and opinion about narcissism useful for their research. At the same time, some of the suggestions made in the book might serve as hypotheses for conducting more research. One example among dozens of possibilities is whether an optimum degree of narcissism predicts leadership effectiveness and career success.

STRUCTURE OF THE BOOK

To achieve its purposes and goals the book is divided into ten chapters. Chapter 1 explains the meaning of narcissism as a personality trait, including its components and associated behaviors. Also included is a discussion of the narcissistic personality disorder. (Although it is now dropped as an official personality disorder by the American Psychiatric Association, the disorder is still widely recognized by mental health professionals.) Chapter 2 closely examines the behaviors and demands of workplace narcissists, such as uncivil treatment of others, arrogance, and a feeling of entitlement. Also explained is how strongly narcissistic workers attempt to manipulate others to accomplish their ends. Chapter 3 examines the roots of workplace narcissism, and therefore focuses more on personal life and early-life influences than do other chapters. The chapter includes a discussion of how generational values and personal branding contribute to narcissism.

Chapter 4 shifts attention to the healthy, productive narcissist – a category of worker that seems to have gone under-recognized in writings about narcissists. The role of healthy self-esteem in contributing to productive narcissism is emphasized, as well as the contribution of narcissism to workplace creativity. Chapter 5 again emphasizes the positive side of narcissism with an explanation of how this personality trait contributes to leadership effectiveness. For example, narcissism often contributes to vision formation. Chapter 6 shifts to how narcissism can often contribute to dysfunctional leadership through such means as an excessive desire for power, wealth, and admiration. Also, the narcissistic leader will sometimes promote a vision that fits his or her need for grandiosity.

Chapter 7 describes strategies and tactics for dealing with the many potential problems created by narcissistic coworkers. Emphasis is placed on such communication tactics as giving ample feedback and offering constructive criticism. Chapter 8 is about the delicate problem of dealing with a narcissistic manager, including the technique of using good emotional intelligence, maintaining your professionalism, and flattering him or her. Chapter 9 describes tactics and strategies for dealing with the narcissistic subordinate, including focusing on the relationship with the subordinate as well as the tasks performed. This chapter also explores the issue of how a narcissistic organization can trigger workers into behaving narcissistically.

Chapter 10 describes how social media, mobile phones, and email are forces for encouraging narcissistic behavior among their users. Emphasis is placed on how negative mobile phone behavior often includes an element of narcissism, such as accepting a call during a work conversation.

All chapters include several features in addition to a description of the subject material: a checklist in the form of a self-quiz; a chapter summary; a section about guidelines for application and practice in relation to the chapter topic; and a case history of a workplace narcissist that includes a brief analysis of the narcissism displayed.

ACKNOWLEDGMENTS

A project as complicated as a scholarly book requires the cooperation of a group of dedicated and talented people. First, I thank the many people working in organizations as well as public figures whose behavior has given me an opportunity to observe both the positive and negative aspects of narcissism. Second, I thank the anonymous manuscript reviewer who saw the merit in this project.

Thank you also to the editorial and production staff at Edward Elgar who helped make this book possible, as follows: Alan Sturmer, Executive Editor; Alexandra Mandzak, Assistant Editor; and Tom Fryer, Project Manager at Sparks Publishing Services Ltd.

Writing without loved ones would be a lonely task. My thanks therefore go to my family members: Drew, Douglas and Gizella, Melanie and Will, Drake, Rosie, Clare, Camila, Sofia, Eliana, Carson, Julian, and Owen.

ABOUT THE AUTHOR

Andrew J. DuBrin is a Professor of Management emeritus at the E. Philip Saunders College of Business at the Rochester Institute of Technology, where he has taught courses and conducts research in leadership, organizational behavior, influence processes, and career management. He also served as department chairman and team leader in previous years. He received his PhD in industrial/organizational psychology at Michigan State University.

Professor DuBrin has business experience in human resource management, and consults with organizations and individuals. His specialties include leadership, organizational politics including influence tactics, and career development. He is an established author of both textbooks and trade books, and also contributes to professional journals. He has written textbooks on leadership, organizational behavior, management, human relations, organizational politics, and impression management.

1. Who is a workplace narcissist?

A person's chances for success in the workplace increase when he or she has high self-confidence and self-esteem. Yet some people push these characteristics so far that they annoy and irritate many work associates. *Narcissism* is an extremely positive and inflated view of the self combined with limited empathy for others. The term narcissism derives from a Greek myth that has been widely circulated. Narcissus was the unusually handsome son of a minor god. His handsomeness prompted the nymphs who lived in woods where he hunted to fall in love with him, but Narcissus shunned them all. One of the shunned maidens prayed that Narcissus would at some time feel what it was like to love, and not have that love returned. An avenging goddess heard and granted the prayer. One day, shortly thereafter, when Narcissus was out hunting he came upon a clear fountain with water that resembled silver. As he bent down to drink some fountain water, Narcissus saw his own image in the water. Concluding that the image was a beautiful water spirit living in the water, Narcissus fell in love with himself.

When Narcissus attempted to reach in the water and embrace the image, it dispersed but returned when the water was calm again. Narcissus was transfixed with the image, and could not tear himself away. Little by little, Narcissus lost his color, vitality, and the handsomeness that had previously charmed the nymphs. Eventually Narcissus pined away and died. The nymphs mourned for Narcissus, and wanted to bury him. However, his body was nowhere to be found. In its place was a beautiful flower which bears his name and preserves the memory of Narcissus.[1]

The carry over to modern life is that a narcissist is a person with intense self-love.

Quite often extreme narcissism can hamper success because the narcissist irritates and alienates others in the workplace as well as in personal life. Yet, the right amount and type of narcissism can at times facilitate success because the narcissist appears to be charismatic and self-confident.

A major purpose of this book is to describe both the positive and negative features of narcissism, and also to present strategies and tactics for dealing constructively with narcissistic traits and behaviors in oneself and others. One example is that a person might capitalize on his or her narcissism to become a successful leader. Another example is that if you better understand the traits and behaviors of narcissistic work associates, including managers, you are likely to develop better working relationships with them.

Where possible we will base the findings and prescriptions presented in this book on scientific research and the opinion of professionals in the field of human behavior and mental health. At other places we will rely on less systematically gathered evidence and opinion to provide descriptions and recommendations to the reader.

As a starting point in our study of narcissism, you are invited to take the questionnaire, Tendencies toward narcissism, presented in Exhibit 1.1. As with other self-quizzes presented in this book, its purpose is to stimulate your thinking rather than to provide you with a professional diagnosis of some aspect of workplace narcissism. Nevertheless, the self-quizzes and other questionnaires are based on known traits and behaviors of narcissistic people rather than conjecture.

Exhibit 1.1   Tendencies toward narcissism

Instructions: Many narcissists exhibit some of the behaviors and hold some of the attitudes described below. To help you understand your tendencies toward narcissism, rate how strongly you agree with each of the statements below on a scale of 0–4, with 0 meaning not at all and 4 meaning very much.

1.	When I am in a gathering of people I am usually the best looking person in the room.	0	1	2	3	4
2	When I am in a gathering of people I am usually the smartest person in the room.	0	1	2	3	4
3.	I love me more than I love anybody else.	0	1	2	3	4
4.	If my stomach were upset, I would post that information on a social media website such as Twitter.	0	1	2	3	4
5.	I think it is important that my contacts receive updated photos of me.	0	1	2	3	4
6.	I don't think anybody has the right to criticize me.	0	1	2	3	4
7.	I don't think I should have to wait an entire year for a salary increase.	0	1	2	3	4
8.	If I were dating, I would expect the person I am dating to fall in love with me by at least our fourth meeting.	0	1	2	3	4
9.	I am destined for greatness.	0	1	2	3	4
10.	If I wanted a consumer product or a vacation, and I didn't have the money, I would use my credit card without a second thought.	0	1	2	3	4
11.	I get really upset when somebody criticizes me.	0	1	2	3	4
12.	When I fail on a task, it is almost always because somebody else messed up.	0	1	2	3	4
13.	I talk loudly on my cellphone or smart phone when in public places.	0	1	2	3	4

14.	During a meeting (or in a classroom) I answer my phone even if the call is not urgent.	0	1	2	3	4
15.	I would feel uncomfortable if a day went by without being admired by somebody.	0	1	2	3	4
16.	You don't find too many people as good looking and smart as me.	0	1	2	3	4
17.	I rarely worry about other people's problems.	0	1	2	3	4
18.	People who know me are readily influenced by me.	0	1	2	3	4
19.	I am a natural leader.	0	1	2	3	4
20.	I enjoy being the center of attention.	0	1	2	3	4
21.	I look at myself in the mirror almost whenever the opportunity presents itself.	0	1	2	3	4
22.	When I read about famous people, I usually realize that I am equally good or better than they are.	0	1	2	3	4
23.	I check search engines almost every day to see if there is a new mention of my name.	0	1	2	3	4
24.	I am a very special person.	0	1	2	3	4
25.	I am destined for outstanding success in career and personal life.	0	1	2	3	4
26.	Rather than discuss current events with other people, I like to talk about myself and my accomplishments.	0	1	2	3	4
27.	If I were not rated outstanding in a performance evaluation, I would regard it as an insult.	0	1	2	3	4
28.	I don't take most rules seriously because I make my own rules.	0	1	2	3	4
29.	I am hot.	0	1	2	3	4
30	I am special and unique.	0	1	2	3	4

Scoring and interpretation:

91 or over: You have strong narcissistic tendencies to the extent that your work associates and personal contacts probably perceive you to be self-centered and preoccupied with your own importance. Some people most likely label you as a narcissist.

61–90: You have average narcissistic tendencies to the extent that you have high self-esteem and self-confidence. Some people may regard you as self-centered but not to an annoying, bothersome level.

31–60: Your narcissistic tendencies are below average to the extent that there are situations in which you appear too humble and modest. You could stand to focus attention on yourself a little more.

0–30: Your narcissistic tendencies are well below average, to the extent that your self-esteem and self-confidence could be suffering. You might develop a stronger appreciation of your good points and strengths.

Source: The idea for a few of the questions stem from Raskin, Robert and Howard Terry (1988), "A Principal-Components Analysis of the Narcissistic Personality Inventory and Further Evidence of Its Construct Validity," *Journal of Personality and Social Psychology*, **54** (5), 894.

A VARIETY OF DEFINITIONS OF NARCISSISM

As mentioned above, a general definition of narcissism focuses on a positive and inflated view of the self, combined with a lack of empathy for others. For a more complete understanding of narcissism, it is helpful to also examine a variety of definitions of narcissism. Many of these definitions imply that the narcissist has pushed a positive attitude toward the self too far, thereby experiencing a personality problem. Following are 15 definitions of narcissism, grouped into those with a positive connotation versus those with a negative connotation. Most of the definitions presented are different wordings of the same theme of self-love and self-admiration.

Definitions of Narcissism Suggesting Positive Qualities

1. A broad psychological continuum related to healthy self-esteem at one pole and maladjusted self-functioning at the other.[2] (As will be explained later, narcissism is regarded basically as a personality factor or trait that leads to many positive and negative behaviors in the workplace.)
2. *Primary narcissism* refers to the love of self which must precede the ability to love others (the psychoanalytic definition). The psychoanalytic perspective has prompted the belief that to love other people, you must first love yourself.
3. *Secondary narcissism* refers to identifying with and incorporating characteristics of a person into one's psyche. A *narcissistic object choice* involves identifying with another person based on that person's similarity to oneself.[3]
4. A normal stage in the development of a child characterized by self-absorption (from psychoanalysis). When narcissism extends into puberty, it is classified as secondary narcissism and can lead to a personality disorder. (Narcissists in the workplace are often perceived to be child-like because of their constant self-focus.)
5. A primary ingredient for the development of self-esteem (as analyzed by Freud).[4]

Definitions of Narcissism Suggesting Negative Qualities

1. A pattern of behaviors or fantasies that show a pervasive need for attention, admiration, and exhibit a lack of concern for others.[5]
2. Self-love and egoism; excessive love or admiration of oneself. (This is an everyday, useful definition.)
3. A state of looking at oneself with undue favor, self-love, conceit, pride, and vanity.

4. A psychological state characterized by preoccupation with the self, lack of empathy, and unconscious deficits in self-esteem.[6]
5. An attribute of the human psyche characterized by admiration of oneself but within normal limits.[7] (Workers in fields where personal appearance is an asset, such as store associates in upscale stores, or models, would therefore benefit from this version of narcissism.)
6. Narcissism includes self-absorption, self-love and self-aggrandizement as attempts to gratify infantile needs (Freud). The narcissist therefore may act immaturely in order to bring attention to himself or herself, such as continually making jokes during a serious meeting.[8]
7. A pattern of behavior that emphasizes feelings of superiority, entitlement, and a constant need for attention and admiration. (A narcissist can therefore be an annoying coworker, manager, subordinate or customer because he or she demands so much.)[9]
8. *Overt narcissism* involves tendencies toward grandiosity and exhibitionism. *Covert narcissism* involves interpersonal hypersensitivity and vulnerability. (Whether overt or covert, the narcissist can come across as an annoying work associate.)[10]
9. A personality disorder in which a person is self-absorbed to the point that the needs and feelings of others do not matter. (This is a useful definition for classifying people who are at the high end of the continuum of narcissism.)
10. A personality disorder characterized by extreme self-absorption, an exaggerated sense of self-importance, and a strong need for attention and admiration from others. (This reflects the standard psychiatric definition of people who suffer from a *narcissistic personality disorder*, and will be explained more fully later in the chapter.)

NARCISSISM AS A PERSONALITY TRAIT

A practical approach to understanding narcissism in the workplace is to regard narcissism as a personality trait ranging from being lowly narcissistic to highly narcissistic. This conception of narcissism is can be inferred from the questionnaire, Tendencies toward Narcissism, presented above (see Exhibit 1). Our approach is consistent with research that shows narcissism as a personality dimension, not exclusively a personality disorder. As a dimension of personality, people can be reliably arrayed on this continuum.[11] Being arrayed on a continuum means that individual differences in narcissism exist, just as people differ in intelligence and height.

Personality psychologist Scott Barry Kaufman reports that narcissism is a stable trait that varies in degree among people. Several aspects, including self-confidence and self-sufficiency, are healthy and adaptive. Only at the extreme end of the continuum does narcissism become a disorder. The reason is that toxic levels of vanity, entitlement, and exploitativeness are displayed at the extreme end of the personality trait of narcissism.[12]

It is therefore more accurate to specify that a person is strongly narcissistic than simply labeling him or her as *narcissistic*. Similarly, people vary on personality traits such as conscientiousness, rather than being *conscientious* versus *not conscientious*. So when we refer in this book to a person being narcissistic, we are really referring to a high standing on the trait of narcissism.

The High and Low Ends of the Narcissism Continuum

Many people at the highest end of the personality trait of narcissism suffer from a personality disorder. A synthesis of studies about the topic suggests that those with a narcissistic disorder are unable to regulate their self-esteem. As a result they become dependent on social sources for affirmation. These high-end narcissists engage in activities and behaviors that help them maintain their inflated sense of self. At the beginning of a business meeting, the extreme narcissist may occupy five minutes describing his or her recent vacation.

Highly narcissistic people are preoccupied with receiving attention, and expect special treatment from others. They are so intent on having their needs met that they lack empathy for others. This is one reason that narcissists often interrupt others, and hog conversations.

At the low end of the continuum is healthy narcissism. People classified as healthy narcissists have a positive self-image resulting from a realistic assessment and acceptance of their strengths and weaknesses. The moderate narcissist thus has high self-esteem. The apparent high self-esteem of strongly narcissistic individuals is a façade used to cover up and compensate for an underlying sense of worthlessness and inadequacy. A false sense of self-esteem makes the person vulnerable to slights and failures.[13] You may have noticed that highly narcissistic people become defensive and angry when criticized – providing they listen to the criticism.

The late Steve Jobs, the co-founder of Apple Inc., exemplified a person with healthy narcissistic tendencies in the sense that he is widely admired for his success, yet also noted for his egomaniacal tendencies and wanting to control others closely.[14] Before his health problems forced him into the background, Jobs was at the center of every product launch and controlled intimate technical details of the presentations.

The Trait Components of Narcissism

As a personality trait, narcissism consists of both a general trait and sub-traits or components. The general trait of narcissism reflects the definition of narcissism presented at the outset of the chapter: an extremely positive and inflated view of the self combined with limited empathy for others. Based on extensive studies with the Narcissistic Personality Inventory (NPI), Robert Raskin and Howard Terry characterize the high NPI scorer as "being relatively dominant, extraverted, exhibitionistic, aggressive, impulsive, self-centered, subjectively self-satisfied, self-indulgent, and nonconforming."[15]

The NPI has been the basis for considerable quantitative research about narcissism, based on investigations in a variety of settings, with college students the population most frequently studied. A sampling follows of 4 of the 40 items on the most widely used version of the Narcissistic Personality Inventory. The respondent essentially agrees with the item or the opposite of the item. (An *item* is a psychometric term for a question or a statement on a test.)

- *Item number 7*: I know that I am good because everybody keeps telling me so.
- *Item number 8:* If I ruled the world, it would be a much better place.
- *Item number 12:* I like to be the center of attention.
- *Item number 32:* Everybody likes to hear my stories.

Use your intuition and common sense to guess whether responding "agree" or "disagree" would be in the narcissistic direction for the four sample questions above.

Studies based on the NPI have revealed seven sub-traits or components. The components are referred to statistically as factors, as revealed by factor analysis. Each one of these sub-traits is presented next, along with a brief interpretation of what a very high score would mean in terms of the individual's behavior.[16]

Authority
Authority refers to a person's leadership skills and power. People who score high on authority like to be in charge and gain power, often for power's sake alone. A person who scored particularly high on authority would have the self-image of a leader, and would be someone who values power.

Self-sufficiency
As implied in its label, self-sufficiency refers to how much a person relies on others versus his or her own abilities to meet his or her needs in life. A person who scores high on self-sufficiency would behave independently, such as not frequently consulting others before taking action or making a decision.

Superiority
This trait refers to whether a person feels he or she is superior to others in close contact. The higher the score the haughtier and more superior the person thinks

that he or she is in comparison to others. (For many extreme narcissists, this opinion is unjustified.)

Exhibitionism
This trait refers to a person's need to be the center of attention, and willingness to ensure that they are the center of attention – even at the expense of the needs of others. A person with a high standing on exhibitionism might take up coworkers' time explaining how he or she narrowly escaped an accident on the way to work.

Exploitativeness
This trait refers to how willing a person is to exploit others in order to meet his or her own needs or goals. Exploiting could take many forms such as stealing ideas from others, asking a coworker to do some of your work when you are overloaded, and borrowing money without repaying,

Vanity
Vanity refers to a belief in one's own superior abilities and attractiveness compared to others, thereby fitting the usual definition of being vain. A manager who placed high on the trait of vanity would typically think that his or her suggestions and creative ideas were superior to those from the group.

Entitlement
This trait refers to the expectation of the amount of entitlement a person has in his or her life. In this context entitlement refers to unreasonable expectations of especially favorable treatment or automatic compliance with one's expectations. People with a high standing on this trait generally have a greater expectation of entitlement, whereas those who score lower expect little from others or life. A worker with a high standing on entitlement would think that he or she should unquestionably receive a very positive performance evaluation and above-average salary increase.

The components of the broader trait of narcissism just listed are widely accepted, yet other research suggests that narcissism has only two main components or factors. Nida Corry and her research associates administered the 40-item Narcissistic Personality Inventory to 843 female and 843 male college students, most of whom were Euro-American. The purpose of the study was to identify the key components or factors within the broader trait of narcissism. Two factors were identified: Leadership/Authority and Exhibitionism/Entitlement. Furthermore, Leadership/Authority and Exhibitionism/Entitlement were positively correlated.[17] In practice this means that people who score high on one

Exhibit 1.2   A sampling of specific beliefs and attitudes incorporated into the narcissistic factors of leadership/authority and exhibitionism/entitlement

Leadership/authority	Exhibitionism/entitlement
I have a natural talent for influencing people.	I would do almost anything on a dare.
I will be a success.	I know that I am good because everybody keeps telling me so.
I see myself as a good leader.	I like to show off my body.
People always seem to recognize my authority.	I will usually show off if I get the chance.
I would prefer to be a leader.	I get upset when people don't notice how I look when I go out in public.
I am a born leader.	I really like to be the center of attention.

Source: Compiled from information presented in Corry, Nida, Rebecca Davis Merritt, Sylvie Mrug, and Barbara Pamp (2008), "The Factor Structure of the Narcissistic Personality Inventory," *Journal of Personality Assessment*, **90** (6), 596.

factor would tend to score high on the other, and people who score low on one factor would ten to score low on the other.

A basic interpretation of the two-factor structure of narcissism is that a big chunk of being narcissistic is composed of a person having two self-beliefs. First, the person believes that he or she can exert leadership and authority over others. Second, the person believes that he or she should be the center of attention and is entitled to major rewards. Exhibit 1.2 presents a few more specifics about these two factors based on the research under discussion. We emphasize strongly that self-beliefs and attitudes do not necessarily translate into behavior and accomplishments. For example, some highly narcissistic people believe that they are natural leaders, yet they inspire nobody and have not been appointed to a leadership position. A key characteristic of narcissists is an inflated opinion of their talents.

KEY SYMPTOMS OF NARCISSISM

Many of the symptoms of narcissism have already been identified because the traits and definitions of narcissism either mention directly or imply the symptom. One of many possible examples is that if a narcissistic person has high standing on the trait of *superiority* he or she will attempt to act superior to others, such as casually mentioning the names of powerful people in his or her network, or bragging about personal accomplishments. The checklist presented in Exhibit 1.3 gives you an opportunity to think through your own symptoms of narcissism.

Exhibit 1.3   The narcissism checklist

Listed below are 25 symptoms experienced by people who have varying degrees of narcissism. Check whether each symptom is something that applies to you in the sense that you have had such a symptom. People who are highly narcissistic, however, often do not clearly perceive their symptoms. To verify the accuracy of your responses to the checklist, have a person who knows you well help you respond to the checklist.

Symptom of narcissism	Applies to me	Does not apply to me
1. Patronizes and criticize others.		
2. Hates to be criticized.		
3. Strongly dislikes disagreements with others.		
4. Becomes quite upset when cannot control a situation.		
5. Very little concern for others.		
6. Thinks of self first.		
7. Works hard at maintaining a false self.		
8. Thinks more about extraordinary achievements than carrying out daily responsibilities.		
9. Works hard to maintain a façade of wealth.		
10. Convinced of own superiority.		
11. Dependent on others for frequent doses of admiration and affection.		
12. Invests a disproportionate amount of personal income into clothing and other attire.		
13. Own or leases a vehicle that he or she thinks will impress others by its luxury.		
14. Abuses and insults others without feeling the least bit guilty.		
15. Believes that he or she can accomplish anything with proper effort.		
16. Believes that he or she should receive special treatment because of his or her wonderful qualities.		
17. Believes that other people are envious of him or her.		
18. Acts like a snob.		
19. Will often say something to the effect of "Oh, how nice" when someone else describes a personal accomplishment.		

The symptoms to be described next overlap with and reinforce those listed in Exhibit 1.3. For convenience, the symptoms are classified as mostly behavioral versus mostly emotional. *Behavioral* refers to how the narcissistic person acts and talks, whereas *emotional* refers to how he or she feels.

Symptom of narcissism	Applies to me	Does not apply to me
20. Often bullies others.		
21. Intense envy about the accomplishments and possessions of others.		
22. Poor team player because of need to be the center of attention.		
23. Frequently finds fault with other people and other things.		
24. Quick to blame somebody else for own mistake.		
25. Feels uncomfortable when another person receives praise and recognition in his or her presence.		

Scoring and interpretation: The more of these symptoms you have demonstrated or felt, the more that your level of narcissism is creating problems for you in the workplace. If you have 15 or more of these symptoms, you may need to take corrective action to become less of an annoyance to others so you can improve your interpersonal relations with work associates. Attaining work goals often requires collaboration, so if you decrease your symptoms of narcissism you will most likely become more productive.

Mostly Behavioral Symptoms of Narcissism

People with a high standing on the trait of narcissism display certain behaviors, or behavioral symptoms, that reveal their narcissistic attitudes and traits. Narcissists have many of these symptoms in common, but not every narcissistic person exhibits all the behaviors listed below.

Self-admiration

Almost by definition, the highly narcissistic person engages in self-admiration both alone and in the presence of others. Exaggerated statements about self-importance are included in self-admiration. Self-admiring statements in the office include the following:

"If I do say so myself, this budget I have prepared is almost flawless."

"The CEO just loved my report."

"Have you noticed what a perfect match this suit is for me?"

"As a confidant of the CFO (chief financial officer), I must tell you that…"

"It is gratifying to know that I have played such a key role in the success of our team."

Statements of superiority

The narcissist will often speak as if he or she is superior to others, whether in terms of intellect, accomplishment, appearance, education, or other aspects of life. Bragging about the past is typical, as in: "When I was studying at Harvard Business School..."

Incessant talking and monologues

Narcissists are often insensitive to the impact their actions have on other people. One of the key indicators of this insensitivity is a compulsion to keep talking, often at the expense of listening to other people. One-on-one meetings with an incessant-talking narcissist are difficult because it is very hard to find a chance to present your opinions or develop a point. The narcissist will often dominate time at meetings expressing his or her opinion on every point raised in the meeting. The incessant talking often takes the form of a monologue because the highly narcissistic worker requires no feedback from others, being a self-perceived expert on a wide range of subjects.

Interrupting others

Although the high-end narcissist prefers to keep talking and not be interrupted, the same person frequently interrupts others while they are talking. Often this interruption takes the form of correcting the other person, such as saying "You have it wrong," or "Let me explain it better." Interrupting others appears to be based on two motives. First is the desire for the narcissist to monopolize the conversation; it is difficult to talk when somebody else is talking. Second, the interruptions are yet another way for the narcissistic person to demonstrate superiority, particularly when the interruption involves correcting the speaker.

Temper tantrums

The extreme narcissist is prone to temper tantrums or avoidance when he or she cannot figure something out or things do not go his or her way. Steve Jobs was mentioned above as a successful person who had narcissistic tendencies. One of his behaviors was to become vehement when criticized or when he disagreed with a subordinate. He was particularly prone to swearing at journalists and other authors who criticized him.

Expects special attention

Therapist Wendy T. Behary writes that some narcissistic personalities expect special attention from everyone or act as though rules do not apply to them. A representative statement might be, "What do you mean I have to *wait* two days for my order to be processed?"[18]

Dependent on others for reinforcement of the self-image
Although the outward bragging of the high-end narcissistic personality suggests that the person is self-contained and self-assured, the opposite may be true. The narcissist often seeks outside approval to reinforce the idea that he or she is a highly effective person. This is one reason why the person with a high degree of narcissism frequently fishes for compliments. To obtain reinforcement of the self-image and fish for compliments, the narcissistic person might ask questions such as the following:

"What did you think of the cool PowerPoint presentation I gave this morning?"

"Do I look great today, or what?"

"How many people do you know who are as good as I am in terms of…?"

"Who else do you know who has made such a steady contribution to the success of our company?"

The narcissistic person, of course, is expecting only positive answers or affirmations in response to the above questions. Negative feedback will not receive careful listening.

Perfectionism and compulsivity
A narcissist is often a perfectionist because he or she likes to appear in total control through such means as minimizing errors in speech, writing, and appearance. Perfectionism can also manifest itself in correcting small errors of other people. During a meeting one of the members said, "I like this new candidate. She's very practical minded. That's one reason she studied business administration at Ohio State University." A narcissist in the group responded with a smirk, "I think you are referring to *The* Ohio State University."

Perfectionism is closely tied to compulsive behavior because compulsivity facilitates attending to small detail. For example, if the narcissist wants to demonstrate perfection in dress, he or she has to be compulsive about small details such as a broken button or a scuffed shoe.

Limited empathy
As oft-repeated here and in most research about narcissism, the highly narcissistic person has limited or no empathy for others. The limited empathy contributes to many of the behavioral symptoms already described. For example, if the narcissist were more empathic he or she would recognize the need for other people to talk without being interrupted. With more empathy the narcissist would also understand that frequently talking about one's own superiority irritates most people.

Being a dandy

For those readers who want a refresher on the study of logic, consider this statement: "All dandies are narcissists, but not all narcissists are dandies." A *dandy* is a man who places heavy importance on physical appearance, refined language, and the cultivation of leisure activities. Dandies were apparently first recognized in the late 18th and 19th centuries, but still exist today in modern form.[19] The men depicted in Ralph Lauren advertisements give the appearance of being dandies, but many of them are simply playing a paid role. The dandy-style narcissist often works as a sales representative either in upscale stores or for investment firms. Being a dandy is quite effective in such positions for selling $15 000 watches and $200 000 sports cars.

Dandyism illustrates the point that many symptoms and behaviors of narcissism are interrelated. The dandy is often filled with self-admiration, and may also have feelings of superiority, as well as being a perfectionist.

Healthy self-regard

As will be described at length in Chapter 4, the right degree of narcissism can facilitate a person having a healthy self-regard and a healthy level of self-esteem. The person might be proud of his or her accomplishments, yet at the same time recognize the accomplishments of others and share in their glory.

Mostly Emotional Symptoms of Narcissism

The emotional symptoms of narcissism are often less evident to work associates of narcissistic people than are the behavioral symptoms. Yet when emotional symptoms drive behavioral symptoms, as they often do, the emotional symptoms become indirectly evident. For example, if the highly narcissistic person has the emotional symptom of fragile self-esteem, this symptom can result in the person frequently asking others for compliments.

Fragile self-esteem

The self-esteem of many highly narcissistic people is fragile because it does not have a solid foundation. In general, sturdy self-esteem develops from attaining legitimate accomplishments and then receiving recognition for those accomplishments. The prototypical example would be working hard to perform well in math and reading in elementary school, then receiving high grades, then being complimented by parents, teachers, and relatives. Fragile self-esteem might stem from being lavished with compliments and praise for modest accomplishments or even for no accomplishment. Parents have been widely condemned in recent years for giving inappropriate praise to children, resulting in high narcissism in later life.[20]

Fragile self-esteem is a troublesome emotion to the narcissist because he or she has lingering doubts about deserving all the praise that he or she demands. A narcissist might expend huge amounts of time collecting followers, friends and contacts on the social media as an affirmation of personal popularity. Yet the person might have the disturbing thought, "Do all these people really like me or care about me? Or are these just very shallow contacts?"

Acquired situational narcissism
Related to fragile self-esteem is the emotional problems of developing narcissistic behavior because of being thrust into celebrity. According to professor of psychiatry, Robert B. Millman, *acquired situational narcissism* is a form of narcissism that develops in late adolescence or adulthood, brought on by the wealth, fame, and adulation associated with celebrity. The person may have had pre-existing tendencies toward milder narcissism. Acquired situational narcissism will often take the form of a full-blown narcissistic personality disorder. The emotional symptoms are confusion and self-questioning that result in the behavioral symptoms of unstable relationships, substance abuse and erratic behavior.[21] Many young actors, actresses, and sports stars suffer from these problems, as recorded in the media almost daily.

Rationalization to justify own behavior
Rationalization is a cognitive mechanism but also has an emotional component because the rationalization is linked to a feeling about wanting to feel important. The narcissist rationalizes such feelings as wanting to feel important or receive special treatment through such beliefs as (a) "I really deserve a break in life," (b) "If not me, who?" and (c) "Much lesser people than me get what they want in life."

Emotional detachment
An extreme narcissist will often stay emotionally distant from those whom his or her behavior affects. A person who is emotionally detached has an inability to connect with others on an emotional level. The emotional detachment contributes to the limited empathy shown by the narcissist. The emotional detachment, or emotional distance, also makes it easier for the narcissistic worker to ignore others while he or she attempts to be the center of attention. The attitude is "Who cares what you think or feel. It is me who is important."

NARCISSISM AS A PERSONALITY DISORDER

A person at the highest level of the personality trait of narcissism may be on the borderline of having a true narcissistic personality disorder. Yet there is no strict drop-off point where the trait of narcissism becomes a personality disorder. As a trio of narcissism researchers explain, "…one would not expect to see substantial qualitative differences in the behavior of an individual with clinical narcissistic personality disorder (NPD) versus an individual with high subclinical narcissism."[22] For example, Bruce in customer service might be an avid body builder who talks frequently about his great body, and every week posts updated body shots on Facebook. In the office he frequently tells coworkers how hard he works, and the tough problems that he has resolved. Yet he almost never asks how or what coworkers are doing. Bruce might be close to having a true NPD, or he might simply be a high narcissist. Bruce would have to exhibit many of the symptoms to be described next before he can be diagnosed as having an NPD.

The Nature of a Personality Disorder

To understand an NPD, it is helpful first to understand that the condition is but one of many possible personality disorders. A *personality disorder* is a pervasive, persistent, inflexible, maladaptive pattern of behavior that deviates from expected cultural norms. The disorder is learned early in life and causes distress to the person and/or conflicts with others. Individuals with personality disorders range from harmless eccentrics to dangerous, aggressive individuals.[23]

A personality disorder can also be regarded as a pattern of deviant or abnormal behavior that the individual does not change even though it causes emotional upsets and difficulties with others in the workplace and in personal relationships off the job. Personality disorders usually stem from both upbringing and inherited tendencies but are not caused by drug or alcohol use, head injury, or physical illness. NPD is but one of ten personality disorders recognized by the American Psychiatric Association. All the disorders show up as deviations from normal (culturally acceptable) behavior in one or more of the following four domains:

1. *Cognition.* Perception encompasses thinking, as well as interpretation of oneself, other people, and events. For example, a person with a paranoid personality disorder might think that a bank has singled out his account for creating errors.
2. *Affectivity.* Included here are quality of emotional responses in terms of intensity, lability, and appropriateness. (Lability refers to openness to change.) A deviation from the norm in terms of affectivity would be for a worker to laugh during a ceremony honoring a coworker killed in a industrial accident.
3. *Interpersonal functions.* A person with problems in interpersonal functions would have difficulty getting along with others.

4. *Impulsivity*. Impulsivity relates to not being able to hold back words and actions even if the consequences are severe, such as a worker with an *antisocial personality disorder* punching a coworker or using a company credit card to make an unplanned purchase.[24]

A personality disorder may not always be easy to diagnose. Yet the behavior of a person who appears to have such a disorder can be difficult to cope with, including the behavior of someone with an NPD.

The Narcissistic Personality Disorder

A person with a true NPD has a pervasive pattern of grandiosity in fantasy or behavior, a strong need for admiration, and lack of empathy. The disorder begins in early adulthood and is present in a variety of situations. An NPD translates into a pattern of self-centered or egotistical behavior that manifests itself in thinking and behavior in many situations and activities. People with an NPD will not or cannot change their behavior even when it causes friction at work, or when their behavior creates emotional distress for others.

A person is diagnosed as having an NPD when he or she exhibits five or more of the following nine criteria:

1. *Has a grandiose sense of self-importance*. For example, the person exaggerates achievements and talents, or expects to be recognized as a superior person without commensurate achievements.
2. *Is preoccupied with fantasies of unlimited success, power, brilliance, or ideal love*. For example, an operator of a franchise pool-cleaning service might be preoccupied with how he is going to become the next US Senator for his state although he has never held any political office.
3. *Believes that he or she is "special" and unique and can only be understood by, or should associate with other special or high-status people or institutions*. True narcissists think that everyone who is not special and superior is much inferior to them. The narcissist will often brag about how famous people are his or her "friends" or "followers" on Facebook or Twitter.
4. *Requires excessive admiration*. People with an NPD desire praise, compliments, deference, and expressions of envy continually. They also want to be told that everything they do is better than what others are capable of doing. Sincerity is not an issue; all that matters is the frequency and intensity of the admiration.
5. *Has a sense of entitlement*. He or she is likely to have unreasonable expectations to receive especially favorable treatment or automatic compliance with his or her expectations. A person with a full-blown NPD expects you

to drop what you are doing to help him or her, even when he or she is not your boss.

6. *Is interpersonally exploitative.* The extreme narcissist will take advantage of others to achieve his or her ends including blaming errors on others.

7. *Lacks empathy.* Among the manifestations of lacking empathy is unwillingness to recognize or identify with the feelings and needs of others. The boss with an NPD might ask a subordinate to reschedule her oral surgery until after a key project is completed.

8. *Is often envious of others or believes that others are envious of him or her.* Instead of sharing in the joy of a coworker getting promoted, the narcissist might envy that promotion. When a full-blown narcissist does not receive a compliment about his or her appearance, he or she will often think the other person is envious.

9. *Shows arrogant, haughty behaviors and attitudes.* He or she might be quite disrespectful of personal service workers such as restaurant servers or the custodial staff.

As with physical disorders and other emotional disorders, the NPD presents itself at different levels of severity. For example, a person with a mild NPD might have dissatisfying and disruptive interpersonal relationships but still function satisfactorily as a worker and parent. Another person with a severe NPD might spend so much time in self-admiration and grooming that he or she cannot work or build relationships with other people. Three levels of impairment for the NPD have been identified, as described next.[25]

1. *Mild impairment* occurs when the self-centered or egotistical behavior leads to minor problems but the person is generally functioning at a satisfactory level. Tim, a website designer, might monopolize too much time in meetings making jokes about what others are saying so he can be the center of attention. Tim encounters some difficulties because he is reprimanded by the team leader for his immature behavior. Yet Tim holds on to his job despite occasional admonitions about his office clown behavior.

2. *Moderate impairment* occurs when self-centered or egotistical behavior results in such negative consequences as (a) missing days from work, household responsibilities, or school, (b) significant performance problems as a wage-earner, homemaker, or student, (c) frequently avoiding or alienating friends, or (d) significant risk of harming self or others. The risks of harm can occur because the person who has a NPD becomes enraged when it appears that he or she is not receiving the admiration he or she desires.

3. *Severe impairment* occurs when the self-centered or egotistical behavior results in such behaviors as (a) staying in bed all day, (b) totally alienating all friends, family, and work associates; or (c) repeated attempts at harming

self or others. An attempt at self-harm might be a suicide gesture with a tweet, of this nature: "Not received enough compliments today to keep living." The gesture itself might take the form of jumping into a river from a bridge, yet swimming safely to shore or being rescued.

Psychologist and narcissism specialist Elsa F. Ronnington observes that narcissistic people can be suicidal or express suicidal intentions without being clinically depressed. Suicide or thoughts of suicide are driven by motives such as anger or revenge or to save themselves from an intolerable life situation.[26] An intolerable situation would include being shamed or degraded or feeling something that is disgraceful. A particularly degrading statement to a severely impaired narcissist would be to say, "You look terrible today. Are you ill?"

An important insight into an NPD is that a traumatic situation can trigger the disorder when a person already has narcissistic tendencies. The clinical term is *trauma associated narcissistic reactions*. People can react with narcissistic traits and behaviors in a stressful situation such as job loss, divorce, or death of a loved one. Suddenly the covert symptoms will surface. The stress associated with the trauma can overwhelm the self and trigger symptoms such as shame, humiliation, and rage. Furthermore, a person's self-esteem might fluctuate in response to the trauma. The problems just mentioned can happen to people with relatively healthy self-esteem as well as people who have tendencies toward narcissism.[27]

The Changed Categorization of the Narcissistic Personality Disorder

Many mental health professionals continue to diagnose and treat the NPD, yet the disorder has been eliminated from the fifth edition of the *Diagnostic and Statistical Manual of Mental Disorders* (DSM-5) to be published in 2013. The revision of the manual will replace the NPD with a measure of impairment in personality functioning. Clinicians will also be given a list of pathological traits that they might choose from when diagnosing a client with a personality disorder.[28] An example relevant to narcissism would be "preoccupation with the self to the exclusion of the welfare of others."

The chair of the revision committee, Andrew E. Skodol, said, "There is a fair amount of literature suggesting that narcissism is a dimension varying amongst people and across disorders, not necessarily a disorder in and of itself." Skodol also points out that the verdict on the status of the NPD is far from final, and that the revised status of the NPD could revert back to the original.

An example of dissension about the changed status of the NPD comes from Thomas Arthur Widiger, a University of Kentucky psychology professor who served on the committee revising the status of the personality disorder. He says, "By turning narcissistic personality disorder into a list of traits that will lack official coding within a medical record, you are essentially turning it into a sidebar that will unlikely draw much research or diagnostic interest."

Whether or not an extreme workplace narcissist has a true personality disorder, or simply a group of traits that make working with him or her difficult, the challenge remains the same. The manager or coworker must recognize the problem of narcissism and learn techniques for counteracting the problem.

GUIDELINES FOR APPLICATION AND PRACTICE

1. Enhance the value of your study of workplace narcissism by recognizing that narcissism is a personality trait that drives both constructive and destructive behaviors in terms of interpersonal relationships. Two important examples are that successful sales representatives and leaders usually have above-average standing on narcissism because of their high self-esteem and self-confidence.

2. Narcissism can also affect the work itself as well as interpersonal relationships. If you admire your own work too much you might not ask for feedback, listen to feedback, or critically evaluate your own work. Assume that a person with an optimum degree of narcissism completes a work product, such as a report or website. The person might ask, "What can I do to make this decent job even better?" The person with too high a degree of narcissism might not engage in critical self-evaluation. Instead, the person might say, "I am so proud of this wonderful piece of work. I know everybody will love it."

3. One of the most dysfunctional aspects of narcissism is limited empathy for others. If you think that you might have insufficient empathy, take the time to ask people questions about themselves. Ask them to give you more details about their point of view so you can better understand their perspective. A representative questioning statement would be, "I'm interested. Tell me more about why you think that…"

4. Assume that you believe you have become too narcissistic in your interpersonal relationships based on both self-reflection and feedback from others. For example, more than one work associate might have told you that you talk too much about yourself and that you seem disinterested in others. The self-recognition of your problem may have already placed you on the road to recovery. The next step is to learn from additional experiences. During one-on-one encounters, as well as group meetings, observe how people react more positively to you when you talk less about yourself and ask more questions about others. Be alert to nonverbal indicators such as smiles, nods, and facial expressions suggesting that you now have more harmonious relationships with others.

5.   Assume that after studying the section in this chapter about narcissism as
     a personality disorder you think that the description fits you well. Further-
     more, assume that you had close to a maximum score on Tendencies toward
     narcissism (Exhibit 1.1), and almost all the symptoms on the Narcissism
     checklist (Exhibit 1.3) applied to you. It would be appropriate to discuss
     your concerns with a mental health professional.

SUMMARY

Narcissism has various definitions, centering on the idea that narcissism is an
extremely positive and inflated view of the self combined with limited empathy
for others. The term narcissism stems from the Greek myth about a handsome
young man who fell in love with his own image in the water, and eventually died
because of his preoccupation with the self-image.

A practical approach to understanding narcissism in the workplace is to
regard narcissism as a personality trait ranging from low to high. Many people
at the highest end of the narcissism trait suffer from a personality disorder.
Highly narcissistic people are preoccupied with receiving attention and expect
special treatment from others. People classified as healthy narcissists have a
positive self-image resulting from a realistic assessment, and acceptance of their
strengths and weaknesses. The moderate narcissist thus has high self-esteem.

The general trait of narcissism has sub-traits or components, identified as
follows: authority, self-sufficiency, superiority, exhibitionism, exploitativeness,
vanity, and entitlement. Other research indicates that these seven sub-traits can
be reduced to two factors, Leadership/Authority and Exhibitionism/Entitlement.

The mostly behavioral symptoms of narcissism identified here are as follows:
self-admiration, statements of superiority, incessant talking and monologues,
interruption of others, temper tantrums, expects special attention, dependent on
others for reinforcement of self-image, perfectionism and compulsivity, limited
empathy, and being a dandy. A healthy self-regard is also possible.

The mostly emotional symptoms of narcissism identified here are as follows:
fragile self-esteem, acquired situational narcissism, rationalization to justify
own behavior, and emotional detachment.

A person at the highest end of the personality trait of narcissism may be
on the borderline of having a true narcissistic personality disorder (NPD). A
personality disorder is a pervasive, persistent, inflexible maladaptive pattern of
behavior that deviates from expected cultural norms. The NPD is but one of ten
recognized such disorders.

A person is diagnosed as having an NPD when he or she exhibits five or more
of the following nine criteria: (1) has a grandiose sense of self-importance; (2)
is preoccupied with fantasies of unlimited success, power, brilliance, or ideal

love; (3) believes that he or she is special or unique; (4) requires excessive admiration; (5) has a sense of entitlement; (6) is interpersonally exploitive; (7) lacks empathy; (8) is often envious of others or believes they are envious of him or her; and (9) shows arrogant, haughty behavior and attitudes.

A person with an NPD can show mild, moderate, or severe impairment. A traumatic situation can sometimes trigger an NPD when a person already has narcissistic tendencies. The status of the NPD as a formal psychiatric diagnosis (or syndrome) is changing toward a focus on the specific personality traits associated with the problem.

The study of workplace narcissism has practical implications. For example, a highly narcissist person might learn to become more sensitive to feedback about his or her behavior and make some adaptations.

CASE HISTORY OF A WORKPLACE NARCISSIST[29]

Our first case history deals with the story of a businessperson whose narcissistic traits and behaviors facilitated his outstanding success for many parts of his career, but eventually led to his downfall.

Kenneth Starr: Financial Advisor to the Stars

During the high points of his career, Kenneth Starr was a financial advisor to celebrities including actors Wesley Snipes and Sly Stallone. Starr was charged by federal prosecutors in 2010 of stealing $30 million from clients. He allegedly spent a lot of the money on a luxury apartment and jewelry.

Starr, who operated through his firm, Starr and Co., was charged with wire fraud, fraud by an investment advisor, money laundering, making false statements to the IRS and lying to federal agents. Ten days after his arrest, a grand jury indicted Starr for cheating 11 clients. When agents came to arrest him, Starr hid behind coats in a closet at his home, forcing the agents to yank him out by the collar. (Starr's lawyer said that his client was petrified by the loud knocking and smashing, and hid in the closet to escape harm.)

A major accusation against Starr was that he promised his clients that their money would be invested in "sure deals." Instead, Starr diverted the money from clients to himself and his colleagues in high-risk investments, according to a lengthy indictment. Among the clients bilked by Starr and his colleagues were a former hedge fund manager and well-known philanthropist, an actress who was a long-time friend of Starr's, and a prominent New York City jeweler.

A major technique Starr used to build relationships with powerful people was through repeated name-dropping. A former lunch companion said that dining with Starr meant listening to him reel off names of successful people as he drank Diet Cokes.

Starr's wife, Dianna Passage, a former exotic dancer, was also involved in the financial scams. She was accused by federal officials of operating a company named Colcave, LLC. Starr was proud that his new wife was a former pole dancer, and would frequently use his iPhone to display photos of her pole dancing to friends. Starr transferred much of his client's money to Colcave. In a manner similar to Bernard Madoff, Starr became friends with some of his highest-investing clients. "He made it a point to seem it was a very exclusive thing, creating a mystique about what it means to be a client of Mr Starr," said US Attorney Preet Bharara. The aura of exclusivity about Starr appealed to his elite clients.

Starr developed such a close relationship with his clients that he was granted access to their bank accounts. Yet Starr would often make unauthorized transfers from their accounts to Starr and Co. When a client wanted to receive a payment as a return on investment, Starr would resort to the Ponzi scheme of paying them with money from another client's account. Starr attempted to withdraw $750,000 from one client's account but was blocked when a suspicious bank official alerted the investor. A long-time professional acquaintance of Starr's said that he had high-level skill in ingratiating himself to others.

Because Starr and his colleagues had access to many of their clients' bank accounts, Starr was able to use some of the money to purchase a $7.6 million apartment in Manhattan. The five-bedroom apartment contains a recreation room with a wet bar, a 32-foot granite lap pool, and a 1500-square-foot garden. The complaint against Starr also states that he used client money to purchase a $32 000 wedding band and a $13 000 pair of diamond earrings. Also, in 2006 Starr bought more than $400 000 in jewelry from a firm owned by an investment client.

The SEC lawsuit indicates that Starr and Co. provides financial services to more than 30 wealthy individuals, "many of whom are

socialites or luminaries in the entertainment and business worlds."
The company manages assets in excess of $700 million.

A Starr employee said that "Kenneth was a great person work
for. I'm disappointed and shocked by all of this."

Narcissism Analysis

Tip-offs to Starr's narcissism include his high-level name dropping,
his heavy emphasis on looking impressive, such as his expensive
apartment, and how he showed off his flashy wife to personal
contacts. The large sums Starr spent on jewelry for his wife also
reflect his emphasis on making a glitzy appearance. Starr's lack
of empathy is reflected in his willingness to bilk his clients even
though he considered them to be his friends.

REFERENCES

1. This version of the story is based on Carter, Les (2005), *Enough About You, Let's Talk About Me*, San Francisco: Jossey-Bass, pp. 3–4.
2. Soyer, Renate B., Janet L. Rovenpor, Richard E. Kopelman and P. J. Watson (2001), "Further Assessment of the Construct Validity of Four Measures of Narcissism: Replication and Extension," *Journal of Psychology*, **136** (3), 246.
3. Definitions two and three are from Marshall, Gordon, *A Dictionary of Sociology* (http://www.encyclopedia.com/doc/1088-narcissism.html). See also Fenichel, Otto (1945), *The Psychoanalytic Theory of Neurosis*, New York: W. W. Norton, p. 420.
4. Freud, Sigmund, "On Narcissism," in J. Strachey (ed.) (1957), *The Standard Edition of the Complete Works of Sigmund Freud*, vol. 144, London: Hogarth Press, pp. 69–102. Original work published in 1914.
5. Ritala, Jean and Gerald Falkowski (2007), *Narcissism in the Workplace*, United States: Red Swan Publishing for IT Service Management Institute, p. 1.
6. "Narcissism," *Answers.com*, http://.answers.com/topic/narcissm (accessed November 10, 2010).
7. "Narcissism," *Answers.com*.
8. Freud, Sigmund, in Strachey (1957).
9. Bogart, L.M., E.G. Benotsch, and J.D. Pavlovic (2004), "Feeling Superior but Not Threatened: The Relations of Narcissism to Social Comparison," *Basic and Applied Social Psychology*, **26**, 35–44.
10. Soyer *et al.* (2001), p. 245.
11. Chatterjee, Arjit and Donald C. Hambrick (2007), "It's All About Me: Narcissistic CEOs and Their Effects on Company Strategy and Performance," *Administrative Science Quarterly*, **32**, 353.
12. Kaufman, Scott Barry (2011), "The Peacock Paradox," *Psychology Today*, **44** (4), 59.
13. Bergman, Jacqueline Z., James W. Esterman and Joseph P. Daly (2010), "Narcissism in Management Education," *Academy of Management Learning & Education*, **9** (1), 119–20.
14. Leonard, Devin (2010), "The Last Pitchman," *Bloomberg Business Week*, June 14–20, pp. 4–5; Barbara Kiviat (2008), "Steve Jobs," *Time*, May 12, p. 120.

15. Raskin, Robert and Howard Terry (1988), "A Principal-Components Analysis of the Narcissistic Personality Inventory and Further Evidence of Its Construct Validity," *Journal of Personality and Social Psychology*, **54** (5), 899.
16. Raskin, Robert and C. S. Hall (1979), "A Narcissistic Personality Inventory," *Psychological Reports*, **44**, 590; "Narcissistic Personality Quiz," *PsychCentral*, htto://psychcentral.com/cgi-bin/narcissisticquiz.cgi (accessed November 16, 2010).
17. Corry, Nida, Rebecca Davis Merritt, Sylvie Mrug, and Barbara Pamp (2008), "The Factor Structure of the Narcissistic Personality Inventory," *Journal of Personality Assessment*, **90** (6), 593–600.
18. Behary, Wendy T. (2008), *Disarming the Narcissist: Surviving & Thriving with the Self-Absorbed*, Oakland, CA: New Harbinger, p. 17. Points two through six on the list are from the same source.
19. "Narcissism," *Answers.com* (www.answers.com/topic/narcissism), p. 15 (accessed November 20, 2010).
20. Twenge, Jean M. and W. Keith Campbell (2009), *Living in the Age of Entitlement: The Narcissism Epidemic*, New York: The Free Press, pp. 73–88.
21. Cited in "Narcissism," *Answers.com*, p. 11.
22. Bergman *et al.* (2000), p. 120. *Manual* (IV-TR), Washington, DC: American Psychiatric Association.
23. American Psychiatric Association (2000), "Personality Disorder," in *Diagnostic and Statistical Manual* (IV-TR), Washington, DC: American Psychiatric Association.
24. The four deviations noted are from Ashmun, Joanna M., "What Is a Personality Disorder?" www.halycon.com/jmashmun/npd/dsm-iv.html, pp. 1–6 (accessed November 21, 2010). © 1998–2004.
25. The levels of impairment, but not the examples, are from Ashmun, "What Is a Personality Disorder?" p. 3.
26. Cited in "Psychologist Is Leader in Narcissism Research, Treatment," *nePsy.com*, www.masspsy.com/leading/0612_ne_qa.html, p. 2 (accessed December 2006).
27. "Psychologist Is Leader in Narcissism Research, Treatment," *nePsy.com*, p. 2.
28. The information and quotes are from Dingfelder, Sadie F. (2011), "Narcissisms and the DSM," *Monitor on Psychology*, February, p. 67.
29. The facts in this case are derived from Helyar, John and David Glovin (2010), "Like Candy from a Baby," *Bloomberg Businessweek*, June 21–7, pp. 78–83; Neumeister, Larry (2010), "Ken Starr Charged with Fraud, Hid In Coat Closet Before Arrest," www.huffingtonpost.com, May 27, pp. 1–3; Weis, Murray, Lachlan Cartwright, and Bruce Golding (2010), "Manhattan Financial Adviser to Celebs Is Charged with Scamming Clients," *New York Post*, May 28, pp. 1–2.

2. The behavior and demands of the workplace narcissist

Much of our understanding of narcissism in the workplace stems from how workers with strong narcissistic tendencies behave toward others including the demands that they make. Visualize a pension fund manager, Karen, who has highly narcissistic tendencies. Her narcissism is of concern to others mostly when it affects her relationship with work associates and the investments she makes. In dealing with superiors, subordinates, and coworkers Karen might talk too much about herself and her accomplishments, and be a poor listener. Of greater consequence, some of her financial decisions are influenced by her narcissistic tendencies. She often invests company funds into sources of investments when the financial consultant has lavished her with praise and entertained her splendidly. Several of the investments she makes are less profitable for the pension fund than those represented by consultants who have not catered to her narcissism. Karen's narcissism has interfered with her professional judgment in the realm of making the best possible investments for the pension fund.

In this chapter we emphasize the behaviors and demands of workers with strong narcissistic tendencies. Much of the rest of the book also deals with narcissistic behavior and demands because the impact of narcissism in the workplace cannot be understood without mention of behavior and demands. For example, if we describe highly narcissistic leaders, much of the discussion deals with how these leaders behave and the demands they place on others.

IDENTIFYING THE WORKPLACE NARCISSIST

In reference to quality as well as pornography, it is has often been said, "It is hard to define, but you know it when you see it." The same might be said of workplace narcissism. We cannot always readily define narcissism (despite all the definitions presented in Chapter 1), yet we can recognize the behaviors and demands of narcissists on the job. Knowing what type of behaviors and demands to look for, and then directly observing people can provide useful diagnostic information about their narcissistic tendencies. The checklist presented in

Exhibit 2.1 provides a representative sampling of how a workplace narcissist is likely to act. The symptoms of narcissism presented in Chapter 1 would also provide clues to identifying a narcissist. Among the key symptoms mentioned were self-admiration, statements of superiority, interruption of others, and, of course, lack of empathy.

Exhibit 2.1   Checklist of narcissistic workplace behaviors and demands
Below is a list of frequent behaviors and demands, both negative and positive, of workplace narcissists. Keep in mind one individual, and indicate whether the particular behavior or demand fits that person.

No.	Narcissistic workplace behavior or demand.	Fits person
1.	Charismatic, including being charming and witty.	
2.	Patronizing toward others in the sense of condescension.	
3.	Creates conflict by pitting one coworker versus another.	
4.	Expects special treatments and privileges.	
5.	No matter what the subject, seems to say he or she is already familiar with it.	
6.	Fishes for compliments frequently, such as saying, "What do you think of my cool new smart phone?"	
7.	Can be cruel and abusive toward peers, but usually charming toward higher-ranking people.	
8.	Poor at listening to the problems of others.	
9.	Doesn't seem to "get it" when someone else attempts to explain his or her position or concern about an issue.	
10.	Extremely well dressed, often to the point of being over-dressed for the occasion or setting.	
11.	Gives warm smiles, particularly when the subject of the conversation deals with him or her.	
12.	Expresses strong appreciation and warmth when he or she is complimented.	
13.	Asks others for small favors, such as bringing coffee or refreshments.	
14.	Acts quite negatively when his or her ideas are criticized.	
15.	Is rarely friendly toward someone who does not give him or her compliments.	
16.	Strong tendency to take personal credit when something works well, and blame others when things go wrong.	
17.	Mentions frequently that management does not give him or her enough respect and recognition.	
18.	Often interrupts others even when the other person seems quite busy.	

No.	Narcissistic workplace behavior or demand.	Fits person
19.	While talking with someone else will take phone call without apologizing.	
20	Sends and receives text messages while attending group meetings.	
21.	Often ends a one-on-one meeting by showing the other person an internet photo album of photos of self, family, and friends.	
22.	Doesn't appear to recognize own limitations.	
23.	Makes frequent contributions to a meeting, even if the quality of the idea is not the best.	
24.	At his or her best, a warm and gracious individual.	
25.	At his or her worst, a rude and disruptive, self-centered person.	
26.	Brags about possessions and accomplishments.	
27.	Will often shift the focus of any discussion to self, such as saying, "Something quite similar happened to me."	
28.	Holds a grudge against another person if wronged in any way by him or her.	
29.	Will often not carry fair share of the workload.	
30.	Almost never admits being wrong.	

Scoring and interpretation: Some of the workplace behaviors and demands would apply to many people who have few narcissistic tendencies. Yet if 25 or more of the above applied to the person you have in mind, that person is most likely a true workplace narcissist.

Source: Ten of the above statements are based on Ritala, Jean and Gerald Falkowski (2007), *Narcissism in the Workplace*, United States: Red Swan Publishing for IT Service Management Institute, pp. 1–2, 14–15; Harvey, Paul and Mark J. Martinko (2009), "An Empirical Examination of the Role of Attributions in Psychological Entitlement and Its Outcomes," *Journal of Organizational Behavior*, **30** (4), 459–76; Brown, Nina (2002), *Working with the Self-Absorbed*, Oakland, CA: New Harbinger, p. 150.

A study of CEOs conducted by Arjit Chatterjee and Donald C. Hambrick demonstrates how direct observation of behavior can be useful in detecting workplace narcissism.[1] At the same time, the study is useful in showing how a variety of behaviors can be an indicator of narcissism. The researchers empirically studied 111 CEOs in the computer and software industry by using five unobtrusive measures of narcissism, as described next.

1. *Prominence of the CEO's photograph.* The company annual report provides an opportunity for the CEO and other officials to report on the company's progress and prospect, as well as its financial standing. The annual report

can also be used to showcase the CEO, including photographs of him or her. The researchers believed that the highly narcissistic CEO will strive for considerable visibility in the annual report, as an exercise of vanity. The photos can also dramatize the importance of the CEO in comparison to others in the firm. The photo indicator of narcissism was rated as follows:

- Four points if the CEO's photo was of him or her alone and took up more than one-half a page.
- Three points if the photo was of the CEO alone and took up less than half a page.
- Two points if the CEO was photographed with one or more fellow executives.
- One point if the annual report did not contain a photo of the CEO.

2. *Prominence of the CEO in company press releases.* The content of press releases is entirely under the CEO's control even if communication specialists prepare the releases. The highly narcissistic CEO will demand to be mentioned as often as possible, both to be vain and to communicate who is in control. The quantitative measure of this aspect of narcissism was calculated as the number of times the CEO was mentioned by name in the company's press releases divided by the total number or words in thousands in all the company's press releases. The ratio is as follows:

$$\frac{\text{CEO Name}}{\text{Thousands of words in report}}$$

3. *CEO's use of first-person singular pronouns.* The frequent use of first-person singular pronouns (I, me, mine, myself) reflects self-absorption and is therefore an indicator of narcissism. Chaterjee and Hambrick used digital transcripts of interviews of CEOs conducted by journalists or financial analysts to isolate direct quotes. Then they counted the number of first personal singular pronouns used by CEOs, divided by the sum of those pronouns plus all first person plural pronouns (we, us, our, ours, ourselves). This measure of narcissism was the percentage of all first person pronouns that were singular.

4. *Two measures of relative pay.* According to the researchers, the highly narcissistic CEO believes that he or she is far more valuable than any other employee in the firm, and this belief is reflected in his or her relative pay. Relative pay was measured by (a) the CEO's cash pay relative to the second highest paid executive in the firm, and (b) the CEO's non-cash compensation, such as deferred income, relative to the second highest paid executive.

The narcissism index was calculated as the simple mean for the five measures (measure 4 counts double). The researchers then found a novel method for ascertaining whether they had a valid (true) measure of CEO narcissism. Five security analysts who specialized in the information technology sector were asked to rate the degree of narcissism of the 40 CEOs with whom the analysts had the most contact. Ratings were made on a 1-to-4 scale: (1) not at all narcissistic, (2) slightly narcissistic, (3) moderately narcissistic, and (4) highly narcissistic. Instructions to the analysts included the following:

> We would like you to rate the degree to which, in your estimation, the CEOs listed below have narcissistic personalities. Narcissism is the degree to which an individual has an inflated sense of self that is reflected in feelings of superiority, entitlement, and a constant need for attention and admiration. Some of the specific manifestations of narcissism include: enjoying being the center of attention, insisting on being shown a great deal of respect, exhibitionism, and arrogance.
>
> In rating the CEOs, please draw upon your first-hand familiarity with them, as well as what you have learned about them from their close associates. Please rate only those CEOs whose personalities you are fairly sure about.

The researchers found that their ratings of CEO narcissism based on the five measures described above corresponded well with the ratings of the outside financial analysts. The correlation between the average analyst rating for each CEO and the unobtrusive narcissism index was 0.82. This unusually high correlation coefficient indicates that the analysts' perceptions and the unobtrusive ratings of the CEO conformed closely to each other.

The point of reporting this research methodology in detail is to suggest that narcissism in the workplace can be reliably spotted through a variety of behaviors exhibited by the person with narcissistic tendencies. We will return to that study again in discussion of leadership and narcissism in Chapter 5.

UNCIVIL TREATMENT OF OTHERS

Uncivil treatment of others is a workplace behavior of narcissists that creates discomfort and stress for many people. Not all uncivil people are highly narcissistic but many narcissistic people exhibit incivility such as being outright rude toward others. Incivility among work associates is a problem with notable consequences. Christine Pearson, a professor of management at the Thunderbird School of Global Management in Arizona, notes that her research during the recent decade indicates that many workers voluntarily left their jobs because of continuing incivility. Yet many of these workers did not reveal that incivility drove them for their job and company.[2]

A major problem with incivility is that a person with low empathy may fail to recognize that it hurts. In the words of Richard Boyd, an associate professor of government at Georgetown University, "To fail to be civil to someone – to treat him or her harshly, rudely or condescendingly – is not only to be guilty of bad manners. It also, and more ominously, signals a disdain or contempt for them as moral beings. Treating someone rudely, brusquely or condescendingly says loudly and clearly that you do not regard him or her as your equal."[3]

Why Narcissists are Often Uncivil

In their book about the narcissism epidemic, Jean M. Twenge and W. Keith Campbell include an analysis of why narcissistic people are so often uncivil and aggressive – both verbally and physically.[4] The two authors reason that in a culture of self-admiration it seems paradoxical that the self-loving narcissist would hurt someone else. However, narcissists are aggressive precisely because they love themselves so much and believe that their needs take precedence over those of others. Narcissists lack empathy for the pain their incivility might cause, and often act aggressively when they feel they are not getting the respect they deserve.

A person with strong narcissistic tendencies might be civil and non-aggressive most of the time. The aggressiveness and incivility is most likely to surface when they are criticized or corrected. For example, a self-adoring administrative assistant received an e-mail from a member of the department indicating that she had misinterpreted some sales forecasts in her recent report. The administrative assistant lashed back with an e-mail message stating, "Who do you think you are? You are a young jerk, and you wear cheap polyester suits."

Narcissists can also be aggressive and uncivil when someone attempts to restrict their freedom. This is true because highly narcissistic people often believe that they are beyond the restrictions placed on others. Restriction of freedom in the workplace includes such constraints as limiting a budget, placing controls on photocopying, restricting access to recreational websites, and forbidding the use of overtime.

Several times in the last few years flight attendants have been subject to severe verbal abuse when a passenger was told that his smart phone must be put away because the plane was about to take off. The passengers in question had already received the same general warning about the use of electronic devices as had the other passengers on the aircraft. In all of the instances referred to here, the rule-violating passenger said something to the effect, "Who do you think you are to tell me not to use my phone?" One of these passengers was a business executive, one a professional football player, and the other a United States Senator.

Another plausible explanation for the incivility of narcissists is that their anger is readily triggered when they are frustrated. Although it is difficult to measure accurately today's levels of frustration in comparison to previous times, many workers suffer substantial frustration in the present environment. Among the frustrations are concerns about being downsized, being forced to work harder and longer because the company is understaffed, and having fewer opportunities for promotion. The latter occurs because business firms, government agencies, and non-profit organizations operate with fewer layers of management than in the past.

Narcissistic workers are likely to overreact to these frustrations by verbally abusing coworkers and subordinates. Verbal abuse is often regarded as bullying, and includes such behaviors as (a) unwarranted or invalid criticism, (b) blame without factual justification, (c) being sworn at, (d) being shouted at or humiliated, and (e) being the target of practical jokes.[5]

A Study about the Narcissistic Personality Traits of Uncivil and Difficult Coworkers

A team of researchers set out to identify the personality traits associated with the workplace incivility of coworkers perceived to be difficult people. *Workplace incivility* was defined as "low-intensity deviant behaviors that are rude, discourteous, displaying a lack of respect with ambiguous intent to harm the target, in violation of workplace norms for mutual respect."[6] A difficult employee was regarded as one who exhibits workplace incivility by engaging in behaviors that are in violation of workplace norms for mutual respect.

The purpose of the study was to develop an empirically based profile of the difficult employee based on the model of a personality disorder (as described in Chapter 1). The ten personality disorders described in the *Diagnostic Statistical Manual of Mental Disorders* (4th edition) were the basis for the study. As you may recall, the narcissistic personality disorder is included among the ten. A questionnaire was developed for the study that asked questions related to the ten personality disorders. More than 300 working professionals from seven different organizations described difficult coworkers they knew by checking descriptive phrases such as (a) "Shows emotional instability as evidenced by marked emotional reaction," and (b) "Has a grandiose sense of self-importance."

For the final sample of 312 respondents, 58 percent described a difficult employee who was a former coworker, and 42 percent described a current coworker. The respondents were approximately equally divided between males and females. Among the difficult employees described by study participants, there were slightly more females (51.6%) than males (48.4%).

Exhibit 2.2 presents the percentage of times mentioned for the top seven traits in response to the statement, "The trait most responsible for my negative

Exhibit 2.2 Behaviors most responsible for negative emotional reaction to workplace associate based on study of 312 respondents

Behavior based on trait	Percent*
1. Arrogant or haughty (directly narcissism related).	42.6
2. Takes advantage of others to achieve his or her own ends (directly narcissism related).	40.7
3. Shows emotional instability as evidenced by marked emotional reactions.	38.1
4. Has a sense of entitlement, i.e. has unreasonable expectations of especially favorable treatment or automatic compliance with his or her expectations (directly narcissism related).	33.0
5. Has a grandiose sense of self-importance (directly narcissism related).	32.7
6. Is preoccupied with details, rules, lists, order to the extent that the major point of the activity is lost.	29.8
7. Lacks close friends or confidants.	28.8
8. Shows rigidity and stubbornness.	28.2
9. Consistent irresponsibility, as indicated by repeated failure to sustain consistent work behavior or honor financial obligations.	24.4
10. Lacks empathy (directly narcissism related).	23.7

* Refers to the percentage of time the behavior was mentioned based on the total number of mentions of behaviors and traits.
Source: Adapted from information presented in Kemelgor, B., L. Sussman, J. Kline, and Jozef Zurada (2007), "Who Are the Difficult Employees? Psychopathological Attributions of Their Co-Workers," *Journal of Business & Economic Research*, **5** (10), 51.

reaction to this employee was…" (For example, "The trait most responsible… was deceitfulness as indicated by repeated lying or conning others.")

A striking finding based on these data is that five of the behaviors most annoying to the working professionals surveyed are behaviors directly related to narcissism, as follows:

- arrogance and haughtiness;
- taking advantage of others to achieve own ends;
- sense of entitlement;
- grandiose sense of self-importance; and
- lack of empathy.

The team of researchers concluded that within their sample, traits of the narcissistic personality disorder were the most frequently chosen descriptors. Narcissism emerged as the dominant disorder in terms of an employee being regarded as difficult. The overrepresentation does not mean that narcissistic workers are necessarily far more abundant in the workplace than people with the other nine personality disorders. The authors offer the interpretation that narcissistic traits may evoke more intense negative emotional reactions from others than do other negative personality traits. The narcissist is the person in the workplace exhibiting the most obvious incivility.

Another possible interpretation of the findings is that workers have less sympathy for extreme narcissists than they might for coworkers with another type of personality disorder, such as someone who is paranoid or obsessive–compulsive. For example, a paranoid personality might be regarded as mentally ill, and would therefore receive sympathy from many other workers. However, a narcissistic coworker might be regarded as quite difficult based on such traits as arrogance and attention-seeking – rather than as having a valid mental illness.

Observations by psychiatrists highlight why narcissists might be regarded as so difficult. Individuals with a narcissistic personality disorder might expect intense dedication from others without regard to the impact on their lives.[7] When the person with a narcissistic personality disorder is in a position of authority, the problem becomes intensified. This is true because it is more difficult for people in a hierarchy to ignore the demands of a boss than a coworker.

ARROGANCE, HAUGHTINESS, AND CONDESCENSION

As indicated in the study just described, arrogance and haughtiness are characteristic of a person with strong narcissistic tendencies. Condescension is a closely related behavior because the arrogant individual is often condescending as part of being arrogant and haughty. Haughtiness refers to being scornfully and condescendingly proud – and therefore being perceived as arrogant.

Arrogance

Work associates who act with pride are often admired, but when pride becomes arrogance the person's behavior is annoying. By definition, the arrogant person displays exaggerated self-importance as well as overbearing self-worth. A proud tech-support person might say to a staff member needing help, "The problem with your mouse creating dozens of copies of the same line on the screen is one I have seen many times before. I've been there before so I can help you." The arrogant tech-support person in the same situation might say, "Your problem is so simple to solve, I wouldn't even consider it a problem."

The arrogance of narcissists may come about because they want to show their superiority. By acting arrogantly, the narcissist gives the impression of being tough and in control, even if the arrogance creates distress for others. For example, the arrogant person might say to the person attempting to cope with a work problem, "Here, let me do it for you. At least I know what I'm doing."

Another manifestation of workplace arrogance is seeing oneself as unusually gifted. A representative statement from a manager with a self-perception of giftedness is, "I'm so capable that I should be CEO. The board just doesn't get me."[8]

In order to establish a client relationship, financial advisors sometimes display arrogance in the form of bragging about being gifted. A frequently used statement describing his or her investment prowess is "I'm really good." The advisor then goes on to explain some favorable returns on investment he or she has obtained for clients. The advisor may be telling the truth, but a careful analysis of the claims of superior investing acumen might be close to the industry average for such investments. Arrogance does not necessarily imply fabrication, but a self-image distorted in an upward direction.

Arrogance can also take the form of making preposterous claims about one's importance or exclusivity. The financial advisor proclaiming to be really good is a lesser degree of arrogance than claiming to be the "best in the business." An advertising claim about being the best is usually not interpreted as a sign of arrogance because most people expect advertising to exaggerate in a positive direction. In recent years, thousands of people have emerged who claim to be experts in assisting companies make effective use of the social media. Some of these consultants claim in person, as well as on their websites, that they are outstanding experts. With so much competition, many of these claims of world-class expertise appear to be products of arrogance.

Donald Trump represents a specific example of arrogance expressed by a highly narcissistic – and highly successful – executive. (A case history of Trump will be presented later in this book.) Trump himself, as well as his organization, has such inflated self-importance that at one time you were not supposed to write "Donald Trump" without the registered trademark, as in Donald Trump®. One example of the arrogance of Trump took place in a dispute over the use of the title, "You're Fired." In 2004, a Chicago pottery store with the name You're Fired challenged Donald Trump's attempt to trademark the tagline used in the reality TV show, *The Apprentice*.

The You're Fired pottery store owner, Susan Brenner said, "Every person who walks into the store now says, 'Oh you're copying Donald Trump.' And I say, 'No he's copying me.'" As Brenner's lawyer put it, "People are associating her with Donald Trump and want to know why she's using his mark. All the money she spent on advertising, all that good will now will be taken away from her."[9]

As described in *Kramer's Law*, Donald Trump filed a trademark application for the catchphrase that placed his reality TV show, *The Apprentice*, on top of the prime-time ratings. According to the US Patent and Trademark Office, the famous real estate developer wants the exclusive right to use these parting words in games, toys, casinos and clothing.[10] The legal test to obtaining the trademark would be for Donald Trump to establish that the slogan "You're fired" has a secondary meaning which identifies America's most flamboyant entrepreneur.[11] "The Donald" has appeared on television explaining that he feels he is right in seeking trademark protection for "You're Fired."

Attempting to block other people from using a generic phrase such as "You're fired" might be regarded as arrogant and narcissistic. It will be up to the US Patent and Trademark Office to decide on Trump's legal right to trademark the term.

False self-esteem

Arrogance is sometimes tied in with a false sense of self-esteem because, by behaving arrogantly, the person projects a strong sense of self-esteem that patches over the reality. William J. Dorgan III, a management consultant, writes that narcissistic managers frequently do not understand that they have modest authentic self-esteem. They compensate for this problem by creating a false front that takes the form of an inflated, somewhat pretentious, grandiose self-image characterized by arrogance. Many narcissistic managers conduct themselves as if they are the most important and valuable people in their area of expertise. Often this behavior is driven by a self-perception of having unusual expertise. The same managers insist that everyone should recognize their privileged status.[12] As one narcissistic manager often told his contacts, "My name is high on the list of executive placement firms when there is an opening in my field."

Dorgan further explains that many narcissistic managers show modest ability outside their fantasy lives. Those with advanced skills and ability often squander their capabilities and lose sight of their objectives. Blocking their progress is the fact that their goals become success and achievement for their own sake rather than concentrating on the quality of the work.

Managers with strong narcissistic tendencies often cause their own downfall on the job because their arrogance and conceit blind their judgment. They may even create scandals that humiliate and undo them in the process. A common example is that the arrogance of a narcissistic executive will lead him to believe that he can violate corporate policies (and employment law) prohibiting sexual harassment. The executive's narcissism blinds him to the fact that lower-ranking people have many tools to combat sexual harassment.

On the positive side, narcissistic managers can be charming despite the occasional arrogance. They can mesmerize and convince others of their special abilities. (As will be described in Chapter 5, narcissism in the right dose contributes to charisma.) Highly talented managers are often tolerated as "gifted but difficult" people.

The arrogance of narcissistic managers often leads them to reject criticism. Some of them react inwardly with distress and humiliation when criticized, with intensity disproportionate to the gravity of the criticism. Other narcissistic managers react with inappropriate rage, even tantrums. In the process they manipulate others to acquiesce to their demands.[13] The scenario is much like a young child throwing a temper tantrum in a supermarket to influence the parent to purchase a box of his or her favorite cereal.

Inflated self-estimate of skills

Arrogance can be irritating when a worker has an estimate of his or her skills and capabilities that is much higher than the perception of coworkers or superiors. Based on his research about narcissism, Timothy Judge, a professor of psychology and management at the University of Florida, observes that people who think highly of themselves are unlikely to have coworkers who share that opinion.[14]

Conceited, vain, and self-absorbed workers often have an inflated estimate of their job skills. Often this inflated self-image is inaccurate because the same workers are below-average performers in the view of the supervisors and coworkers. "It's one thing to think you're better than other people when in fact you're no better, quite another to think you're better when you're actually worse," said Judge. "Not recognizing your own limitations in the workplace is going to keep you from trying to develop skills that would help you improve and make your organization more effective."

Judge also observes that because people with a high-standing on the narcissism trait lack empathy and have self-serving motives, they are less likely to contribute positively to the office social climate. Among the missing contributions are helping others, being a good sport, and going above and beyond the call of duty for the greater good.[15] (The behaviors just mentioned are key aspects of *organizational citizenship behavior.*)

Exaggerated claims of knowledge

A curious behavior of highly narcissistic people is to claim knowledge they do not really have, referred to as *over-claiming*. The person who over-claims knowledge can be considered arrogant because pretending to have knowledge you lack shows arrogance. Over-claiming is also regarded simply as overstating knowledge – some people think almost everything they encounter is familiar to them. You suggest a good idea, and the over-claimer says, "Oh, I've heard of that idea before. We tried it once a few years ago with mixed results." Besides being related to narcissism, the problem of over-claiming could be a memory quirk.

Research on this topic was conducted by Del Paulhus, a professor of psychology at the University of British Columbia in Vancouver, Canada. He asked 211 students to rate their knowledge of events or concepts such as The Lusitania or Pygmalion. In addition, students were asked to rate their knowledge about nonexistent items such as "El Puente" or "1966 Glass Animal." Students with narcissistic character traits as indicated by a personality test taken earlier, more frequently expressed familiarity with all items, including the fake references. Participants in the study were then asked to view the same items as well as new ones, and indicate their certainty about what they had already seen. Subjects given more time to ponder the items were just as likely to falsely claim familiarity with them. An interpretation of the false claims even after being given more time is that over-claiming is an unconscious process.

Paulhus concluded that "People who over-claim are likely not aware of their behavior. Perhaps the behavior becomes more habitual over time and thus becomes a default reaction in relevant situations."[16]

The workplace implication of this small experiment is that workers with strong narcissistic tendencies are likely to exaggerate how familiar they are with ideas and things. As a result they may appear arrogant because they are difficult to impress.

Condescension and Haughtiness

In this context condescension refers to dealing with others in a patronizing, superior manner. A condescending manager might make such statements to a subordinate such as the following:

> "I am so happy that you arrived on time for this morning's meeting. I appreciate your effort in acting like a responsible adult."

> "I wish you would read your e-mails more carefully so as to minimize mistakes. After all, you are a college graduate."

> "It looks like you actually got a good night's rest. I'm proud of you."

> "Your reports are still not as good as I need, but I do like the fact that you are showing a little progress."

Condescension can have negative workplace consequences because many people perceive condescension to be insulting. The person with less power in a work relationship is more likely to shrug off a condescending remark. In contrast, the person with more power in the relationship might retaliate, such as a customer walking away from a condescending vendor. H. Williams, a business intelligence consultant from St Louis, provides the following anecdote that illustrates the point in question:

I've also worked for a very unproductive narcissist who inherited a good-sized family business. Two or three condescending remarks he made during an important presales meeting with Intel cost our company millions in sales.

Fortunately, he had a "sidekick" who patched things up in his wake. It wasn't enough, and I left. In two years since, the company has suffered 80% turnover in front-office staff.[17]

Condescension is perceived as insulting also because its recipient senses that he or she is being treated in a child-like manner. (Children, of course, may also dislike condescension.) The workplace narcissist might be condescending as a way of gaining control and power over the other individual by making him or her feel less competent. Here is a sampling of condescending comments that might be interpreted by the recipient as being treated as if he or she were a child requiring direction:

"Please remember to bring your driver's license on the trip to San Francisco. Airport security requires that all passengers carry appropriate identification."

"Get a good night's rest before our meeting tomorrow morning. I want you to be alert for the entire meeting."

"Do you need to use the restroom before our trip to the other office? We could get stuck in traffic."

"Please remember to use the spell check before you submit that team report to our boss."

The *haughtiness* observed among narcissistic people is close in meaning to condescension. The haughty workplace associate has an air of superiority often combined with a disdain for others. *Haut* is the French word for high, implying that the haughty person acts as if he or she is higher than others. To be haughty is also to be a snob, or to *ride a high horse*. It also implies being a little phony and pretentious, as exemplified by the worker who says, "I received my *baccalaureate* from Princeton" rather than saying, "I have a bachelor's degree from Princeton." Here is a sampling of haughty behaviors than can annoy work associates:

- A financial analyst asks the department administrative assistant, "You didn't really buy your children back-to-school supplies at Wal-Mart, did you?" (The implication is that the administrative assistant must be living on a tight budget.)
- A manager says to a candidate for transfer into his department, "I take it then that all your experience has been in the domestic side of the

business." (The implication is that a candidate without overseas experience is unsophisticated.)

- An information technology specialist tells other members at a meeting, "For those of you still clinging to email, I will hold yet another seminar on the use of modern communication technology." (The implication is that workers who still use email, in preference to newer technology that resembles an internal social network, are out of date and require special assistance. The statement also implies that the IT specialist is smarter and more up-to-date than people who still use email.)

FEELINGS OF ENTITLEMENT

A key aspect of the arrogance of workplace narcissists is that they expect special treatment and privileges, or believe they are entitled to something special.[18] Younger people, especially members of Generation X and Generation Y, are widely perceived to feel entitled to privileges whether or not they have worked hard for these privileges and rewards. Yet it is unfair and subjective to think that only young people have a feeling of entitlement. A higher proportion of young people may have strong feelings of entitlement, yet narcissistic people of all ages feel entitled to undeserved rewards.

The term *entitlement* has different interpretations, with social assistance of any kind often being labeled as entitlements. College students who bombard their professors with email in an effort to have a grade change upward are said to have strong feelings of entitlement. And the ten-year-old who expects a trophy just for being a member of the local soccer team is also said to have feelings of entitlement. Here are a few workplace examples of entitlement:

- A CEO expects a $3 million performance bonus even though the company lost money in the previous year, and the company stock price plunged 15 percent.
- An inventory specialist, who has accomplished nothing unusual for his unit, demands a performance rating of outstanding because, "It will look good in my personnel file."
- A store associate demands that she be able to talk on her cell phone while serving customers because, "My friends and family are important to me."
- A CEO demands that the board purchase a corporate jet because, "I shouldn't have to travel like ordinary people."
- A labor union demands a cost-of-living adjustment for its members even though inflation for the previous year has been close to zero.

These five examples all support the idea that an entitlement really means that a person wants to receive a reward or privilege without his or her accomplishments or circumstances having justified that reward or privilege. The example about the labor union refers to the idea that external circumstances – the Consumer Price Index – did not justify the cost of living adjustment.

Less Work for More Pay

The point above about undeserved rewards is reinforced strongly by Twenge and Campbell in their analysis of the narcissism epidemic. They contend that, in business, entitlement often boils down to the demand of less work for more pay. At the same time many workers demand flexibility, balance, meaning, and frequent praise for their work. Many managers in white-collar businesses have complained that workers want to know what the company will do for them, rather than what they will do for the company. The worker demands include benefits such as an on-site gym, childcare facilities, and generous time off.

High expectations have also become more frequent with many employees wanting to change established business practices within their first week on the job, or believing that they will be the CEO within five years. The new employee mantra might be, "I want a job that is fulfilling, flexible, and pays six figures."[19]

Although these reports of workers demanding less work for more pay may be correct, during the Great Recession worker demands became more subdued. Employees complained less about having to work hard, and were much less prone to be absent from the job.

Work–Life Choices and Entitlement

A continuing debate exists over whether a person can give equal balance between work and family life, and still advance far in his or her career. Workers with a strong sense of entitlement believe they should be able to be highly successful in their careers without sacrificing almost any aspect of family and personal life. The reality is that if becoming successful in one's field requires 60 hours per week of hard work, that person might not be able to meet that demand and still be a full contributor to family life. Jack Welch, former GE Chief Executive and now business writer and educator, told participants at a human resources conference, "There are work–life choices, and you make them, and they have consequences."[20]

The narcissistic person might think that the world owes him or her an outstanding career and personal life at the same time. Only the most talented jugglers of responsibilities will be able to achieve outstanding satisfaction in both career and home life, and they have to work quite diligently to attain the balance.

Resistance to Negative Feedback

A major workplace behavior of narcissists with strong feelings of entitlement is that they want almost all their feedback from their managers and coworkers to be positive. Earlier in life many of these workplace narcissists were deluged with words of praise and stickers, to the effect, "You are great," "You are the best," "You're the boy," and "You're the girl." When deserved, such feedback functions as contingent reinforcement and is therefore effective. Too much undeserved praise in early life appears to be linked to expecting mostly all-positive feedback later in life.

According to Paul Harvey, a professor of management at the University of New Hampshire, managers have considerable problems with workers resisting negative feedback as well as constructive criticism. Entitlement involves having an inflated view of the self, and many managers find that younger employees are often strongly resistant to any feedback that doesn't involve praise and rewards.[21] Part of the reason that narcissistic workers often experience low job satisfaction is attributed to not receiving all the positive feedback and adoration that they want. Negative feedback strongly dampens their job satisfaction.

One approach the workplace narcissist uses to resist negative feedback is to challenge its accuracy. A manager of packaging design might say to a package designer with strong feelings of entitlement, "Those last few label designs you proposed for our dog food client just aren't good enough. I don't see much originality or sparkle in your proposed labels." The package designer in question might reply, "How do you really know what the consumer will like? Where is your evidence? I showed my label designs to a few friends, and I received all praise." The manager who believes she has the authority and expertise to provide critical feedback now feels frustrated. She must now deal with a subordinate's anger.

Another approach the narcissist might use to resist negative feedback is to treat it with denial, as if the negative feedback did not take place. After hearing (not really listening) to the criticism about the dog food labels, the package designer might say, "Oh yeah. I'm glad you didn't see any big issues with my designs."

Demand Stretching as Entitlement

Even when the treatment demanded is not unusually special, the demand is stretched to the maximum allowable, such as taking every possible personal leave day and vacation day possible. Tina, a narcissistic marketing assistant, went on a week's vacation with her family. Tina became sick for two days during her vacation. She sent a text message to her boss, Nina, the marketing director, demanding that her vacation be extended for two days because she wanted to count her two days of being ill as *sick days* rather than *vacation days*. Nina carefully evaluated the request, and then rejected Tina's request stating that because Tina became sick during vacation sick leave did not apply. Tina was outraged but nevertheless returned to work as scheduled without taking two days of unauthorized vacation to compensate for losing two vacation days to illness.

Feelings of Entitlement and Self-Serving Attributions

A potential problem linked to workers who feel entitled to undeserved preferential treatment is that they are more prone to get into workplace conflict and experience low job satisfaction. As the number of younger workers with strong feelings of entitlement increases, more of these conflicts could surface. Harvey, and professor of management Mark Martino at Florida State University, found that people who feel entitled to preferential treatment are likely to exhibit a *self-serving attributional style*. This style refers to a tendency to take credit for favorable outcomes and blame others when things go wrong.[22]

A sales representative with a self-serving attributional style would boast about surpassing his sales quota by 24 percent, claiming to be really effective at closing big sales. In contrast, should the same sales representative fall 24 percent below quota for a given period, he might blame a poor economy for the poor results. A manager who kept turnover below the company average during a one-year period might attribute the successful figures to her engaging and supportive leadership style. In contrast, if the turnover in her department exceeded company norms one year, she might blame the high turnover on "pitiful wages in comparison to the competition."

MANIPULATION OF OTHERS

As described by psychotherapist Les Carter, narcissists are so self-absorbed that they focus exclusively on manipulating other people to accomplish their own ends.[23] In a psychological sense, to *manipulate* is to influence another person or persons in such a way that the manipulator attempts to get what he or she wants or makes the other party believe something in a calculating and devious way. To influence a subordinate to work extra hours, a manipulating manager might say, "I will need you to work five consecutive Saturday mornings, and don't forget that I am a senior member of the promotion committee."

Some manipulators gain the compliance of another person by making untrue statements or faking certain behaviors. For example, a leader might imply that if a colleague supports his position in an intergroup conflict, the person *might* be eligible for a superior performance evaluation. Another manipulative approach is to imply dire consequences to innocent people if the influence target does not comply with demands of the influence agent, such as, "Even if you don't want to put in extra effort for me, think of the people with families who will be laid off if we don't make our targets."

A widely used manipulative approach is the *bandwagon technique,* in which one does something simply because others are doing likewise. An example is a manager who informs the vice president that she wants an enlarged budget for attendance at the latest technology seminars because "all other companies are doing it."

The bandwagon technique can be combined with peer pressure to influence a group member. If one person is not stepping forward to work well as a team member, the manager will say, "Bob, everyone in the department is committed to developing a team atmosphere and we'd like you to be a part of it."[23]

Passive-aggressive behavior is a widely-used manipulative technique by the person with strong narcissistic tendencies. The passive-aggressive person masks pent up aggression by agreeing to do something and then not following through, or by creating problems through inaction. Passive-aggressive behavior is another form of manipulation because the narcissist attempts to create a more favorable outcome for him or her by not taking action. The person literally takes out his or her aggression by not taking appropriate action. Kent, a passive-aggressive, might agree to take on the assignment of ordering refreshments for Louise, the leader of an upcoming meeting. The atmosphere of the meeting turns quite negative when the refreshments do not arrive, and most of the participants blame Louise. Despite his blunder, Kent derives some satisfaction from having created problems for Louise.

Passive-aggressive narcissists resent responsibilities imposed on them. As a result they will engage in unpleasant acts to avoid personal accountability. This type of narcissist is stubbornly unreliable, often lazy, and difficult to change. As observed by Carter, specific behaviors of the passive-aggressive narcissist are as follows:

- Being deliberately evasive. (In this way you do not know whether a task has been done or will be done.)
- Giving the silent treatment as a means of expressing disapproval. (In this way you are kept guessing a little as to whether he or she is one your side.)
- Promising to do something and then not doing it. (This type of passive-aggressive is dreadful when collaboration among workers is needed.)

- Saying what another person wants to hear, then acting contrary to what was said. (You thought you had agreement on a work issue, but you soon become frustrated because the agreement was violated.)
- Complaining behind other people's backs, but refusing to discuss problems openly. (Backstabbing is sometimes included in a narcissist's tool kit of nasty tricks.)[24]

A final approach to manipulation to be described here is telling another person you want him or her to engage in one behavior, but really hoping he or she will do the opposite – because the opposite is what you really want. *Reverse psychology* is the convoluted term given to the behavior in question. The father concerned about his 10-year-old's math skills might say, "Please don't practice math more 30 minutes a day because your eyes will become tired." The father's hope is that the child will study more than 30 minutes per day. The workplace narcissist expecting a below-average performance evaluation might say to the boss, "Please zap me with a terrible evaluation for this period. Because of illness in the family, my performance has been dreadful, so give me what I deserve." (Notice how the narcissist attempts to evoke a little sympathy.)

Reverse psychology is a weak and often naïve tactic of manipulation and influence. More sophisticated workplace narcissists therefore will make only infrequent use of reverse psychology. Instead, they will use many of the more refined techniques described throughout this book.

GUIDELINES FOR APPLICATION AND PRACTICE

1. A recommended way of identifying a workplace narcissist is to observe the behavior directly, including the statements and actions, of the person whom you suspect is narcissistic. The Checklist of Narcissistic Workplace Behaviors and Demands presented in Exhibit 2.1 can provide useful clues to identifying a workplace associate who is highly narcissistic. Armed with careful identification, you are less likely to take the behavior of the narcissistic individual personally. For example, if you think that a person who is rude, disruptive, and self-centered is acting out his or her narcissism, you will be less likely to take this behavior personally.
2. Chapters 7, 8, and 9 deal specifically with approaches to dealing with narcissistic work associates. As a preliminary thought, it is helpful to set limits to the uncivil and rude behavior exhibited by many workplace narcissists. Explain that you refuse to be treated in a particular manner, such as being interrupted during a meeting, or the person sending text messages while you are discussing a work problem with him or her. When

a narcissistic worker strongly objects to following a rule or procedure, it can be helpful to explain that he or she is not being singled out – that the rule or procedure applies to everyone.

3. Do not be discouraged when a work associate you believe to be highly narcissistic does not empathize with a work or personal problem you are facing. Look elsewhere for compassion and understanding. One of the most consistent observations about narcissistic people is that they lack empathy for others.

4. A major challenge in dealing with narcissistic work associates is that they feel entitled to so many privileges and rewards without having earned them. In dealing with a narcissist it may therefore be necessary to explain patiently that performance precedes a reward. As a manager, for example, a narcissistic worker must explain that exceeding goals is the only way to attain a performance rating of outstanding. Another example is that a highly narcissistic customer demanding a large discount must be informed that the discount must be earned through a high-volume purchase or through longevity as a customer.

5. Self-serving attributional styles are more likely to be present in work environments with a high level of ambiguity, according to Paul Harvey and Mark Martinko. One approach to lessen a coworker's self-serving bias is to collect and document evidence that may be useful in establishing who is responsible for positive and negative results. "If you fear that a coworker might take credit for something good that you've done, it's smart to keep evidence of your involvement in the outcome. For example, an email from a stakeholder thanking you for your effort or performance on a task can be used to refute the claims of a coworker trying to take credit for what you have accomplished."[25]

    It is also important to remember that even relatively objective people often have a slight self-serving bias. So before engaging a coworker for blaming you for a problem you feel you did not create or taking credit for a good outcome you think you are responsible for, it might be smart to make sure you're being totally honest with yourself, too, says Harvey.[25]

6. Passive-aggressive behavior is a manipulative technique widely used by narcissists. A passive-aggressive person can create problems because of his or her inaction despite a promise to take action. If you are dealing with a passive-aggressive person you will need to follow up frequently to verify if the person is going to deliver as promised. For example, you might have to ask the field technician several times, "Did you visit the customer yet with the noisy gear in their milling machine?"

SUMMARY

Knowing what type of behaviors and demands to look for, and then directly observing people, can provide useful diagnostic information about their narcissistic tendencies. The checklist presented in Exhibit 2.1 provides a representative sampling of how a workplace narcissist is likely to act. A study of CEOs in the computer and software industry demonstrates how direct observation of behavior can be useful in detecting workplace narcissism. Among the behaviors observed are the following: the prominence of the CEO's photos in the company annual report; the prominence of the CEO in company press releases; the CEO's use of the first-person singular pronouns; and two measures of relative pay.

Uncivil treatment of others is a workplace behavior of narcissists that creates discomfort and stress for many people. Incivility among work associates is a problem with notable consequences, such as voluntary turnover. Narcissists are often aggressive because they love themselves so much and believe that their needs take precedence over those of others. The aggressiveness and incivility of narcissists is most likely to take place when they are criticized or corrected. Narcissists can also be aggressive and uncivil when someone attempts to restrict their freedom because they believe that they are beyond the restrictions placed on others. Another plausible explanation for the incivility of narcissists is their anger is readily triggered when they are frustrated.

A study attempted to develop an empirical profile of the difficult employee based on the model of a personality disorder, with the ten psychiatric personality disorders forming the basis for the study. Respondents rated difficult employees they knew based on behaviors related to the personality disorders. Five of the seven most annoying behaviors were those directly related to narcissism: arrogance and haughtiness; taking advantage of others to achieve own ends; sense of entitlement; grandiose sense of self-importance; and lack of empathy.

Work associates who act with pride are often admired, but when pride becomes arrogance the person's behavior is annoying. The arrogance of narcissists may come about because they want to show their superiority. By acting arrogantly, the narcissist gives the impression of being tough and in control, even if the arrogance creates distress for others. Another manifestation of workplace arrogance is seeing oneself as unusually gifted. Arrogance can also take the form of making preposterous claims about one's importance or uniqueness.

Arrogance is sometimes tied with a false sense of self-esteem because by behaving arrogantly the person projects a sense of self-esteem that patches over the reality. An irritating aspect of arrogance is when a worker has a self-estimate of skills and capabilities that is much higher than the perception of coworkers or superiors. Conceited, vain, and self-absorbed workers often have an inflated estimate of their job skills. Because highly narcissistic people lack empathy and have self-serving motives, they are less likely to contribute positively to the office social climate. Some evidence suggests that highly narcissistic people claim knowledge they do not really have, or over-claim.

The condescension of narcissists refers to dealing with others in a patronizing, superior manner. Many people perceive condescension to be insulting, or being treated in a child-like manner. The haughtiness observed among narcissistic people is close in meaning to condescension because it refers to an air of superiority often combined with a disdain for others.

A key aspect of the arrogance of workplace narcissists is that they expect special treatment and privileges, or feel they are entitled to something special. A higher proportion of young people may have strong feelings of entitlement, yet narcissistic people of all ages feel entitled to undeserved rewards. In business, entitlement often boils down to the demand of less work for more pay. Workers with a strong sense of entitlement believe they should be able to be highly successful in their careers without sacrificing almost any aspect of family and personal life.

A major workplace behavior of narcissists with strong feelings of entitlement is that they want almost all of their feedback from managers and coworkers to be positive. Too much undeserved praise in early life appears to be linked to expecting mostly all-positive feedback later in life. One approach the workplace narcissist uses to resist negative feedback is to challenge its accuracy. Even when narcissists do not demand unusual treatment, the demand might be stretched to the maximum allowable, such as taking every possible personal leave day. People who feel entitled to preferential treatment are likely to exhibit a self-serving attributional style, or a tendency to take credit for favorable outcomes and blame others when things go wrong.

Narcissists are so self-absorbed that they manipulate other people to accomplish their ends. Some manipulators gain the compliance of another person by making untrue statements or faking certain behaviors. A widely used manipulative approach is the bandwagon technique in which one does something simply because others are doing likewise.

The passive-aggressive person masks pent-up aggressions by agreeing to do something and then not following through, or by creating problems through inaction. Manipulation is involved because the person attempts to create a more favorable outcome for himself or herself by not taking action. Another form of manipulation is *reverse psychology*, which involves telling another person to engage in one behavior because you really hope he or she will do the opposite.

CASE HISTORY OF A WORKPLACE NARCISSIST[26]

The following case history is about a world-famous executive who is well known for his self-adoration, and has been labeled a narcissist in the press.

The Flamboyant Larry Ellison of Oracle

Larry Ellison, the co-founder and CEO of Oracle Corp., had a humble beginning in life. Born in New York City, he was raised in Chicago by an uncle and aunt who adopted him. Today he is one of the world's richest people and he is known for his voracious appetite for luxury, beautiful women, dangerous sporting activities such as jet flying, sailboat racing, and fame. Several years ago, his home in Atherton, California was placed on the market for $16 million.

His colorful exploits are frequently reported in gossip columns, and he has a reputation for living life in the fast lane, with a preference for ultra-expensive suits, sports cars, and celebrity friends. When Ellison appeared on the Oprah Winfrey Show, 4000 women wrote to the show proposing marriage to him. The title of his biography was *The Difference Between God and Larry Ellison: God Doesn't Think He's Larry Ellison.* In the book, Ellison is described as a "crazy visionary" and an "uncontrolled adolescent."

In addition to flying and sailing, Ellison also supports causes to protect gorillas. One of his driving business passions has been competing against Microsoft Corp. Oracle's foundation product was database software for companies to store their information. Ellison's vision, beginning in 1996, was the presence of network computers that could retrieve data and software stored on a large central computer elsewhere. Ellison explained over a decade ago, "Our early commitment to internet computing has enabled us to extend our lead in world database market share. The internet changes everything, especially the software business."

Oracle plays a key role in the information technology revolution. Along with technology titans such as IBM, Hewlett-Packard, and Cisco Systems, Oracle makes the technology that runs major corporations throughout the world. Under Ellison's direction, Oracle has continued to modernize, and has flourished and grown more rapidly and consistently than its primary rivals. Between 2005 and 2010 alone, Oracle acquired more than 65 technology firms, including an attempt to move into the hardware business on a grand scale by purchasing Sun Microsystems.

Ellison is well known for his candor in expressing disagreement with other executives and companies. In 2010 he said that the HP board members were idiots for dismissing Mark Hurd. (Hurd was accused of expense account irregularities and sexual harassment.) Ellison then hired Hurd as a co-president, and ridiculed HP's directors when they chose a former SAP director as their new CEO. Ellison basically says to all competitors, "I am your enemy." Ellison believes that he sets himself up for criticism because of his forward thinking. He says, "When you innovate, you've got to be prepared for everyone telling you you're nuts."

Ellison cares about the image he projects. Born in the mid-1940s, he is tall and trim, and keeps himself in excellent shape. His hair is dark with a reddish tint. He has brown eyes and a short beard that helps to camouflage his long jaw. Ellison radiates enthusiasm and charm. He's animated and engaging on stage and at his best in informal question-and-answer sessions where he can rap with the crowd. He has also been described as a fan of and expert on Japanese culture. Ellison perceives himself as a samurai warrior. He likes to quote Genghis Khan: "It is not sufficient that I succeed. Everyone else must fail."

In 2010, Ellison closely associated himself and Oracle with a comic-book hero whose fictional life parallels his own. In the film, *IronMan 2* Ellison suddenly makes a cameo appearance playing the real Larry Ellison. The film is about Tony Stark, a highly intelligent, eccentric, excessive billionaire CEO of a high-tech defense contractor. Stark invents a metal suit that converts him into a formidable weapon. Ellison is presented as but one of thousands of people who fawn over the Stark character.

In 2010, Oracle, and Larry Ellison, had a major triumph in terms of defending itself against copyright infringement in the form of illegal downloading of its software. Oracle was awarded $1.3 billion from SAP, after an 11-day jury deliberation. The case had its origins in 2007 when Oracle sued SAP for illegal downloading of its software for resale to Oracle customers. The downloading was executed by TomorrowNow, an SAP subsidiary. TomorrowNow was accused of using the downloads to sell software to Oracle customers for half the price charged by Oracle. SAP was disappointed with the decision, and planned to pursue all possible options to get the decision overturned.

Fans of Ellison describe him as charismatic, candid, brave, and not hesitant to tell the unvarnished truth. His detractors describe him as brash, arrogant, rude, and flamboyant. He has also been described as "... a bad listener and a big talker, whose brash, take-no-prisoners approach tends to alienate employees and customers alike."

Narcissism Analysis

Larry Ellison merits the title of a narcissistic leader of extraordinary financial accomplishment. Among his many narcissistic traits and behaviors are his brashness, vision creation, disdain for people he disagrees with, and flamboyance. Despite his incredibly busy work schedule, Ellison makes ample time to have an extreme social life including extensive dating, jet flying, sailboat racing, and even appearing in a film. Ellison also shows an immense quest for power as he continues to build Oracle into one of the world's leading companies. It is also characteristic of famous narcissistic personalities to accumulate intense fans as well as intense detractors. Note carefully that we have not even hinted that Larry Ellison suffers from a narcissistic personality disorder.

REFERENCES

1. Chatterjee, Arjit and Donald C. Hambrick (2007), "It's All About Me: Narcissistic CEOs and Their Effects on Company Strategy and Performance," *Administrative Science Quarterly*, **32**, 351–86.
2. Cited in Tugend, Alina (2010), "The Cost of Incivility Is More than Hurt Feelings." *The New York Times* (www.nytimes.com), November 19, p. 1. Some of the earlier supporting research is found in Pearson, Christine M. and Christine L. Porath (2005), "On the Nature, Consequences and Remedies of Workplace Incivility: No Time for 'Nice'? Think Again," *Academy of Management Executive*, February, pp. 7–30.
3. Quoted in Tugend (2010), p. 2.
4. This section is based on Twenge, Jean M. and W. Keith Campbell (2009), *Living in the Age of Entitlement: The Narcissism Epidemic*, New York: The Free Press, pp. 195–210.
5. Washington State Department of Labor & Industries (2008), "Workplace Bullying: What Everyone Needs to Know," Report prepared by the Safety & Health Assessment and Research for Prevention (SHARP) Program, Washington State Department of Labor & Industries, April, p. 1.

6. Kemelgor, B., L. Sussman, J. Kline, and Jozef Zurada (2007), "Who Are the Difficult Employees? Psychopathological Attributions of Their Co-Workers," *Journal of Business & Economic Research*, **5** (10), 47–61. The definition quoted appears on page 47.

7. American Psychiatric Association (1994), *Diagnostic and Statistical Manual of Mental Disorders,* 4th edn, Washington, DC: American Psychiatric Association, p. 659.

8. Quote extended and adapted from Sulkowicz, Kerry (2008), "Analyze This," *Business Week*, March 10, p. 19.

9. Dehnart, Andy (2004), "Pottery Store Wants Donald Trump to Stop Trying to Trademark 'You're Fired,'" *Reality Blurred* (www.realityblurred.com), March 31.

10. Kramer, Irwin R. (1998–2010), "Getting Trumped," *Kramer's Law* (www.kramerslaw.com).

11. Kramer, Irwin R. (2004), "The Donald's new Game of Trademark Monopoly," *Kramer's Law* (www.kramerslaw.com), March 29.

12. Dorgan, William J. III (2000), "Narcissus on the Job," *Modern Machine Shop*, September.

13. Dorgan (2000).

14. Judge, Timothy A., Jeffery A. LePine, and Bruce L. Rich (2006), "Loving Yourself Abundantly: Relationship of the Narcissistic Personality to Self- and Other Perceptions of Workplace Deviance, Leadership, and Task and Contextual Performance," *Journal of Applied Psychology*, **91** (4), 762–76.

15. Quoted in "Unrequited Love," *Industrial Engineer*, November 1, 2005.

16. Perina, Kaja (2003), "You Say You Know it All: Duping Ourselves Into Overclaiming," *Psychology Today*, January–February.

17. Williams, H. (2000), "Letter to the Editor," *Harvard Business Review*, March–April, p. 187.

18. Twenge and Campbell (2009), p. 235.

19. Twenge and Campbell (2009), p. 235.

20. Quoted in Schaefer Riley, Naomi (2009), "Work and Life – and Blogging the Balance," *The Wall Street Journal*, July 17, p. W11.

21. "Prima Donnas Cause More Conflict at Work; Ranks Rising Among Younger Workers," *Newswise* (www.newswise.com), April 27, 2009.

22. Harvey, Paul and Mark J. Martinko (2009), "An Empirical Examination of the Role of Attributions in Psychological Entitlement and Its Outcomes," *Journal of Organizational Behavior*, **30** (4), 459–76.

23. Anonymous (2003) "Create an Arsenal of Influence Strategies" *Manager's Edge*, March, p. 1 [staff written, no author attributed].

24. Carter, Les (2005), *Enough About You, Let's Talk About Me*, San Francisco: Jossey-Bass, pp. 64–5. The bracketed information is original.

25. Harvey's advice is quoted in "Prima Donnas Cause More Conflict at Work; Ranks Rising Among Younger Workers," *Newswise* (www.newswise.com), April 27, 2009.

26. The facts in this case are from Tuna, Cari (2010), "Jury: SAP Owes Oracle $1.3 Billion," *The Wall Street Journal*, November 24, pp. B1; Crum, Chris (2010), "Verdict: SAP to Pay Oracle $1.3 Billion: SAP Pays Big Time For Illegal Downloads," WebProNews (www.webpronews.com), November 24; Hamm, Steve and Aaron Ricalda (2009), "Oracle Has Customers Over a Barrel," *Business Week*, September 21, pp. 52–5; Posted by Andrews, David (2010), *Under The JD Edwards Advisor*, "Iron Man Ellison," andrewseg.wordpress.com, May 11; Ahmed, Mubbisher (2010), "Larry Ellison's (CEO Oracle) Management Style and CIOs," http://mubbisherahmed.wordpress.com, November 24; Carnevale, Chuck (2011), "Larry Ellison: Oracle's Profit Oracle," http://seekingalpah.com, October 6; "Larry Ellison: A Profile," *BBC News: World Edition*, http://news.bbc.co.uk (accessed February 10, 2000).

3. The roots of workplace narcissism

Narcissism in the workplace, just as in any other setting, has its roots and contributing factors somewhere. The start could begin in the fetus if narcissism is created by genetic factors. More evidence suggests that strong narcissistic tendencies have their roots during childhood development. Generational values and practices could also encourage a teenager or young adult to behave narcissistically. A tee shirt worn by Rugby players in England has this declaration printed on the front: "It's not narcissism if you truly are better than everyone else!" Who else but a narcissist could design or wear the shirt? Another possibility is that events in later life, including workplace pressures, could trigger narcissistic behavior as a way of coping with the world.

At various places in this book we will point to the positive aspects of narcissism in the workplace, yet we emphasize that most observers of narcissism in a work environment view it negatively. At the beginning of the 21st century a business journalist in London wrote:

> Do you constantly check your appearance in your office window? Do you think you're right and everybody else is stupid? Chances are you're suffering from narcissism. This term describes people who only see their own point of view. At home it makes them selfish bastards; at work their ruthlessness can propel them to executive levels. As a leader, the narcissus is self-absorbed and untrustworthy. "Me" is the only word they understand.[1]

Whether workplace narcissism has negative or positive outcomes, understanding its origins can lead to dealing more effectively with the workplace narcissist. For example, if you believe somebody is acting in an unrealistically self-centered manner due to *acquired situational narcissism* you might be able to coach the person to recognize that the sudden attention he or she is receiving is but temporary.

In this chapter we explore various roots of narcissism as well as other contributing factors. Workplace narcissism usually stems from a combination of the factors described in this chapter, such as parenting practices, generational values, and societal values. For example, a boy might have doting parents and received trophies in early life for accomplishing virtually nothing. As a teenager he reads about Wall Street executives who earn $50 million dollars per year despite their firms laying off thousands of workers. The combination of factors makes the boy, who is now a young adult, think, "I want more, more, more and I don't care about others."

As a starting point in thinking about the early life origins of narcissism, go through the checklist in Exhibit 3.1.

Exhibit 3.1   Checklist for developing narcissistic children and adults
Below is a list of practices and attitudes that can facilitate a child developing narcissistic traits and behaviors. Included also are behaviors and attitudes that might heighten any narcissistic tendencies in an adult. You would need to have an unusually strong memory to check those that have applied to you in your lifetime, but do the best you can.

Item no.	Narcissism facilitating action or attitude	Done to me
1.	Child told frequently, "You are the best."	
2.	Child told frequently, "You are really special."	
3.	Parent raves when child does something ordinary such as washing his or her hands.	
4.	Dozens of framed photos of the child adorn the house.	
5.	Child is regularly shown hundreds of photos of him or her posted on Facebook or other social media sites.	
6.	Child receives giant trophy just for being a member of an athletic team.	
7.	Child is yelled at because he or she gets stain on clothing while eating or playing.	
8.	Child is almost always the subject of conversation at family gatherings.	
9.	Child is frequently told by parents or relatives that he or she is the most important person in the world.	
10.	Child is ridiculed when he or she does not receive an A or its equivalent on a report or course grade.	
11.	Parents almost never have harsh words for the child even when child makes a big mistake like throwing a rock against a window.	
12.	Parent or parents ridicule child for physical feature such as prominent eyeballs or large nose.	
13.	Child is frequently ignored while parent is occupied with watching television, using the computer, or talking on phone.	
14.	From early adolescence forward person is told that "feeling good about yourself" should be a major life goal.	
15.	Practically all gift-giving during holidays is centered on the child.	
16.	Grandparents talk about almost nothing but the child.	
17.	Parents do most of the work when the child has to write a report for school.	
18.	Parents or teachers mock child when child makes factual or grammatical error.	

Item no.	*Narcissism facilitating action or attitude*	*Done to me*
19.	Child is told repeatedly that the whole world loves him or her.	
20.	Early in career person receives only praise from managers to the exclusion of negative feedback on performance and constructive criticism.	

Scoring and interpretation: The more of the above statements that are identical or similar to something a person has experienced, the greater the probability that he or she will show narcissistic tendencies in work and personal life. The checklist does not come with a precise answering key because several of the statements are mutually exclusive in the sense that it would be rare for several of them to happen to the same person. For example, it would be relatively rare for one person to have experienced the following two parental behaviors: No. 2, "Child told frequently, 'You are really special.'" and No. 10, "Child is ridiculed when he or she does not receive an A or its equivalent on a report or course grade." Nevertheless, it is conceivable that a combination of being doted over most of the time, and being harshly criticized at other times could contribute to narcissistic behavior in later life.

DOTING PARENTS AND OTHER FAMILY MEMBERS

Many observers and researchers believe that narcissism in general, as well as workplace narcissism, has its roots during infancy. Parents and other family members who give the infant too much unwarranted praise and other rewards are thought to be the major contributors to planting the seeds of narcissism.

A social learning theory of narcissism is that special treatment and overindulgence by parents can result in the child strongly valuing himself or herself regardless of real attainments. For example, a child might pick up a toy spontaneously, and then be lavishly praised for having helped the parent clean the room. As a result of the overindulgence the child builds expectations for automatic admiration and praise. Later in life, on the job, the narcissistic-leaning worker expects admiration for having completed an ordinary task.

A cognitive theory perspective emphasizes that idealizing parents may cause the child to develop an overactive view of the self that includes inflated beliefs of personal uniqueness and self-importance. In this approach to child rearing, the parents may systematically deny or distort negative feedback to their child. If a friend, or perhaps store associate, should criticize the child, the parent might respond with a statement to the effect, "Don't listen to her. You did nothing wrong." The insulation from such feedback probably contributes to the hypersensitivity to negative feedback so frequently observed among narcissists – both as students and workers.

Doting parenthood is not limited to dealing with infants. The term *helicopter parents* refers to members of the current generation of mothers and fathers who hover over their children, protecting them and taking over some of their tasks, or sharing these tasks.[2] The helicopter parent might intrude in such situations as writing essays for college applications, preparing job résumés, and cover letters. Parents have also been observed accompanying adult children to job interviews, and helping with salary negotiations. One applicant demanded a staring salary 10 percent more than was offered because in his words, "My father told me that's what I should do. He knows because he's a CEO."

The link between helicopter parenting and later workplace narcissism is relatively weak. A plausible link is that the doted over young adult has further reinforcement that he or she is special, and therefore deserves special treatment. When faced with a difficult problem, the recipient of helicopter parenting expects that the manager, or some other influential person, will intervene in a positive way.

Psychotherapist Wendy T. Behary has analyzed the type of young children who become narcissists as adults. Here we describe three types that appear to be the product of doting, overindulgent parents.[3]

1. *The spoiled child.* One explanation is that a narcissist may have been raised in a home where the idea of being better than others and having special rights and privileges was reinforced. Typically this takes place in a home where few limits were set and negative consequences did not result from overstepping boundaries and breaking rules. Have you ever visited a home (or lived in one) in which the parents do not intervene when the child in the high chair keeps throwing food on the floor?
2. *The dependent child.* Another potential way of breeding a narcissist is for parents to be heavily involved in making a child's life as pain free as possible. Instead of teaching and encouraging the child to develop age-appropriate skills for managing tasks and interacting with others, the parents attempt to do everything for the child. The 18-month-old might be attempting to climb the stairs, and a parent intervenes by picking up the child and carrying him or her up the stairs. As a result of this type of intervention, the child does not develop a strong sense of personal competence, and learned instead that he or she was weak and dependent. Later in life, on the job, the former dependent child expresses narcissism is such ways as demanding that others perform simple tasks for him or her, such as reloading the desktop printer with paper or replacing its cartridge.
3. *The spoiled-dependent child.* The narcissist in the making often has a combination of origins, consistent with the idea that most complex behavior patterns have multiple causes. The narcissistic worker early in life may have been spoiled as well as made dependent. With this dual parenting thrust, the

adult may act entitled as well as superior. The superiority stems from the family attitude, of "we're better than others." The same person might also feel dependent and incompetent because the parents were waiting on him or her instead of helping to develop self-reliance. As an adult worker he or she may feel entitled and expected to be doted on and indulged, such as the administrative assistant who informs work associates that she expects flowers on her desk at least once a month as well as generous gifts at holiday time.

Another potential adult problem with the spoiled dependent is that the person may avoid taking the initiative and making decisions for fear of exposing weaknesses. A supervisor with this decision-making weakness was approached by a production technician who said, "I can't find one of my small hand wrenches. I'm wondering if it fell down into the door of one of the vehicles I worked on in the last hour. What should I do?" Faced with this difficult decision, the supervisor said, "I have no idea. Do what's best."

Not Required to Submit to Authority

Carter provides another useful explanation of how parental doting can encourage narcissism in later life.[4] In some families children do not learn the value of deferring to others because they are encouraged to think that they do not have to follow the same rules or standards as do others. When the child attempts to clean his or her room in the best way he or she can, the parent intervenes and takes over the task. Related to this type of doting parents, some young children are led to believe that they are exempt from accepting the authority of adults.

Assume that a teacher or nursery school aide disciplines a child, and the child balks. Parents who respond to the situation by excusing the child instead of demanding obedience communicate the message that the child does not have to submit to authority. As these types of experiences accumulate, the child learns that submission to broader goals or general principles of fair conduct is not necessary. As an adult worker, the same child might engage in such behaviors as (a) ignoring limits on travel expenses, (b) rebelling against rules for promptness in arriving at work, (c) getting around smoking regulations on company property, and (d) ignoring rules about turning off electronic equipment when not in use.

HARSH PARENTING

Although considerable opinion exists that doting parents create conditions that lead to narcissism among their children, the polar opposite type of parents also contribute to the later-life narcissistic behavior of their children. In general, narcissism may develop from parents who lacked empathy, were neglectful, or devalued their children.[5] The general idea is that if you lacked certain things or experiences as an infant, you will compensate for the problem in later life. For example, the manager who did not receive enough empathy from her parents, and was also neglected, will demand that subordinates pay attention to her and frequently acknowledge her contributions.

Here we focus on two overlapping categories of parenting behavior that help to shape a child into a narcissistic adult: forces that contribute to low self-esteem for children, and not meeting the psychological needs of children.

Forces Contributing to Low Self-Esteem in Childhood

The same experiences that contribute to low self-esteem in early life may lead to narcissism during adulthood. *Self-esteem* has various connotations. As used here, the term refers to the experience of feeling competent to cope with the basic challenges in life and of being worthy of happiness.[6] Low self-esteem contributes to narcissism because a person might compensate for low self-esteem by developing exaggerated self-love and self-admiration. With so much emotional attention invested in the self, the feelings of others will often be neglected. According to research synthesized at the Counseling and Mental Health Center at the University of Texas, childhood experiences that lead to low self-esteem include the following:[7]

- being harshly criticized
- being yelled at or beaten
- being ignored, ridiculed or teased
- being expected to be "perfect" all the time
- experiencing failures in sports or school
- often being given messages that failed experiences (losing a game, getting a poor grade, and so forth) were failures of one's whole self.

Other adults, as well as teenagers, can also engage in behaviors that lower the self-esteem of children. A teacher or coach who ridiculed a child for an unintentional error might also damage the child's self-esteem. In contrast, delivering constructive feedback might help bolster the child's self-esteem.

Unmet Psychological Needs and Conditional Love

Children are born as narcissists in the sense that they are so demanding and self-centered, thinking nothing of depriving their parents of a good night's sleep just so they can be fed or cry. Eventually most infants become less selfish as they mature. Yet if psychological needs are frustrated, narcissism that continues from the earliest stage of life endures.

Children who lack a true intimate connection with their parents are likely to become later-life narcissists, as explained by Carter. Starting with their relationships with their mother and father, young children need consistent messages of affirmation and compassion. If children receive consistent messages of love and caring from their primary caregivers, they gradually come to recognize that there is a big external world in which their emotions and needs do not always receive primary attention. Narcissists rarely think about the feelings and needs of other people, which strongly implies that they did not receive enough nurturing to respond to the needs of others as adults.[8]

Another aspect of having unmet psychological needs is to have grown up feeling conditionally loved, meaning that love was based on performance. The interpretation the child makes is, "I am not being loved for me, but rather for what I can accomplish." According to Behary, conditional love is the major factor contributing to adult narcissism. Conditional love often translates into parents expecting the child to be the best. As a result, any performances short of perfect mean the child was flawed, inadequate, and unlovable. The child learns that love is tentative and contingent on performance demanded by parents. For example, a three-year-old might be rejected for hours because she failed to put her socks on correctly. A child experiencing conditional love may have been manipulated into believing that he or she could get his or her emotional needs met only by striving for perfection.[9] As a workplace narcissist, the person might strive for perfection in an attempt to be loved and admired by work associates.

Exhibit 3.2 presents a list of early life influences that includes both doting and harsh treatment of young children. The exhibit is therefore relevant to this and the previous section of the chapter.

Exhibit 3.2   Early life influences that can contribute to narcissism

---

Many early life influences can contribute to narcissism including the following:

- Abuse (physical, sexual, emotional, verbal, psychological)
- Idealization as a child
- Devalution as a child
- Conditional love and acceptance during early childhood
- Overly protective parenting
- Bullying (both victim and perpetrator)
- Low self-esteem
- Poor or inadequate setting of boundaries when young
- Misplaced priorities displayed and portrayed by parental figures or role models

---

Source: Derived from the research of mental health professionals, and presented in "Kick Off: Tracking Mental Health for Rugby League," www.kickoff.net.au/Narcissism.html (accessed November 30, 2010).

The link between parenting practices (both doting and abusive) and work-place narcissism in adults is based on clinical experiences and logical reasoning. An experiment about the link between the type of parenting received and workplace narcissism would have to resemble the following design: First, a group of children would have to be studied with respect to the parenting they received. Trained observers would have to spend time in the children's homes, and rate the parents on the dimensions of doting and harshness. Second, the children would have to be followed up about 30 years later, and their degree of narcissism would have to be carefully studied, again using trained observers. Third, the workplace narcissism would have to be compared to that of a comparable group of workers raised in homes where the parenting was in the mid-range – neither doting nor harsh. The comparison group could come from the first step in the experiment, using the children who received parenting that was neither doting nor abusive.

Given that probably nobody would fund such a study, and few researchers would be willing to conduct a 30-year study, we have to rely on clinical experience and logical reasoning to arrive at conclusions about the link between parenting and later-life narcissism.

GENERATIONAL VALUES

A widely accepted observation about young people, such as members of Generation X and Generation Y, is that they are more self-centered and narcissistic than previous generations. As a sweeping generalization about millions of people, there are hundreds of thousands of exceptions. The best we can safely say about a stereotype is that it fits the modal member of the generation. W. Keith Campbell contends that by looking at individual scores on narcissism, or on data of the lifetime prevalence of the narcissistic personality disorder, or at cultural trends, they point in the same direction: "Narcissism is on the rise."[10]

Empirical data published by narcissism expert Jean M. Twenge and her colleagues demonstrated that scores on the Narcissism Personality Inventory have increased over time.[11]

The researchers synthesized 85 samples of American college students who completed the 40-item version of the NPI between 1979 and 2006. The total number of students in the sample was 16 475. The mean narcissism scores were significantly related to the year in which the data were collected. Since 1982, NPI scores have increased by one-third of a standard deviation. This indicates that approximately two-thirds of college students in the mid-2000s were above the mean narcissism score for students in the period from 1979–1985, a 30 percent increase in the score. The results of this synthesis complement previous studies that found increases in other individualistic personality traits such as assertiveness, agency, self-esteem, and extraversion. (*Agency* is the extent to which a person believes that one exists as an individual, emphasizing such concepts as self-protection and the creation of a unique identity.)

The finding of Twenge and her colleagues that college students also rate higher on other individualistic traits than their counterparts of the past is notable. It suggests that generational values are indeed pushing people in a narcissistic direction.

We assume also that the samples of more recent college students are based on people older than in previous generations, because the age of college students has increased over the years. Students also take longer to complete their college studies, meaning that the average age of students is increasing by a couple of years. The interpretation to be drawn is that both young college students and those slightly older are influenced to be more narcissistic by generational values.

Note that scores on the NPI are but one measure of narcissism. The direct observation of behavior, as described in Chapter 2, is also a meaningful way of measuring narcissism. The data presented by Twenge and her colleagues are useful because they provide empirical support for the observation that over time many people have developed a more narcissistic personality. These findings suggest that the heavy emphasis on teamwork in the workplace and in schools has not overcome core attitudes toward being self-serving.

Beyond the statistical data, Twenge has presented an analysis of narcissism among young people that adds to an understanding of the topic.[12] When asked how to reconcile the fact that young people are doing more volunteer work with the increase in narcissism scores, Twenge replied, "Volunteering among young people has gone up. However, over that same time, high schools began to require community service. And colleges started to either require, or like to see in applications, volunteer work. They're doing this because it's required, not necessarily of their own volition."

According to Twenge, young people are showing their narcissism in the social media. For example, the slogan of YouTube is "Broadcast Yourself." Data about young people collected from the Pew Research Center also suggest self-centeredness. When asked, "What are your generation's most important goals?", eight in ten said getting rich, whereas only four in one hundred said becoming more spiritual.

As analyzed by Twenge, a major factor in the increased narcissism among young people is the rise in individualism. Many young people believe that "the greatest love of all is loving yourself."

Twenge contends that the increase in narcissism is related to rising depression, anxiety, and loneliness. She reasons that individualism may cause people not to value close relationships. The problem is that close relationships are the most effective inoculators against depression and anxiety. The unrealistically high expectations of narcissists have a strong potential negative consequence. If people with heavy narcissistic tendencies are disappointed, that could eventually lead to anxiety and depression.

In her earlier work Twenge concluded that during Generation Me focusing on the self was not only tolerated, but actively encouraged. (Generation Me cuts through a wide swathe of the population because it includes people born in the 1970s, 1980s, or 1990s.) Many members of Generation Me were the recipients of constant praise and self-esteem boosting. Phrases typifying Generation Me include: "Be yourself," "Believe in yourself," and "You must love yourself before you can love somebody else." School systems across the country instituted programs aimed at elevating the self-esteem of students. Many of the attempts at self-esteem building may have focused too much on self-esteem building for its own sake, rather than stemming from legitimate accomplishment.[13]

One result of all this self-esteem building appears to have resulted in a generational value of focus on the self, thereby encouraging narcissism.

SOCIETAL VALUES

Generational values are a subset of societal values, because a particular generation is a chunk of society. Parenting practices that lead to narcissism in adults are also often a reflection of generational and societal values. For example, if society values self-esteem highly, some parents might be prompted to exaggerate the importance of self-esteem building in their children. Two specific societal or cultural values that would tend to encourage narcissism if carried to extremes are individualism at the expense of collectivism, and materialism at the expense of concern for others.[14]

1. *Individualism versus collectivism.* At one end of the continuum is individu-
    alism, a mental set in which people see themselves first as individuals and
    believe that their own interests take priority. Members of a society who
    value individualism are more concerned with their careers than with the
    good of the firm. Members of a society who value collectivism, in contrast,
    are typically more concerned with the organization or the work group than
    with themselves. An example of individualistic behavior would be to want
    to win an employee-of-the month award; an example of collectivisitic
    behavior would be to want to win an award for the team. Highly individu-
    alistic cultures include the US, Canada, and the Netherlands. Japan and
    Mexico are among the countries that strongly value collectivism. However,
    with the increasing emphasis on teamwork in American culture, more US
    workers are becoming collectivistic.

A high standing on the cultural value of individualism would encourage narcissism in the workplace because personal welfare would supersede the importance of group welfare. For example, a highly individualistic person would object strongly to taking a 10 percent pay reduction so the company could avoid downsizing. (The objection would of course disappear if his or her job were at stake.)

2. *Materialism versus concern for others.* In this context, materialism refers to an emphasis on assertiveness and the acquisition of money and material objects. It also means a de-emphasis on caring for others. At the other end of the continuum is concern for others, an emphasis on personal relations, and a concern for the welfare of others. Materialistic countries include Japan and Italy. The US is considered to be moderately materialistic, as evidenced by the high participation rates in charities. Scandinavian countries all emphasize caring as a national value.

    A high standing on materialism lends itself naturally to workplace narcissism, because the narcissist cares much more about personal aggrandizement than caring for others. A materialistic financial services sales representative would see no problem with selling an expensive variable annuity to a client whose financial situation did not warrant owning this type of investment.

Thirty-five years ago Christopher Lasch, a history professor at the University of Rochester at the time, reasoned that the student unrest surrounding the Vietnam War during the 1960s was followed by a period of national disillusionment. A major consequence was the beginning of a culture of narcissism. Lasch believed that the youth of the US:

*   had become unusually self-centered and demanding;
*   wanted immediate gratification, and were incapable of tolerating delay;
*   were excessively focused on materialistic consumption;
*   had an inability to see their own lives or relationships in extended time;
*   experienced quick boredom and short attention spans; and
*   lacked the capacity for sustained intimacy.[15]

All of these charges are made about the youth of today, and if deeply ingrained in the psyche lead to narcissistic behavior in work and personal life.

LIFE AND WORKPLACE PRESSURES THAT ENCOURAGE NARCISSISM

The concept of narcissism was first popularized by psychoanalysts including Sigmund Freud, so it is natural that much of narcissistic behavior is attributed to early-life influences, particularly parenting. We have explained in the previous two chapter sections that two other major forces, generational and societal values, can also encourage people to behave narcissistically in the workplace. Narcissism is also fostered by other pressures that are more likely to be experienced in adulthood than in childhood. A few of them are examined here, as well as the next section about personal branding.

Acquired Situational Narcissism

As described in Chapter 1, acquired narcissism is a form of narcissism that develops in late adolescence or adulthood, brought on by the wealth, fame, and adulation associated with celebrity. We mention the concept again here because acquired situational narcissism explains how a life or workplace pressure can trigger narcissistic behavior. According to Helen Kirwan-Taylor, a person with acquired situational narcissism develops symptoms including anxiety and substance abuse when, for example, the person is promoted to CEO unexpectedly. Suddenly, coworkers act like sycophants, competing to capture his or her attention.[16]

Soon the newly appointed CEO becomes accustomed to special treatment, and even demands such treatment. Acquired situational narcissism is typically thought of in relation to people suddenly promoted in a major position, but it could easily apply to a person in a more modest position who just became the supervisor. An amusing example of mild situational narcissism is when football players receive special treatment in the form of assistant coaches and trainers squirting water into their mouths as they come off the field for a pause on the bench. Such coddling can contribute to football players thinking that they merit special treatment off the field also.

Playing Misery Poker

As explained by Elizabeth Bernstein, coworkers have always whined to each other about nagging bosses, lazy spouses, and malfunctioning equipment. But during difficult times, such as the Great Recession, complaining intensifies. Feeling overly stressed and desperate for others to understand their heavy pressure, many workers are attempting to outdo each other with the intensity of their complaints. The mechanism is referred to as *misery poker*, in which instead of sharing misery, we use it as a competitive weapon. Points are scored when coworkers brag about their workloads.[17] The more complaints and misery you have, the more points you score.

One coworker might say to another, "My life is a mess today. I just got demoted from supervisor to order-fulfillment specialist." The other coworker wins this hand of misery poker by retorting, "You think things are bad for you? I just got laid off."

Work pressures that lead us to complain – and encourage the playing of misery poker – are turning us into narcissists. For self-protection we push others away. The theme is "Hey, I'm tap dancing as fast as I can, so if you think you have problems, take a look over here," says Ed Dunkelblau, a psychologist and director of the Institute for Emotionally Intelligent Learning.[18]

Misery poker is much like a temper tantrum, attempting to draw attention to a person's plight. The mechanism is counterproductive because the more time you spend complaining about your life (and therefore acting like a narcissist) the less time you have to fix it. "Congratulations, you have the worst job on earth – how is that two seconds of validation going to help you?" says Robyn Landow, a clinical psychologist in private practice. The solution, she observes, is to focus on what you can do when you are with your partner to relieve your stress.[19]

Being a Business Student

A person who studies business at the undergraduate or graduate level might be more narcissistic than the general population. Or the reverse might be true: Studying business places a person in an environment that encourages narcissistic thought and behavior. A similar issue is whether working for an investment banking firm might appeal mostly to people who seek power and wealth. Or might working for an investment banking firm encourage a person to seek power and wealth? Another possibility is that a person with slight narcissistic tendencies might be interested in the field of business. After enrolling in business school, the tendencies toward narcissism are intensified. A similar analysis could be made for the field of investment banking. The field attracts people with narcissistic tendencies, and these tendencies are cultivated further when placed in the field.

Two management professors at Appalachian State University, Joe Daly and Jim Westerman, have conducted research about the rising tide of narcissism in business schools. According to their analysis, members of the millennial generation (born from 1977 to 2000) are a large segment of the student population at business schools. An increasing number of these students have a high standing on the trait of narcissism, as measured by the Narcissistic Personality Inventory. Business students of today were found to be more narcissistic than business students of the past. The business students also had a higher standing on the narcissism trait than psychology students.

As observed by Daly and Westerman, narcissistic students exploit others, are arrogant and haughty, and have limited empathy for others. Furthermore, they are poor team players even though business schools typically emphasize teamwork and collaboration. Narcissistic students often blame others for their failures, take too much credit when a project goes well, and display an exaggerated sense of entitlement. Despite some of these negative characteristics, students with a high standing on narcissism may perform better than less narcissistic students in the classroom because it is a temporary work environment.[20]

Many business students notice that other business students are concerned primarily about their own interests, rather than considering multiple stakeholders. As a result many students in a program of business feel pushed toward a narcissistic attitude. Being a business student is therefore a pressure toward behaving narcissistically.

The study just reported is supported by earlier studies indicating that narcissistic tendencies such as materialistic values and the importance attached to money are strongly evident among business students. A concern is that these types of values and motives may conflict with happiness and well-being because for some people the pursuit of extrinsic rewards is not as satisfying as a focus on helping others. One study found that students majoring in business were more motivated to earn high compensation than were psychology majors. Business students were also more subject to negative mood states, such as anger and depression.[21]

Although Daly and Westerman provide data indicating that business students have higher narcissism scores than previous business students or a comparable group of psychology students, there are many exceptions. As most readers of this book are aware, all business schools emphasize the study of business ethics and social responsibility. As a result, many people who study business and management might become less narcissistic, and more driven toward helping others, as a result of their studies.

Pressures toward Looking and Acting Youthful and Dynamic

A superficial aspect of being narcissistic is going out of the way to have a youthful and dynamic appearance, especially when the person is not chronologically young. The widespread belief is that to be successful in positions that require customer contact, or other meeting with the public, the person should create an appearance matching stereotypes of the image of successful businesspeople. Cosmetic surgery and BOTOX® treatments for business people have increased dramatically in recent years. BOTOX consists of a series of injections which block the nerve impulses that cause facial muscles to generate wrinkles and frown lines. Critics of the procedure claim too much BOTOX can give the person a stiff, expressionless appearance.

Carol Hymowitz, a business reporter for *The Wall Street Journal*, notes that cosmetic surgery, BOTOX, and other de-aging skin treatments have become *à la mode* for baby-boomer managers of both sexes who fear being judged as past their prime. For many executives, plastic surgery is the next step in their rigorous fitness and appearance regimens that include several hours a week at the athletic club, personal trainers, diet consultants, and hair treatments. Many managers color their hair, with many men getting hair transplants to cover bald spots.[22]

Med spa services are a specific approach to appearing more youthful and creating a positive appearance. The several treatments offered are nonsurgical skin treatments aimed at reducing wrinkles, smile lines, and frown lines, as well as restoring volume to the skin. One med spa justifies its services with the explanation that, "In order to gain a competitive edge against other job seekers, many people are turning to cosmetic treatments to provide a more youthful, refreshed appearance. In particular, many middle age job applicants are relying on med spa services which provide effective results with minimal downtime at a fraction of the cost of more invasive plastic surgery procedures."[23]

In addition to vanity, these executives are concerned about job insecurity. They believe that looking older means looking vulnerable, rather than looking experienced and wise. So many managers in their fifties have been downsized that survivors in this age bracket want to appear youthful to hang on to their jobs.

External pressures to make a youthful, attractive look create tendencies toward the aspect of narcissism concerned with appearance. Job candidates over 40 in particular often feel pressured into looking and acting young. This narcissistic thrust toward making a good physical appearance can be misdirected in terms of finding a position or holding on to one. Pat Cook, an executive coach, offers this explanation: "It's a lot less important how old someone is than whether they are young in attitude. I don't care if someone is 55, but I care a lot if he is passionate, enthusiastic and in touch with what is happening in the world."[24]

PERSONAL BRANDING AS A CONTRIBUTOR TO WORKPLACE NARCISSISM

A contemporary contributor to workplace narcissism is the emphasis on personal branding. A *personal brand* is the qualities based on an individual's collection of strengths that make him or her unique thereby distinguishing the person from the competition. The personal brand becomes a person's external identity as perceived by others. According to Peter Montoya and Tim Vandehey, the personal brand is what a person stands for including the values, abilities, and actions that others associate with the person. At the same time the personal brand is a professional alter ego designed to influence how others perceive the person, and turning that perception into opportunity.

The personal brand tells the audience three things: (1) who the person is; (2) what the person does; and (3) what makes the person different, or how he or she creates value for the target market. Montoya and Vandehey also explain that although the term *personal branding* is modern, the phenomenon of people instantly labeling each other based on reputation and behavior has probably always existed.[25]

Personal branding links to workplace narcissism because the idea of a personal brand dictates that the person believes he or she is unique and special. Thus the *branded* warehouse distribution specialist comes to believe that no other distribution specialist has similar personal qualities or adds the same value that he or she does.

The Personal Brand as the Professional Self

Regarding the personal brand as the *professional self* further strengthens its link to narcissism. Daniel J. Lair, Katie Sullivan, and George Cheney explain that within the personal branding movement, people and their careers are marketed as brands. The features of these brands include promises of performance, specialized designs, and tag lines (or slogans) for success.[26]

Judith Sills explains that your reputation is what people think of you, and your résumé is your self-description in written form. Your personal brand includes these two factors but is in total the professional identity you create in the minds of others. Sills regards a personal brand as an important survival tool in a world where job security within a company or industry is difficult to find. Following this reasoning, developing a strong brand pushes a person toward narcissism. The personal branding coach might say, "Think of yourself as Nike or Pepsi Cola – a really strong brand that everybody recognizes." (It would take a narcissist to believe that such branding is possible for him or her.)

The personal brand is part of the impression an individual creates, yet at the same time it makes a person more employable across companies and even industries. Part of the reason that branding contributes to job security is that a person's brand emphasizes his or her expertise. Yet the brand cannot be simply an expression of narcissism. It must be supported by valid capabilities.

An example of terms incorporated into a personal brand that would facilitate job security (if the terms appeared valid) is as follows: "Consistency, reliability, brings projects in under budget, delivers on time, creative thinker, and problem solver." Again, developing a strong brand pushes a person toward narcissism. At the same time, the more narcissistic the person, the easier it is to believe that one has these attributes.

Self-descriptions alone do not constitute a brand. Instead, Sills explains that visibility is important for demonstrating that a person has the capabilities mentioned in the brand. Visible events for displaying a brand include speaking engagements at professional conferences and with groups other than one's own to help solve problems.[27]

Potential Problems with a Personal Brand in the Workplace

A person caught up in the personal branding movement can appear so self-centered and intent on personal gain that he or she irritates people in power. Jerry Wilson, senior vice president and chief customer and commercial officer at Coca-Cola, makes these observations: "The personal branding process can create stress within a corporation. People will see you as merely trying to advance your own career, as opposed to contributing to the success of the organization."[28]

The potential problem with a personal brand can be avoided with sensitivity as to how far the brand can be trumpeted. At the same time the person must be aware of organizational values and make sure that the values align. For example, bragging and self-centeredness might be positive in some organizational cultures but not in others. One example of an executive with a strong personal brand who appears to know how far to push his brand is Scott Monty, the global digital and multimedia communication manager, at Ford Motor Co.

Monty says, "I'm not somebody who can be accused of using Ford's brand to benefit my own. If anything the opposite is true."[29] As a former employee at a business-to-business advertising agency and also at a social-media strategy firm, Monty invested several years developing his reputation in social networking. His specific technique was to write blogs about the convergence of marketing, advertising, and public relations. When Monty was hired by Ford in 2007, he brought with him 3500 Twitter followers. By 2011, he had more than 50 000 followers on Twitter.

Monty has kept his Twitter address as @scottmonty instead of attaching a Ford brand. "I was Scott Monty before I came to Ford, and I'll be Scott Monty after I leave Ford," he says. Monty's large social media following is valuable to his employer. Also, Monty has learned how to balance his own identity with that of the company. His social networking expertise is also quite valuable to the company.[30]

GUIDELINES FOR APPLICATION AND PRACTICE

1. Although narcissism may be partially inherited, similar to having an inborn talent for math or music, or being energetic, it does not mean that a given person is hard-wired to be a narcissist in the workplace or in personal life. A slight natural tendency toward narcissism is not as powerful in determining behavior as learned behavior, and learned behavior can be changed. For

example, suppose a person receives frequent feedback that he or she is too "full of the self," "a poor listener," or an "attention hog." With a little self-discipline and determined effort that person who comes across as a narcissist, can begin to listen more to other people, ask questions, and not talk so much about him- or herself.

2. If you are a parent, or plan to become one in the future, carefully review the items in Exhibit 3.1, Checklist for Developing Narcissistic Children and Adults. The checklist provides a list of practices based on clinical observations that are likely to place a person on a path toward becoming highly narcissistic. If your objective is to foster narcissism, engage in these practices. If your objective is *not* to facilitate the development of high levels of narcissism, *do not* engage in these practices. Item No. 8 provides a potentially useful example. It states, "Child is almost always the subject of conversation at family gatherings." Although it is helpful for the child's self-esteem to be talked about at family gatherings, it is important also to talk about other people and subjects. In this way the child is less likely to develop an egocentric view of the world.

3. A powerful tactic for bolstering the self-esteem of children and work associates is to restrict lavish praise for major accomplishments. The link to narcissism in work and personal life is that too much undeserved praise may create unrealistic demands for praise, and dissatisfaction when not receiving sufficient praise. As a result, the person may fish for compliments in immature ways such as frequently asking questions of this nature: "What did you think of my report?" "How do you like this beautiful suit I just bought?"

4. A difficult-to-handle narcissistic tendency is the adult who believes that many rules and regulations do not apply to him or her, often because of early-life conditioning by the parents. For example, the narcissist who smokes cigarettes may decide to light his or her cigarette before arriving at the designated area outside the building for smokers. Or the same person might violate the rule against using a chair as a ladder. To change this rule-ignoring behavior, the person may need to be reminded frequently when a big or small rule is violated.

5. The practices that are thought to lead to low self-esteem in young children can also adversely affect the self-esteem of working adults. Among these practices are the following: (a) being harshly criticized when the criticism is not justified, (b) being ignored, ridiculed, or teased, and (c) being made to feel that making a mistake such as losing a customer means that the worker is a total failure.

6. Being a member of a young generation does not justify behaving narcissistically in the workplace. Many members of Generation Me are responsive to the needs of other people, and do not demand total attention

and constant praise. In other words, a person cannot excuse his or her narcissistic behavior by saying, "I'm just acting like a Gen Y guy."

7. Playing misery poker can help a person relieve stress from time to time. However, bragging about your problems too frequently might project the image of an annoying narcissist who does not listen to the problems of others. Also, frequent attempts at trying to top other people's problems can project a weak image.

8. The stereotype that people who major in business are greedy, materialistic, and narcissistic is overdrawn. Many people who work in a business environment are interested in the growth and development of others, as well as a strong interest in social responsibility. Also, there is no one-to-one relationship between wanting to earn a good living and being narcissistic.

9. A strong personal brand can contribute to success, yet if carried too far can result in being a caricature of a highly narcissistic person. It is important to think that you have a unique contribution to make to an employer or to customers, but for most people it is going too far to think you have the same commercial impact as Microsoft, Mercedes Benz, or a sports celebrity. Also, telling people that you are heavily branded may communicate the image of an extreme narcissist.

SUMMARY

Workplace narcissism usually has multiple roots or contributing factors, such as parenting practices, generational values, societal values, and life and workplace pressures. Parents and other family members who give the infant too much unwarranted praise and other rewards are thought to be the major contributor to the seeds of narcissism.

Special treatment and overindulgence by parents can result in the child strongly valuing himself or herself regardless of real attainments. Idealizing parents may cause the child to develop an overactive view of the self that includes inflated beliefs of personal uniqueness and self-importance. Helicopter parents dote on children far beyond infancy.

Three types of children who appear to be the product of doting parents are the spoiled child, the dependent child, and the spoiled-dependent child. Not requiring a child to submit to authority is another form of doting that can lead to narcissism.

Harsh parenting can also lead to narcissism, particularly in the form of parents who lacked empathy, were neglectful, or devalued their children. The general idea is that if you lacked certain things or experiences as an infant, you will compensate for the problem in later life. The same experiences that contribute to low self-esteem in early life may lead to narcissism during adulthood. These experiences include being harshly criticized, and being yelled at or beaten.

If psychological needs are frustrated, narcissism that starts from the earliest stages in life endures. Children who lack a true intimate connection with their parents are likely to become later-life narcissists. Another aspect of having unmet psychological needs is having grown up feeling conditionally loved, meaning that love was based on performance or accomplishment. The child might also believe that striving for perfection is the only way to receive love.

It is widely believed that members of Generation X and Generation Y are more self-centered and narcissistic than previous generations. Data published by Twenge and associates indicates that scores on the Narcissistic Personality Inventory have increased over time. The same study also found that college students rate higher on other individualistic traits than their counterparts of the past. The increase in narcissism could be related to rising depression, anxiety, and loneliness. Individualism may cause people not to value close relationships. The focus on self-esteem building experienced by Generation Me appears to have resulted in a generational value of focus on the self, thereby encouraging narcissism.

Parenting practices that lead to narcissism in adults are also often a reflection of generational and societal values, such as a focus on self-esteem building. Two specific societal or cultural values that would tend to encourage narcissism if carried to extremes are individualism and materialism. Over 35 years ago Lasch reported that the youth in the US were caught up in a culture of narcissism through such mechanisms as becoming unusually self-centered and demanding, and an excessive focus on materialistic consumption.

Narcissism is also fostered by pressures that are more likely to be experienced in adulthood than in childhood. Acquired situational narcissism is a form of narcissism that develops in late adolescence or adulthood, brought on by the wealth, fame, and adulation associated with celebrity. Another force toward narcissism is misery poker. This occurs when workers who feel overly stressed and desperate for others to understand their heavy pressure, attempt to outdo each other with the intensity of their complaints. Misery poker is much like a temper tantrum, attempting to draw attention to a person's plight.

Majoring in business might encourage narcissistic thinking and behavior. Research has been conducted about the rising tide of narcissism in business schools, as measure by the NPI, and also by their behavior in terms of exploiting others, being arrogant and haughty, and having limited empathy. Earlier studies have also shown that business students are materialistic. Pressures toward looking and acting youthful and dynamic also contribute to narcissism. Cosmetic surgery and BOTOX treatment for business people have increased dramatically in recent years, particularly for job hunters.

A contemporary contributor to workplace narcissism is the emphasis on personal branding. The personal brand becomes a person's external identity as perceived by others. The personal brand tells the audience three things: (1) who the person is; (2) what the person does; and (3) what makes the person different, or how he or she creates value for the target market. Personal branding links to workplace narcissism because the idea of a personal brand dictates that the person believes he or she is unique and special. A person caught up in the personal branding movement can appear so self-centered and intent on personal gain that he or she irritates people in power.

CASE HISTORY OF A WORKPLACE NARCISSIST

The case history presented this time takes the form of a job interview, which is a natural setting for exhibiting narcissistic tendencies because applicants are almost encouraged to brag about their accomplishments and personal attributes.

The Brand Called Mandy

As Mandy Wildwood navigated the challenging highways toward her job interview in San Francisco, she rehearsed in her mind the importance of communicating that she is a unique brand. "I have to get across the idea that I am special, even if my brand is not as well established as Mercedes or Taco Bell. This administrative assistant position at the airline company will be a good way to launch my career and brand." An excerpt of her job interview with the hiring manager Elena Sanchez follows:

Sanchez: Welcome Mandy, I am pleased that you made it through the online job application and the telephone screening interview. Tell me again why you would like to join our airline as an administrative assistant.

Wildwood: Oh, I really don't want to join you as an administrative assistant. I would prefer a vice president job, but I have to start somewhere. (Smiling) Seriously, I like the airline business. It fits my brand called Mandy. I am a great support person, and a great people person. I'm so unique because I'm great with details and great with people.

Sanchez: Tell me specifically what key strengths would you bring to this job?

Wildwood: As found in my brand called Mandy, I am high info tech and high touch. I'm a whiz at Microsoft Office Suite, and I'm sweet with people. Kind of catchy, don't you think? Come to think of it, have you seen my business card? It contains loads of details about my skills and strengths on the back. The card is laminated so it will last, and it contains my photo, and is even like a hologram with a 3D look.

Another thing you should know is that I have received loads of compliments about my people skills. Just the other day, a little old lady in the supermarket said that I was so kind and nice with the cashier. Many people have told me that I make them feel relaxed.

Sanchez: Yes, Mandy, I do have your card. You gave one to the receptionist, and she gave it to me. And why do you keep referring to yourself as a brand? Is this just a gimmick to get you noticed?

Wildwood: Being a brand is the modern way to tell you that Mandy Wildwood is one of a kind. I've got a skill set that is hard to beat. Besides, I want to build a reputation fast that will propel me to the top as an executive in the hotel field.

Sanchez: On your trip to the top, what do you plan to do for us as an administrative assistant?

Wildwood: I will live up to the brand called Mandy by getting the job done big time. Just ask me to do something, and it will be done. Don't forget I will be building my brand image while in this beginning assignment. With my outstanding people skills, I am sure that employees will bring me ideas for improving the airline. I will then pass on some of these suggestions to the airline executives.

Sanchez: Now let's talk about details like the job assignment, salary, and benefits.

Wildwood: Fine with me. We have to deal with the mundane at some point.

Narcissism Analysis

Mandy Wildwood could be at an early stage in her career as reflected by her enthusiasm for working her way up the corporate ladder from an administrative assistant position. We applaud Mandy for her recognition of the importance of developing a personal brand. It appears that she is headed toward developing a strong personal brand. However, her narcissistic tendencies could create communication barriers between her and Elena Sanchez, the hiring manager.

Mandy makes some highly positive, narcissistic comments about herself which could create the impression that she is too self-absorbed and blindly self-confident. Among such statements are the following: (1) "I am a great support person, and a great people person. I am so unique because I'm great with details and great with people." (2) "As found in my brand called Mandy, I am high info tech and high touch." (3) "I have received loads of compliments about my people skills." (4) "I've got a skill set that is hard to beat." (5) "With my outstanding people skills, I am sure that employees will bring me ideas for improving the airline."

REFERENCES

1. Adapted from Kirwan-Taylor, Helen (2001), "Are You Suffering from… Narcissism?" *Management Today*, October, p. 29.
2. Paragraphs 2, 3, and 4 in this section are based on Bergman, Jacqueline Z., James W. Esterman, and Joseph P. Daly (2010), "Narcissism in Management Education," *Academy of Management Learning & Education*, March, pp. 119–20.
3. Behary, Wendy T. (2008), *Disarming the Narcissist: Surviving & Thriving with the Self-Absorbed*, Oakland, CA: New Harbinger, pp. 14–16.
4. Carter, Les (2005), *Enough About You, Let's Talk About Me*, San Francisco: Jossey-Bass, pp. 32–33.
5. Bergman *et al.* (2010), p. 120.
6. Branden, Nathaniel (1998), *Self-Esteem at Work: How Confident People Make Powerful Companies*, San Francisco: Jossey-Bass.
7. "Better Self-Esteem," www.utexas.edu/student/cmhc/booklets/selfesteem/selfest.html (accessed January 3, 2011).
8. Carter (2005), pp. 27–8.
9. Behary (2008), p. 15.
10. Quoted in Dingfeldler, Sadie (2011), "Reflecting on Narcissism: Are Young People More Self-Obsessed than Ever Before?" *Monitor on Psychology*, February, pp. 64–8.
11. Twenge, Jean M., Sara Konrath, Joshua D. Foster, W. Keith Campbell, and Brad J. Bushman (2008), "Egos Inflating Over Time: A Cross-Temporal Meta-Analysis of the Narcissistic Personality Inventory," *Journal of Personality*, **76** (4), 875–902.
12. Weiss Green, Elizabeth (2007), "It's All about Me." *U.S. News & World Report*, March 12.

13. Twenge, Jean M. (2006), *Generation Me: Why Today's Young Americans are More Confident, Assertive, Entitled – and More Miserable than Ever Before*, New York: The Free Press; *Generation Me*, www.generationme.org/aboutbook.html, 2006.
14. Hofstede, Geert (1980), *Culture's Consequences: International Differences in Work-Related Values*, Beverly Hills, CA: Sage; updated and expanded in "A Conversation with Geert Hofstede," *Organizational Dynamics,* **21** (4), 1993, pp. 53–61; Triandis, Harry (2004), "The Many Dimensions of Culture," *Academy of Management Executive*, February, pp. 88–93; Manasour Javidan, Peter W. Dorfman, May Sully de Luque, and Robert J. House (2006), "In the Eye of the Beholder: Cross-Cultural Lessons in Leadership from Project GLOBE," *Academy of Management Perspectives*, February, pp. 69–70.
15. Lasch, Christopher (1979), *The Culture of Narcissism: American Life in an Age of Diminishing Expectations*, New York: W. W. Norton, as cited in Bergman *et al.* (2010), p. 121.
16. Kirwan-Taylor, Helen (2004), "Are You Suffering from Acquired Situational Narcissism?" *Management Today*, March, p. 16.
17. Bernstein, Elizabeth (2009), "Misery Poker: It's One Game Worth Losing," *The Wall Street Journal*, June 16, pp. D1, D5.
18. Cited in Bernstein (2009), p. D5.
19. Cited in Bernstein (2009), p. D5.
20. Daly, Joe and Jim Westerman (2010), "The Rising Tide of Narcissism: What B-Schools Can Do," *Bloomberg Businessweek*, October 4, www.businessweek.com.
21. Research reported in Bergman *et al.* (2010), p. 120.
22. Hymowitz, Carol (2004), "Top Executives Chase Youthful Appearance, But Miss Real Issue," *The Wall Street Journal*, February 17. The observations of Hymowitz are still accurate today.
23. Lindquist, Courtney (2010), "Med Spa Treatments Become More Popular as Unemployment Rates Climb," *PRWeb*, www.prweb.com, May 6.
24. Quoted in Hymowitz (2004).
25. Montoya, Peter and Tim Vandehey (2005), *The Brand Called You*, Tustin, CA: Peter Montoya Publishing, pp. 11–12, 14.
26. Lair, Daniel J., Katie Sullivan, and George Cheney (2005), "Marketization and the Recasting of the Professional Self," *Management Communication Quarterly*, **18** (3), pp. 307–43.
27. Sills, Judith (2008), "Becoming Your Own Brand," *Psychology Today*, January/February, pp. 62–3. The comments about narcissism in this section are original, and not attributed to Sills.
28. Hyatt, Josh (2010), "Building Your Brand (and Keeping Your Job)," *Fortune*, August 16, pp. 71, 72.
29. Hyatt (2010), pp. 71, 76.
30. Hyatt (2010), p. 76.

4. The healthy, productive workplace narcissist

A realistic perspective about narcissists in the workplace is that some of them are healthy and productive, despite the occasional chagrin they cause for others. With a reasonable dose of narcissism, a person can be productive in a high-level position. Many successful sales representatives, particularly those specializing in consumer products, are self-adoring and flamboyant. Yet their level of narcissism is not so high that it prevents them from empathizing with customers. Many highly successful real-estate sales persons tend toward narcissism with some of them being dandies, or their female equivalent. A large proportion of successful business leaders have sufficient narcissistic tendencies to be flamboyant and self-promoting, yet subordinates respond positively to their leadership. Many entrepreneurs tend toward being narcissistic because their love for the product or service they are promoting is intertwined with self-admiration.

According to Sigmund Freud, one of the reasons that a moderate degree of narcissism in adults can facilitate a person being healthy and productive is that healthy narcissism is an essential part of normal development.[1] Self-love breeds self-confidence. Eventually the healthy child learns to love other people, just as the self-adoring corporate professional also learns to care for coworkers and superiors.

In this chapter we explain how the right degree of narcissism contributes to a person being healthy and productive in the workplace. We will also provide suggestions for attaining the right degree of narcissism, despite the enormous challenge in modifying an aspect of the self as complex as a degree of narcissism.

A starting point in thinking through the potential positive aspects of narcissism in terms of mental health and productivity is to take the quiz presented in Exhibit 4.1.

Exhibit 4.1   A checklist of potentially positive attitudes and behaviors associated with narcissism

Item	Attitude or behavior	Fits me
1.	I am quite proud of my appearance.	
2.	I am quite proud of how I express myself.	
3.	People are drawn to me at networking events.	
4.	I smile frequently because I know that people appreciate it.	
5.	I frequently compliment others so they will like me.	
6.	I feel quite comfortable being photographed.	
7.	I dress much more carefully than most people in my network.	
8.	I am quite confident I can successfully complete almost all assignments given me.	
9.	My mistakes are so few, I hardly use excuse making.	
10.	Negative feedback just gives me another suggestion for being more successful.	
11.	When I receive a compliment, I conclude that the giver of the compliment has good judgment.	
12.	I already own, or would like to own, vanity license plates.	
13.	People who know me well think highly of my potential for promotion.	
14.	My talents are in demand.	
15.	I make a wonderful first impression.	

Scoring and interpretation: If you believe that between 9 and 13 of these statements fit you well, it could be that you have a level of narcissism that is an asset in work and personal life in terms of establishing relationships with people. Yet if you believe that 14 or 15 of these statements fit you well your level of conceit and narcissism could create some interpersonal friction. If you believe that only 8 or fewer of these statements fit you well, you might be experiencing low self-confidence and low self-esteem.

A PROPOSED RELATIONSHIP BETWEEN NARCISSISM AND SUCCESS

As with most dimensions of human behavior, including extraversion and conscientiousness, an optimum level exists for success in many situations. A person who is too introverted might not be successful as a manager or a sales representative. Yet a person who is too extraverted might not appear to be reflective enough to be successful in the two positions just mentioned. Similarly, the personality trait of conscientiousness enhances performance in a wide variety of positions.[2] Yet too much conscientiousness can sometimes result in such strict rule following that the job holder is hesitant to attempt a novel solution to a problem. The super-conscientious worker follows rules so carefully that he or she is hesitant to do something unorthodox and creative.

R. A. Emmons suggested in 1984 that there may be a curvilinear relationship between narcissism and adjustment. (A curvilinear relationship refers to the idea that an optimum relationship between two variables exist: Moderate is better than too high or too low.) Too little of the narcissism trait may be as maladaptive as too much.[3] If you care too little about yourself, your adjustment will suffer. As a result, job and career success might suffer. One of the reasons a moderate degree of narcissism might facilitate success is that narcissists might ingratiate themselves to superiors in order to be well-liked in return.

Figure 4.1 illustrates the curvilinear relationship between narcissism and workplace success. A moderate degree of narcissism might be the most effective because the person would most likely have enough self-esteem and extraversion to impress others and have good interpersonal relationships. When the trait of narcissism is too low, the person might have too many self-doubts and be too low in self-confidence to succeed. When narcissism is too high, the person suffers from many of the problems described throughout this book, such as being

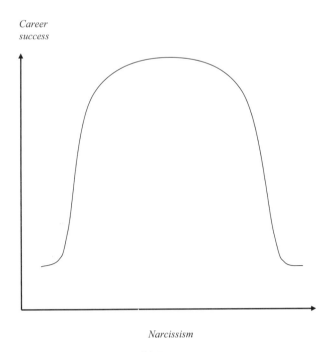

Figure 4.1   A proposed relationship between narcissism and career success

perceived as obnoxious and uninterested in the welfare of others. The curve of the relationship between career success and narcissism is not entirely smooth because many exceptions would exist to the general curvilinear relationship.

THE CHARACTERISTICS OF THE SUCCESSFUL WORKPLACE NARCISSIST

Narcissists in the workplace who are healthy and productive undoubtedly share many of the characteristics of workers who are healthy and productive yet who have less than average narcissism. For example, narcissists who are successful are likely to have good cognitive skills and be conscientious. It is also plausible that healthy and productive narcissists have many of the characteristics of dysfunctional narcissists, yet they possess these characteristics to a lesser degree. Here are a few specific examples based on characteristics and behaviors presented in Chapters 1 and 2.

The healthy, productive narcissist is likely to be a little rather than highly vain. He or she will engage in enough self-admiration to be self-confident but will not obsess about self-admiration. The healthy, productive narcissists will be proud, but not to the point of total arrogance.

For convenience, we organize the characteristics of the successful workplace narcissist into three categories: self-esteem related, enthusiasm, and those specifically associated with the healthy, adult narcissist. The traits may overlap from category to category, reflecting the idea that the same trait can be perceived from slightly different perspectives.

Self-Esteem Related Characteristics

Self-esteem plays a major role in the personality of the healthy, productive narcissist. Here we describe the relationship between narcissism and self-esteem, and the development and enhancement of self-esteem. The Core Self-Evaluations quiz presented in Exhibit 4.2 illustrates a scientifically developed method of measuring self-esteem. Self-esteem is a major component of the core self-evaluations.

The relationship between narcissism and self-esteem
Psychology professors Paul Rose of Union College and W. Keith Campbell of the University of Georgia have synthesized studies about the relationship between narcissism and self-esteem.[4]

Strong evidence exists that the quest for and maintenance of self-esteem is an important part of the narcissistic personality. Narcissism has even been defined as an addiction to self-esteem. Research also indicates that there is a positive

Exhibit 4.2   National Longitudinal Survey of Youth measure of core self-evaluations

No.		True	False
1.	I have little control over the things that happen to me.		
2.	There is little I can do to change many of the important things in my life.		
3.	I feel that I am a person of worth, on an equal basis with others.		
4.	I feel that I have a number of good qualities.		
5.	All in all, I am inclined to feel that I am a failure.		
6.	I feel I do not have much to be proud of.		
7.	I wish I could have more respect for myself.		
8.	I've been depressed.		
9.	I've felt hopeful about the future.		
10.	What happens to me in the future depends on me.		
11.	What happens to me is of my own doing.		
12.	When I make plans, I am almost certain to make them work.		

Scoring and interpretation:
The answers in the high core self-evaluations direction are as follows:

1.	False	5.	False	9.	True
2.	False	6.	False	10.	True
3.	True	7.	False	11.	True
4.	True	8.	False	12.	True

Although there are no specific categories for scores, the more statements you answered in the direction of high core self-evaluation, the more likely it is that you have the type of core self-evaluation that will facilitate high self-esteem and career success.
Source: The statements are from the National Longitudinal Survey of Youth (NLSY79), a study commissioned and operated by the Bureau of Labor Statistics, US Department of Labor. The statements are also reported in Judge, Timothy A. and Charlice Hurst (2008), "How the Rich (and Happy) Get Richer (and Happier): Relationship of Core Self-Evaluations to Trajectories in Attaining Work Success," *Journal of Applied Psychology*, **93** (4), 863.

correlation between narcissism and self-esteem, suggesting that people with strong narcissistic tendencies have high self-esteem. As described earlier, this high self-esteem could be fragile. The positive correlation also indicates that people who have limited narcissistic tendencies also have low self-esteem.

The best evidence of the strong need for self-esteem shown by narcissists derives from studies that examine how narcissists react to self-threatening information.[5] To the extent that narcissistic personalities react defensively to threats to their self-esteem, it can be concluded that it is highly important to narcissists to feel positive rather than negative about themselves. Among the findings of experiments about the link between narcissism and threatened self-esteem are the following:

- When evaluators give narcissists negative feedback about their interpersonal skills, narcissists view the feedback as unfavorable and the evaluator as incompetent and unlikable.
- Narcissists strongly criticize their critics and aggressively punish them, if given the opportunity. The punishment could take the form of a physical attack.
- Narcissists belittle people who outperform them, yet they do not belittle or aggress against people in general. Instead, their hostile reactions appear targeted specifically toward people who insult them, outperform them, or otherwise challenge their self-esteem.

The importance of self-esteem to narcissists is also suggested by their goal to feel powerful, which is probably a manifestation of their goal to feel good about themselves. Considering that a major source of self-esteem is how others view our status – and power brings status – it is natural that people in search of high self-esteem would want to be powerful. A productive narcissist, such as Larry Ellison of Oracle, shows a lifelong pursuit of seeking wealth and fame because the combination of the two bring considerable power.

Dominating others is another source of self-esteem because the dominator feels himself or herself to be above others and have more status. Narcissists are also strongly interested in achievement with the probable reason that more achievement leads to more power and, in turn, to more self-esteem. Productive narcissists, as well as the dysfunctional variety, like to be admired by people in power, which is yet another way of gaining more power and self-esteem.

The development and enhancement of self-esteem

Part of understanding the nature of self-esteem is to know how it develops. Self-esteem comes about from a variety of early life experiences. People who were encouraged to feel good about themselves and their accomplishments by family members, friends, and teachers are more likely to enjoy high self-esteem.[6] The childhood experiences that lead to low self-esteem, including being ignored, ridiculed, or teased, were described in Chapter 3 about the roots of narcissism.

A widespread explanation of self-esteem development is that compliments, praise, and hugs alone build self-esteem. Yet many developmental psychologists seriously question this perspective. Instead, they believe that self-esteem results from accomplishing worthwhile activities and then feeling proud of these accomplishments. Receiving encouragement, however, can help the person accomplish activities that build self-esteem.

Psychologist Martin Seligman at the University of Pennsylvania argues that self-esteem is caused by a variety of successes and failures. To develop self-esteem, people need to improve their skills for dealing with the world.[7] Self-esteem, therefore, comes about by genuine accomplishments, followed by praise and recognition. Heaping undeserved praise and recognition on people may lead to a temporary high, but it does not produce genuine self-esteem. The child develops self-esteem not from being told he or she can score a goal in soccer but from scoring that goal.

Although early-life experiences have the major impact on the development of self-esteem, experiences in adult life also impact self-esteem. David De Cremer of the Tilburg University (Netherlands) and his associates conducted two studies with Dutch college students about how the behavior of leaders and fair procedures influence self-esteem. The study found that self-esteem was related to procedural fairness and leadership that encourages self-rewards. The interpretation given of the findings is that a leader/supervisor can facilitate self-esteem when he or she encourages self-rewards and uses fair procedures.[8] A take away from this study would be that rewarding yourself for a job well done, even in adult life, can boost your self-esteem a little.

To be a productive narcissist it is helpful to enhance self-esteem. Improving self-esteem is a lifelong process because self-esteem is related to the success of your activities and interactions with people. The following are approaches to enhancing self-esteem that are related to how self-esteem develops.

Attain legitimate accomplishments   To emphasize again, accomplishing worthwhile activities is a major contributor to self-esteem in both children and adults. Self-esteem therefore stems from accomplishment.[9] Giving people large trophies for mundane accomplishment is unlikely to raise self-esteem. More likely, the person will see through the transparent attempt to build his or her self-esteem and develop negative feelings about the self. The general-information point of view is the opposite: accomplishment stems from a boost in self-esteem. The two different viewpoints are shown diagrammatically in Figure 4.2.

Another way of framing the attainment of legitimate accomplishments is that, in order to boost your self-esteem, you must engage in behaviors and make choices that are worthy of esteem. To implement this strategy, you must first size up what your reference group regards as esteemed. For most reference groups, or the people whose opinion matters to you, esteem-worthy behavior would include the following:

- successfully completing a program of studies;
- occupying a high-status job and staying long enough to accomplish something worthwhile;
- investing time and money in charitable activities;

The social science perspective

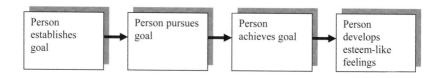

The general information perspective

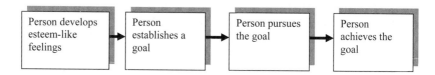

Figure 4.2   Goal accomplishment and self-esteem

- taking pride in your physical appearance and condition; and
- having a social networking web profile (such as Facebook) that is filled with honorable and sensible content.

As you have probably observed, all these esteem-worthy accomplishments reflect values about what is important. For example, a person might have criminals and swindlers in his or her reference group. Self-esteem for this person based on the acclamation of others would therefore stem from such activities as defrauding others of money, and not paying taxes.

Be aware of personal strengths   Another method of improving your self-esteem is to develop an appreciation of your strengths and accomplishments. Appreciating your strengths and accomplishments requires that you engage in *introspection*, the act of looking within oneself. Although introspection may sound easy, it requires considerable discipline and concentration to actually observe what you are doing. A simple example is that we are often not even aware of some of our basic habits such as biting the lip when nervous, or blinking when attempting to answer a difficult question.

The late Leo Buscaglia was a major contributor to emphasizing the importance of people appreciating their strengths in order to boost their self-esteem. Part of his program for enhancing human relationships was for people to love others as well as themselves. A representative example of Buscaglia's advice for being aware of your personal strengths is as follows:

> A wonderful realization will be the day you realize that you are unique in all the world. There is nothing that is an accident. You are a special combination for a purpose – and don't let them tell you otherwise, even if they tell you that purpose is an illusion. (Live an illusion if you have to.) You are that combination so that you can do what is essential for you to do. Don't ever believe that you have nothing to contribute. The world is an incredible unfilled tapestry. And only you can fulfill that space that is yours.[10]

Minimize settings and interactions that detract from your feelings of competence   Most of us have situations in work and personal life that make us feel less than our best. If you can minimize exposure to those situations, you will have fewer feelings of incompetence. The problem with feeling incompetent is that it lowers your self-esteem. An office supervisor said she detested company picnics, most of all because she was forced to play softball. At her own admission, she had less aptitude for athletics than any able-bodied person she knew. In addition, she felt uncomfortable with the small-talk characteristic of picnics. To minimize discomfort, the woman attended only those picnics she thought were absolutely necessary. Instead of playing on the softball team, she volunteered to be the equipment manager. (If this woman were a narcissist, it would be essential to her self-image that she not place herself in situations in which she appeared to be incompetent.)

Talk and socialize frequently with people who boost your self-esteem   Psychologist Barbara Ilardie says that the people who can raise your self-esteem are usually those with high self-esteem themselves. They are the people who give honest feedback because they respect others and themselves. Such high-self-esteem individuals should not be confused with yes-people who agree with others simply to be liked. The point is that you typically receive more from strong people than weak ones. Weak people will flatter you but will not give you the honest feedback you need to build self-esteem.[11]

A related approach to boosting self-esteem is to create a blog in which you enter positive comments, still photos, and videos about you. You invite others to respond with positive comments about you, thereby boosting your good feelings about yourself. A person with strong narcissistic tendencies has to be cautious about appearing to be too self-promoting on a social media site. A downside here, however, is that some people respond to warm invitations with negative and hurtful commentary. An underlying problem here is that many people are quite uninhibited when responding to a blog.[12] Have you ever noticed how nasty and uninhibited people can be on the web?

Model the behavior of people with high self-esteem   Observe the way people who are believed to have high self-esteem stand, walk, speak, and act. Even if you are not feeling so secure inside, you will project a high-self-esteem image if you act assured. Eugene Raudsepp recommends, "Stand tall, speak clearly and with confidence, shake hands firmly, look people in the eye and smile frequently. Your self-esteem will increase as you notice encouraging reactions from others."[13] (Notice here that self-esteem is considered to be about the same idea as self-confidence.)

Choose your models of high self-esteem from people you know personally as well as celebrities you might watch on television news and interview shows. Observing actors on the large or small screen is a little less useful because they are guaranteed to be playing a role. Identifying a teacher or professor as a self-esteem model is widely practiced, as is observing successful family members and friends.

Enthusiasm

A notable positive characteristic of people with a high standing on the trait of narcissism is their enthusiasm. Quite often this enthusiasm is about themselves and the ideas they generate. Visualize a narcissistic woman who develops a new line of high-end women's handbags, which she believes are so unique that she will become a highly successful businessperson through the manufacture and sales of these handbags. The woman needs to be somewhat narcissistic to believe that she has found a new niche in the highly competitive field of luxury handbags. Yet the woman's unswerving enthusiasm gets a few department store buyers and brokers of accessories to listen to her at least.

Eventually the handbag producer gets a few orders based on the stylishness and quality of her handbags, and the enthusiasm she has for them. Feeling encouraged, and not believing that a person of her talent could fail, she launches a website to market her line of handbags. Soon she is actually making a living in a crowded field. She believes that she and her product are so unique and desirable that she will even be able to fend off the counterfeiters of high-end handbags. Without narcissism fueling her enthusiasm, this entrepreneur would never have attempted to launch her small business.

In a study to be described later in the chapter, it was found that study participants who scored high on an abridged version of the Narcissistic Personality Inventory also had a high degree of enthusiasm. The experimental task involved pitching ideas for a movie, and enthusiasm was measured by the ratings of evaluators. Those study participants who generated more enthusiasm for their pitches were the people with high average scores on narcissism.[14]

The Healthy Adult Narcissist

Behary uses the term *healthy adult narcissism* to describe people who, although narcissistic, have achieved recognition and are making a difference in the world or community in which they live. The healthy adult narcissist might be making a positive impact on the lives of many people. Behary observes that many healthy adult narcissists have had stormy and turbulent early childhoods, and their life journey may have taken them across difficult terrain. The same people may have become healthy adults through counseling, psychotherapy, spiritual guidance, or a variety of self-help practices. Another possibility is that people who have struggled in life may have been healed by the gentle kindness of a teacher, friend, mentor, or lover.

Although the self-help movement has been criticized for perhaps contributing to narcissism, certain aspects of self-help can build self-confidence. For example, motivational speakers frequently focus on the theme of helping people become more aware of and confident in their personal resources. Almost all motivational speakers somewhere in their program attempt to inspire people with the theme, "You can do it, if you only try."

A large number of successful people exist within the category of the well-adjusted or healthy narcissism. Many clothing designers with eponymous companies, such as Ralph Lauren, Calvin Klein, and Donna Karen, are on the high end of the narcissism scale, yet highly productive and interpersonally skillful people. Behary proposes eight traits and behaviors that many healthy, productive narcissists share in common:[15]

- *Empathic*: Attuned to the inner world of others. (A rap against most narcissists is that they lack empathy. It could be that the healthy narcissist does have empathy.)
- *Engaging*: Charismatic, socially literate, and interpersonally skilled. (The characteristic of engaging is notable because many charismatic people are tinged with narcissism. For example, the charismatic person might dress and present himself or herself in such a way as to attract admirers and followers.)
- *A leader*: Able to develop a purpose or a vision, and able to point to a direction when collaborating with others. (As will be described in Chapter 5, narcissism can be an attribute for a leader. The description of Donald Trump presented later in this chapter suggests that his high level of narcissism, although widely criticized, has also contributed to his success.)
- *Self-possessed (not selfish)*: Confident and rigorously committed to generosity and authenticity. (One of the great advantages of being a philanthropist is that you get your name attached to colleges, high schools, elementary, schools, hospital wings, even total hospitals, and foundations.

level.)

- *Seeks recognition*: Fueled by approval ratings and motivated to make a difference. (The need for recognition is a natural human need, and the narcissist usually has a much stronger than average need for recognition. Possessing a strong need for recognition, the productive narcissist looks for productive ways to satisfy the need, such as building a successful company, developing a new product, or making a large charitable donation.)
- *Determined*: Able to push beyond opposition, resistance, and an assortment of barriers to success. (The successful and narcissistic sales representative repeats the mantra, "Each rejection just means that I am just one more step closer to receiving a yes." He or she can therefore be gracious when turned down because rejection is brushed off as part of the process of making the next sale. A person of less self-esteem and self-adoration might take the rejection personally and become discouraged from selling.)
- *Confrontational:* Can hold others accountable without harsh criticism. (Although an extreme narcissist is often openly critical of others and enjoys abusing them, the moderate narcissist wants to bring disappointment and disagreement to another person's attention in a constructive manner. The healthy narcissistic team leader might say to a team member, "I want to look good on this project, so I am asking you to rework the numbers you gave me. The numbers are obviously wrong. Here, I will show you what I mean about the numbers being wrong.")
- *Wisely fearful:* Able to tell the difference between an honest attempt at befriending him or her and exploitation. (The extreme narcissist can easily be influenced by ingratiation whereas the productive narcissist will cautiously evaluate flattery. The extreme narcissist might think in response to a lavish compliment about his or her recent PowerPoint presentation, "I am so happy that I have truly made the finest PowerPoint presentation anyone has seen this year." The productive narcissist might think, "It's nice to be complimented, but what is the reason I have been told that I have made the finest PowerPoint presentation anyone has seen this year?")

NARCISSISM AND BUSINESS CREATIVITY

Another key way in which the right dose of narcissism can facilitate productivity is through the potential contribution of narcissism to creativity. As analyzed by Professors Jack Goncalo, Francis J. Flynn, and Sharon H. Kim, a stereotype exists that highly creative people are self-aggrandizing, self-indulgent, and self-absorbed. Some scholars believe that such displays of narcissism may be an inevitable byproduct of creative talent. Creative people are often narcissistic in the sense that they are driven by their own desires and insensitive to the opinion of others. For example, a narcissist is not likely to be dissuaded about the merits of a creative idea just because a coworker or manager says the idea will not work.

Creative workers spend a good deal of time alone, are often absorbed in their work to the point of obsession, and often do not conform to social conventions. As a result, they are likely to project the image of being narcissistic. A stronger link to creativity is that narcissistic workers are motivated to generate novel ideas as a way of standing out and drawing attention to themselves.[16]

Researchers Goncalo, Flynn, and Kim explored a different view of creativity. They hypothesized that narcissists are not necessarily more creative than others, but they think they are, and they are adept at getting others to accept their viewpoint. Based on the ambiguity involved in judging creative work, narcissists may be adept not only at convincing themselves of the high quality of their imaginative suggestions, but also at conveying their ideas with enough enthusiasm and confidence to impress their coworkers. The self-confidence and self-esteem often associated with narcissism may be well suited to selling their creative talents.

The study in question does not denigrate the creativity of narcissistic individuals. Instead, the researchers extended their analysis to the group level to suggest that narcissists are able to contribute to creative outcomes but not acting alone. The researchers reasoned that narcissists may be highly effective at generating novel solutions to complex problems when there is another narcissist in the group who competes with them for attention and support of their opinions.

The predictions about narcissism and creativity were tested in three studies. Narcissism was measured by a short version of the Narcissistic Personality Inventory in all three studies. Different groups of college students constituted the participants for each study.

Study One

In the first study creativity was measured in two ways. First was a measure of the ability to think divergently by imagining different uses for a familiar object, such as a paper clip or a brick. Second was a measure of imaginative thinking such as describing an animal that might live on another planet. Judges were used to evaluate the creative outputs. The results showed that, although the more narcissistic study participants gave themselves higher self-ratings for creativity, the judges did not find their output to be more creative than the less narcissistic participants.

Study Two

The second study investigated whether people higher in narcissism are perceived to be more creative than less narcissistic people because their confidence and enthusiasm matches the stereotypes people have of creative individuals. One student in each pair in the study was assigned the role of the person who pitched an idea, and the other student was assigned the role of the idea evaluator. The "pitcher" role involved (a) coming up with a new movie idea, (2) developing and rehearsing a pitch for the purpose of selling the idea to an evaluator, and (3) actually pitching the idea. Participants were told that the pitcher who received the highest total score across all experimental sessions would receive $50. The evaluators rated the quality of the movie ideas presented as well as the energy of the pitchers.

The results showed that narcissism was significantly correlated with the evaluators' rating of creativity. Narcissism was significantly correlated with the stereotype of a creative personality. However, narcissism was not related to the quality of the movie ideas as rated by outside judges who were not the experimental evaluators. The interpretation of the results was that narcissists may be effective at convincing others that their ideas are creative, partly because they project traits that are closely associated with the stereotype of a creative person. The more narcissistic study participants came across as more charismatic, enthusiastic, and energetic. As a result, they can convince others that their ideas are more novel than those advocated by less narcissistic people who have equally creative ideas.

Study Three

The third study tested the possibility that having a larger number of narcissists in a group can stimulate collaborative energy, until a point at which the number of narcissists becomes a detriment. Each student team was asked to analyze a real organization, making use of the concepts and methods highlighted in an organizational psychology course. The specific assignment was to "adopt the clinical pose of a management consultant, endeavoring to understand the organization, to identify its strengths and weaknesses, and ultimately to propose actions that solve problems and improve performance." Groups were instructed to generate novel plans that the organization could implement to enhance performance.

The average narcissism score for each group was recorded. Group creativity was measured in terms of the creative process used and the action plans developed for organizational improvement. The creativity of each group's product was rated by two outsiders on a 5-point scale, with the following anchor points: 1 = "extremely incremental (no change or almost no change recommended);" 5 =

"extremely radical (a change that would completely overhaul the organization's current approach)."

As predicted, a curvilinear relationship was found between the average narcissism score in the group and the creativity of the action plan suggested for the organization studied. The creativity of the group product increased as the mean level of narcissism in each group increased up to a narcissism score of approximately 6 out of a maximum possible score of 16. After a score of 6, creativity began to diminish. As interpreted by the researchers, the results suggest that the creativity of both group process and product were facilitated by the presence of more narcissistic individuals. Yet, after a point, increasing narcissism becomes detrimental. To paraphrase an old saying, "Too many narcissists spoil the broth."

An important general conclusion to the study is that narcissists can contribute to creativity in groups even if they do not necessarily perform more creatively when working alone. At the same time, narcissists appear to be effective at pitching their ideas. (Idea-pitching is quite important for the entrepreneur seeking funding from venture capitalists, or the corporate professional whose idea needs funding from the company.)

NARCISSISM, WELL-BEING, AND PERSONAL HAPPINESS

An overall reason that many workplace narcissists are healthy and productive is that many are satisfied with their lives as well as happy. We may not know the percentage of narcissists who are happy, but the Rose and Campbell synthesis of studies alluded to earlier in the chapter suggests that the number is higher than most people think. Among these happy narcissists are the small numbers among them who are highly narcissistic to the extent of being delusional. The delusional narcissist will over-interpret small signals from the environment to mean that he or she is a remarkable person. A case in point is the tech support worker who received a handshake and a smile from the CEO because she adjusted a problem with his smart phone. The tech support person proceeded to tell people in her network she had established a good rapport with the CEO, and that she was now a serious candidate for promotion.

The argument that many narcissists experience well-being is built around a model of goal attainment with three major components. First, narcissists strive to attain goals that are self-concordant. (In this context, *self-concordant* refers to pursuing a goal consistent with one's developing interests and core values.) Second, narcissists perceive themselves to be successful in progressing toward their goals. Third, significant progress toward goal attainment enhances their well-being, especially when it fulfills basic human needs.

Here we describe key elements of the model developed by Rose and Campbell, fortified by additional comments and examples.[17] The model under discussion is, in turn, based on the self-concordance model of K. Sheldon and A. Elliot.[18]

Why Narcissists are Often Happy

Previous explanations of why many narcissists are happy have emphasized that self-esteem plays a key role. Because narcissism is linked with positive feelings about the self, and the self is such a key part of life, narcissists experience considerable happiness. *Telic* approaches to understanding well-being underscore the fact that happiness depends on attaining personal goals. (*Telic* refers to tending toward a goal.) However, progress toward some goals yields more personal satisfaction than progress toward others. Specifically, progress toward self-concordant goals yields more satisfaction than progress toward goals that do not fit one's true interests and values. A self-concordant goal for a person who studies accounting might be, "I want to become an accountant because keeping track of finances fascinates me, and I like to help people to understand finances." A self-discordant goal for the same person might be, "I want to become an accountant because my parents said they would not send me to college unless I studied something practical."

A plausible reason that progress toward self-concordant goals yields a better sense of well-being and happiness is that self-concordant goals are more closely linked to the satisfaction of important psychological needs. Among them are needs for competence, autonomy, relatedness, and self-fulfillment.

Following the telic model, there are two major reason narcissists are happy. First, they adopt goals that are consistent with their authentic values, and these goals enable the fulfillment of key psychological needs such as competence. Second, the narcissists are successful in attaining these self-concordant goals.

The Rose and Campbell telic model also emphasizes that the mere perception of success in reaching self-concordant goals is sufficient to produce need-satisfying experiences and increased well-being. Whether a person is making true progress toward a self-concordant goal is not as critical to that individual's happiness as his or her perception of progress.

Assume that Lisa, a business administration graduate with strong narcissistic tendencies, wants to become an executive in a supermarket chain. She is working as an assistant store manager, and wants to become part of a group of managers, labeled "fast-track", who are on a relatively certain path to higher-level management. So far Lisa has not been invited to join this group. Lisa decides to communicate to upper management that she is willing and qualified to join the fast-track group. She chooses to send an e-mail with PDF attached to upper management explaining her interest in and qualifications for becoming a fast-tracker. Within 24 hours, Lisa receives back a bland response thanking her for her interest in becoming a fast-tracker. Lisa now experiences a surge of well-being and happiness, and thinks, "Wow. Upper management now knows of my availability and has expressed interest in me." Lisa's perception that she has made progress toward her important goal has brought her temporary happiness.

The monitoring system for goal attainment does not have to be entirely objective. People with strong motivation to feel good about themselves (an essential characteristic of a narcissist) may perceive themselves to be successfully progressing toward their goals whether or not true progress has been accomplished. Lisa's situation illustrates this point precisely.

The Goals of Narcissists

As a heterogeneous category of people, narcissists pursue a wide variety of goals. A narcissistic NFL quarterback might want to receive (we did not say *earn*) $25 million per year and win a Super Bowl ring. A narcissistic third-grade teacher might want to receive 25 cards at holiday time from her students saying, "I love you, Mrs Rodriguez." The telic model suggests that most of the goals pursued by narcissists can be placed in three categories: the search for power, self-esteem, or excitement. Some narcissists might pursue all three.

Power
Quantitative evidence that narcissists seek power is that scores on the Narcissistic Personality Inventory are positively correlated with test of the need for power. Narcissistic Personality Inventory scores also correlate positively with the need for dominance. Going beyond test measures of narcissism and power, it is evident that narcissists aspire to be influential in politics, and to control vast financial resources. Several of the CEOs who were uncovered during the financial scandals around 2008 were known to have received compensation of over $50 million per year, and had multiple luxury residences, including condominiums in New York City valued at over $25 million.

Narcissists frequently fantasize about winning in competition, gaining revenge against their enemies, being heroes and heroines, and accomplishing great feats. All of these fantasies reflect power-striving. Narcissists also are known to have strong achievement motivation, which is a healthy way of attaining power. For example, entrepreneurs are characterized by a strong achievement motivation and they can attain power as their empire grows. Frank De Luca, the founder of Subway® Restaurants, began modestly at age 17 with one submarine sandwich outlet in 1965. De Luca gradually grew his empire into what has become the world's largest single-brand restaurant franchise based on the number of sites. At the same time he ranks high in a list of the world's richest people.

Self-esteem

As described earlier in the chapter, self-esteem is intertwined with narcissism. Some of the goals narcissistic personalities pursue to experience a feeling of power may also be geared toward feeling good about themselves. Self-esteem also derives from dominance because the feeling of dominating others can make a person feel good about him- or herself. In the workplace, dominating others might take such forms as winning a sales contest, pointing out someone else's errors during a meeting, or harshly criticizing a subordinate during a performance appraisal.

Excitement

Another goal pursued by narcissists is to seek excitement, which often takes the form of thrill seeking. People who score high on the test measure of narcissism also tend to score high on a measure of sensation thinking. The link between narcissism and excitement seeking may not be so evident on the surface. A strong possibility is that engaging in exciting activities and thrill seeking is yet another way of bringing attention to oneself. Previously we mentioned that Oracle CEO Larry Ellison, a widely acknowledged narcissist, is also a physical thrill seeker in terms of such activities as jet flying, and surfing earlier in his life.

Richard Branson, the swashbuckling founder of Virgin Inc., is a world-class celebrity, with hundreds of business firms carrying the Virgin trademark. In addition Branson is a lifelong thrill seeker, including such exploits as balloon flying and descending down the side of a building in Times Square. He is often photographed surrounded by a group of beautiful women. It would be reasonable to conclude that Sir Richard Branson is a productive narcissist.

Frank Farley, a professor of psychology at Temple University, and specialist in the study of thrill seeking, analyzes that Branson fits the type T personality, which is characterized by risk taking, stimulation seeking, and thrill seeking. An individual with this type of personality is also motivated by novelty and change with a high tolerance for ambiguity, is highly self-confident and optimistic. Furthermore, the individual believes fate and destiny is under his or her control. Other traits include creativity, innovativeness, and independence of judgment, such as making up his or her mind. The Type T personality takes naturally to breaking rules, and thrives on challenges.[19]

The activities engaged in by narcissists will often help fulfill more than one of the three goals of power, self-esteem, and excitement. For example, the representative narcissistic behavior of exhibitionism can serve all three basic goals. (Exhibitionism in this context is showing off, not exposing oneself in the nude.) By demonstrating their self-attributed superiority to others, narcissists can satisfy feelings of power, feelings of self-esteem, and the excitation that can result from performing before an audience. Visualize a narcissistic marketing assistant working for an American company. He learns how to read, write, and speak Japanese because he wants to be *cool*. He can now brag to others how smart he is to know Japanese. He feels good about himself because he has developed a skill that others value. In addition, he gets an occasional opportunity to demonstrate his Japanese prowess to coworkers, especially when the company has two visitors from an affiliate in Japan.

The Perception of Narcissists about Goal Attainment

Another characteristic behavior of people with strong narcissistic tendencies is that they perceive themselves as being successful in most endeavors. Research indicates that narcissists perceive themselves to be successful in such varied activities as general intellectual pursuits, committee decision-making tasks, small-group discussions, and in leadership roles. Narcissists are also known to brag. A statement frequently made by narcissists is "I can do anything I set my mind to." Although such a declaration might contribute to self-motivation, it is far too grandiose to be accurate. Could that person win a Nobel Peace prize for economics, become the CEO of a major corporation, or invent a device with a similar impact on society as the internet?

Whether or not narcissists outperform others in most endeavors, it is the perception of being successful that is critical for well-being. Brett, a boastful former industrial sales representative, was laid off from several positions. Totally discouraged with having failed several times as an employee, he decided to operate a food cart, which he runs outside a small office complex when the weather cooperates. Brett ekes out a living and seems happy. Asked how his new business was going, he replied, "I'm a success. My customers like me, and I'm paying my bills." Some people might think that Brett has a failed career because he has slipped down the occupational scale, works only about eight months a year, and barely gets by financially. But Brett is happy because he perceives himself to be successful.

Based on the observation that narcissists perceive themselves to be successful in general, they most likely perceive themselves as being successful in acquiring power, boosting their self-esteem, and finding the excitement they want. Narcissists tend to endorse the following items on a measure of power and influence:

- People see me as a forceful and powerful person.
- I usually know how to get what I want.
- When I'm in charge, people jump when I say jump.

Survey evidence also suggests that narcissists believe that they have high self-esteem. As a result, they feel they have been successful in pursuit of one of their basic goals. A positive relationship found between narcissism and *surgency* indicates that they have attained their excitement goal. (Surgency refers to a sense of liveliness, cheerfulness, and spontaneity.) Narcissism has also been found to correlate positively with mania (or feeling like a manic). Rose and Campbell alert us that narcissists often oscillate between feeling excited and bored. Yet when they do get excited, the feeling is intense. A case in point is Dick Vitale, a well-known television college basketball announcer. He appears to be one of the most narcissistic people in a field populated by narcissists. One of the best known features of Vitale is his exuberance – an observation that can be verified on YouTube. Vitale also oscillates into distraction and boredom with the game during his broadcast, as he discusses restaurants he has patronized, the cooking skill of the wife of a buddy, or the fact that a coach has a beautiful young wife. No doubt, Vitale thinks that his comments about topics extraneous to the game in play add color to the broadcast.

The Narcissist Maintenance of the Illusion of Successful Goal Attainment in the Face of Contradicting Realities

Narcissism is often unrelated to actual performance on many tasks, yet narcissists maintain the perception that they are powerful, competent and filled with excitement. One method they use to maintain this illusion is to blame their failures on others, thereby circumventing the feeling of failure. Another method narcissists use to believe that they have attained their goals is to seek reassurance of their success from others. This mechanism is another example of how the narcissist fishes for compliments. A narcissistic human resource manager, whose plan to operate a company-sponsored diversity training program via social media was rejected, asked a coworker, "Don't you think my cool diversity training effort would have been approved except for the recent budget cut?"

Another tactic narcissists might use to maintain the illusion that they have attained their goals is to set vague goals and deadlines. A narcissistic product developer might say to a coworker, "I have an idea for a product so big it will dwarf anything else the company has released in a decade. I'll be releasing my idea sometime down the pike." Given that the product developer has not committed to anything specific, failure will be difficult to experience.

Basic Need Satisfaction and Narcissism

Another advantage of having narcissistic tendencies for the purposes of well-being is that narcissism helps fulfill the basic needs of feelings of competence, autonomy and relatedness. A study with the Narcissistic Personality Inventory supported this idea because it demonstrated that feelings of autonomy, competence, and relatedness all correlated significantly with narcissism. In general, a variety of studies suggest that narcissists do a reasonable job of satisfying their basic needs. Such data contradict the idea that workplace narcissists inevitably suffer from maladjustment and misery. Some flamboyant narcissists seem to be quite happy, even if they are a little delusional about how much they accomplish and how much they are adored.

Subjective Well-Being and the Fulfillment of Basic Needs

A major contributor to happiness for most people is satisfying basic needs. Competence, autonomy, and relatedness are the basic needs emphasized in the model under consideration. Yet other basic needs, such as recognition, security, and physiological needs, are also mediators of happiness and well-being. We don't need a nationwide poll or controlled experiment to demonstrate that being unemployed or homeless lowers a feeling of well-being and personal happiness.

Despite the contribution of basic need fulfillment to well-being and happiness, a more intense feeling of well-being and happiness stems from self-concordant goal attainment. The narcissist's feeling of power, self-esteem and excitement produces happiness indirectly via need fulfillment. In addition, attaining these goals generates a positive effect that contributes to well-being and happiness. Goal attainment itself contributes to happiness and feeling successful, and the positive feeling that stems from goal attainment gives an additional boost to a feeling of well-being. Imagine meeting your goal today of solving a complex work-related problem. You will be happy about that, but the shot of adrenaline you received from the sudden problem resolution will further increase your well-being.

In summary, the complex model of the association between narcissism and happiness (including well-being) posits that narcissists adopt a unique set of goals (the search for power, self-esteem, and excitement). These goals are extra powerful because they are self-concordant rather than set by others for the individual. The model also suggests that narcissists perceive themselves to be successful in the pursuit of these goals. In turn, these perceptions of success help the narcissist feel competent, autonomous, and related. Having been successful in pursuing both personal goals and fulfilling their basic needs, the narcissists are legitimately and genuinely happy.

NARCISSISM AND PSYCHOLOGICAL OR MENTAL HEALTH

Another explanation as to why many narcissists are healthy and productive is that they enjoy good psychological, or mental, health. A group of five studies indicated that self-esteem is the major mediating factor responsible for positive psychological health among narcissists.[19] To the extent that narcissists have high self-esteem, they are likely to enjoy good mental health. Narcissists are supposedly addicted to self-esteem, and although it seems contradictory, the addiction consequently elevates psychological health. The high self-esteem helps the narcissist ward off worry and gloom.

All five studies used the Narcissistic Personality Inventory to measure narcissism rather than directly observe the behavior of the study participants. A variety of questionnaires were used to measure various aspects of psychological health. College students were the participants for four of the studies, and married couples from the community were the participants for a fifth study. The findings of the five studies, however, would seem to apply well to the workplace. The conclusions of the studies linking narcissism to good mental health are described next. Several of the conclusions are blended from the studies rather than each conclusion stemming from one study. Each study also found that self-esteem was a key factor in sustaining positive psychological health.[20]

1. Narcissism is inversely related to daily symptoms of loneliness. People who are more narcissistic tend to feel less lonely on a daily basis, and have fewer symptoms of depression.
2. Narcissism is positively related to daily and dispositional well-being. Those people who are more narcissistic feel better on a daily basis and they have fewer symptoms of depression.
3. Couples in which both partners had stronger narcissistic tendencies tended to have a higher sense of well-being. (The researchers noted that the majority of the couples studied did not have children, and that perhaps narcissism creates problems in a marriage only when children are present.)
4. Narcissism is inversely related to daily sadness and anxiety, but positively related to psychological health. People who are more narcissistic tend to feel less sad and anxious in their daily lives, two factors that contribute to their positive psychological health.
5. Narcissism is inversely related to neuroticism (emotional instability). Study participants who were more narcissistic tended to be more emotionally stable.

A general conclusion from the studies was that the findings were consistent with the relatively recent portrait of the high narcissist as a psychologically healthy person. High narcissists might be callous, insensitive, and exploitive but they do tend to enjoy good psychological health. (They might derive satisfaction from feeling superior to others.) The high level of self-esteem enjoyed by narcissists contributes to their mental health. Another possibility is that narcissists with high self-esteem enjoy good psychological health because they do not take criticism and other negative feedback seriously. Instead of experiencing anxiety about being criticized, they blame the criticizer for lacking good judgment, or "not getting it."

GUIDELINES FOR APPLICATION AND PRACTICE

1. Suppose that, based on feedback from others, your own observations, and self-quizzes, you conclude that you are moderately narcissistic. Do not be discouraged. The evidence suggests that a moderate degree of narcissism may facilitate success partially because narcissism is intertwined with self-esteem.

2. Given that self-esteem is so important for success, it is helpful to take steps at any stage in life to continue to develop self-esteem. A starting point in building self-esteem as an adult is to appreciate your strengths. You can sometimes develop an appreciation of your strengths by participating in a group exercise designed for such purposes. A group of about seven people meet to form a support group. All group members first spend about 10 minutes answering the question, "What are my three strongest points, attributes, or skills?" After each group member records his or her three strengths, the person discusses them with the other group members. Each group member then comments on the list. Other group members sometimes add to your list of strengths or reinforce what you have to say. Sometimes you may find disagreement.

3. One of the recommendations for building self-esteem is to minimize settings and interactions that detract from your feelings of competence. However, a problem with avoiding all situations in which you feel you have low competence is that it might prevent you from acquiring needed skills. Also, it boosts your self-confidence and self-esteem to become comfortable in a previously uncomfortable situation.

4. A particularly positive trait of narcissists in the workplace is their enthusiasm. Enthusiasm may have a genetic component, yet it is still possible to seek out the positive elements in situations or people and be mindful of making an enthusiastic comment. If you make the right number of enthusiastic comments, you will develop the image of an enthusiastic person.

5. Should you have the opportunity to form a group that faces the task of developing a creative solution to a problem, it is advisable to include as group members several narcissistic people. A couple of narcissists in the group tend to facilitate creativity, but too many of them are detrimental to group problem solving.

6. An important path to happiness and personal well-being is to attain goals that are important to you personally (self-concordant goals), and at the

same time to maintain high self-esteem. Although this suggestion can take years to implement, a little progress each month can move a person toward well-being.

SUMMARY

A realistic perspective about workplace narcissists is that some of them are healthy and productive despite the occasional chagrin they may cause for others. There is most likely a curvilinear relationship between narcissism and workplace success. A moderate degree of narcissism might be the most effective because the person would have enough self-esteem and extraversion to impress others and have good interpersonal relationships.

Self-esteem plays a major role in the personality of the healthy, productive narcissist. The quest for and maintenance of self-esteem is an important part of the narcissistic personality. The best evidence of the strong need for self-esteem shown by narcissists derives from studies that examine how narcissistic personalities react to self-threatening information. Narcissists tend to react defensively to threats to their self-esteem. The goal of narcissists to feel powerful is probably a manifestation of their goal to feel good about themselves.

Self-esteem comes about from a variety of early-life experiences. People who were encouraged to feel good about themselves and their accomplishments by family members, friends, and teachers are more likely to enjoy high self-esteem. A variety of successes and failures also contribute to the development of self-esteem. Experiences in adult life can also impact self-esteem.

Approaches to enhancing self-esteem include the following: attain legitimate accomplishments; be aware of personal strengths; minimize settings and interactions that detract from your feelings of competence; talk and socialize frequently with people who boost your self-esteem; and model the behavior of people with high self-esteem.

A notable positive characteristic of narcissistic people is their enthusiasm. A study showed that participants who generated more enthusiasm for their pitches were those with high average scores on narcissism. Healthy adult narcissists are observed as having the following characteristics: empathic; engaging; being a leader; self-possessed (not selfish); recognition seeking; determined; confrontational; and wisely fearful.

Narcissism often contributes to creativity. One study hypothesized that narcissists are not necessarily more creative than others, but they think they are, and they are adept at getting others to accept their viewpoint. The study found that narcissists are able to contribute to creative outcomes but not acting alone. It appears that narcissists may be highly effective at generating novel solutions to complex problems when there is another narcissist in the group who competes with them for attention and support of their opinions.

The argument that many narcissists experience well-being is built around a model of goal attainment with three major components. First, narcissists strive to attain goals that are self-concordant. Second, narcissists perceive themselves to be successful in progressing toward their goals. Third, significant progress toward goal attainment enhances their well-being, especially when it fulfills their basic human needs.

Self-esteem plays a key role in the happiness of narcissists because narcissism is linked with positive feelings about the self. Key goals of narcissists include power, self-esteem, and excitement. Narcissists tend to perceive themselves as being successful in most endeavors, leading to a feeling of well-being. Narcissism is not often related to actual performance, yet narcissists maintain the perception that they are powerful, competent, and filled with excitement. Despite the contribution of basic need fulfillment to well-being and happiness, a more intense feeling of well-being and happiness stems from self-concordant goal attainment.

Another explanation as to why narcissists are healthy and productive is that they enjoy good psychological health. A group of five studies indicated that self-esteem is the major mediating factor responsible for positive psychological health among narcissists.

CASE HISTORY OF A WORKPLACE NARCISSIST

The following case history is about a celebrity industrialist whose name is often associated with narcissism.

Donald Trump of the Donald Trump Organization

Donald John Trump, born in 1946, first learned about the construction and real estate business from his father, Frederick C. Trump. His mother, Mary MacLeod Trump, and father sent him to the New York Military Academy at age 13, with the expectation that the discipline at the school would help focus his energy and assertiveness in a positive direction. Trump prospered at the Academy, both socially and academically, and became a star athlete and student leader. Trump began college at Fordham University, then transferred to the Wharton School of Finance at the University of Pennsylvania, graduating in 1968 with a degree in economics.

During 2011, Trump made a serious bid to become the 2012 Republican candidate for US President. He made regular media appearances touting his business successes, popularity, and wisdom as key qualifications for becoming president. He frequently challenged President Barack Obama to show his birth certificate to prove he was born in the United States. When Obama did provide the appropriate (long form) birth certificate from Hawaii, Trump contended that he had provided a great service to the US by prompting Obama to give proof of his US citizenship.

A glimpse at some of Trump's business successes and reactions to him

After graduating from college, Trump began his highly successful career as part of the Trump Organization. Trump moved to Manhattan and built a network of influential people. He soon became involved in large building projects in Manhattan. Eventually, Trump was responsible for building the striking Grand Hyatt in Manhattan by renovating an old building. Opened in 1980, the Grand Hyatt was a pivotal moment in Trump's career because he became New York City's best-known developer, and also the most controversial one.

Trump is considered by many business writers and management specialists to be the most famous businessperson in the US, if not the world. A Gallup Organization poll indicated that fully 98 percent of Americans know who he is. The website *Askmen.com* explained why the editors like him: "Not like him, we *love* him. He is funny, smart, and unlike seemingly every other billionaire in the world, he lives the privileged life that we can only dream of."

Trump is regarded as an enormously skilled developer. Associates describe his excellent knack for spotting and ferreting out waste; a memory like a Zip drive; and a grasp of complex zoning laws that he uses to spot opportunities. Trump is also familiar with technical details of construction, such as the energy efficiency of window glass. He often negotiates with subcontractors himself instead of relying on a purchasing department. He will sometimes use his celebrity status to attain better terms. "Donald Trump has the ability to relate to the doorman, to the guy who's carrying the iron or steel, and make that guy important," said the CEO of a real estate financing firm.

In describing his negotiating advantage, Trump explained, "One of the advantages I have by being a superstar is that when I call people, no matter who they are, they're honored to be my partner. And I've done a great job. When Donald Trump calls, you say 'Oh great!' I get to the top immediately. And if he's not in, he calls me back in five minutes."

In a celebrated example of his power and brazenness, Trump convinced New York City officials to permanently close an exit ramp into Manhattan from the West Side Highway to accommodate his $3-billion construction project. Among the properties of the Trump Organization are Trump Towers, Trump Palaces, Trump Plazas, Trump Hotels, and Trump Golf Clubs. His products include men's suits and a direct marketing organization for miscellaneous merchandise. In the present era the Trump Organization owns more than 18 million square feet of Manhattan real estate. During the years of *The Apprentice*, Trump was one of the world's highest-paid TV stars.

Trump's office is decorated with photos of various celebrities, including Ronald Reagan, John F. Kennedy Jr and himself on the cover of *Time* magazine. A letter from the CEO of Barnes & Noble has been framed. It begins, "Dear Donald… to book sellers you are the Harry Potter of business books."

Trump's self-promotion works. He has created a nationally and internationally known luxury real estate brand. Condos in Trump-branded buildings in New York have historically sold well above the per-square-foot average for other condos. His sale of high-price condos in Chicago at one time raised the average price for comparable units in the entire city.

Trump has invested heavily in golf courses, particularly since 2008. In 2010 he began construction on a $1.15 billion golf course and resort in Scotland. Trump says that placing his name on the courses increases the number of members and the fees he can charge.

Some critics say that Trump has devalued his brand because it appears on so many products, including vodka, health supplements, mattresses, suits, cufflinks, shirts, ties, and the seminars. In 2011, Trump claimed that his brand was hotter than ever, and that the popularity of his brand continues to grow and has helped him get through the recession better than most developers. In his words, "If Trump wasn't doing well, the stars don't come up and kiss my ass."

Anna Wintour, a *Vogue* editor, wrote of Trump, "Donald is in cahoots with those who would portray him as a garish, ego-driven mogul. But anyone who has meaningful dealings with him will have invariably caught a glimpse of his good-natured, kind-hearted side."

Gene Marbach, a group vice president at a public- and investor-relations firm, offers the following comment about the impact of Trump: "Whether you like him or not as a person, he's cultivated a brand name that is probably as large as life as a Procter & Gamble. It's a name with an unbelievably high recognition factor. A kind of luxury, fun times – all of the things that you associated with a brand are communicated through the Trump name."

Trump's personal life also reflects his taste for opulence. He lives in one of the most expensive apartments in New York, a three-story penthouse 40 floors above his office. There is a marble fountain in the living room. Trump has an estate in Rancho Palos Verdes, California that went on the market in 2010 for $12 million, which made it the most expensive listing on the market there. The five-bedroom, nine-bathroom home is located at Trump National Golf Course.

The Trump University offers a program, "The Donald Trump Way to Wealth Seminar," that is offered periodically in many cities. The mailer advertising the program begins as follows:

Dear [First Name of Addressee],

You're no doubt familiar with my real estate ventures, but may not realize how successful I've been in business. I have owned more than 100 companies. Based on my extraordinary experience with the hit TV show, *The Apprentice*, I decided to train and educate America's next wave of business entrepreneurs and real estate moguls.

I want to personally invite you to my Donald Trump Way to Wealth Seminar.

Trump problems

In reflecting on a period of time in the 1990s when his organization was close to bankruptcy, Trump said, "I never went bankrupt, but I was in deep trouble and now my company is much bigger, much stronger than it ever was before. So I don't view myself as having made a comeback. But when I speak, I have thousands of people come listen to speeches on success and everything else. Had I had a simple, smooth life, those crowds wouldn't exist." (Some analysts declare that part of the Trump Organization did go bankrupt. In November 2004, Trump Hotels & Casino Resorts filed for Chapter 11 protection in a federal bankruptcy court in New Jersey. The Trump casinos had also filed for bankruptcy in 1992. Also the casinos named the Trump Plaza, Trump Taj Mahal, and Trump Marina did complete a third round of bankruptcy in 2010, yet the Trump Entertainment Resorts Inc. retained control. US Bankruptcy Judge Judith Wizmur ruled in favor of Trump.)

Trump-licensed condominiums in Tijuana, Mexico, and Tampa and Fort Lauderdale, experienced some problems. Approximately 300 people entered into lawsuits against the Trump Organization, seeking refunds on deposits on those projects that were not completed.

Some of Donald Trump's wisdom
Donald Trump is widely quoted not only for the content of his thoughts, but because he is so well known and controversial. Several of Trump's quotes are as follows:

"A little more moderation would be good. Of course, my life hasn't exactly been one of moderation."

"All of the women on *The Apprentice* flirted with me, consciously or unconsciously. That's to be expected."

"I don't make deals for the money. I've got enough, much more than I'll ever need. I do it to do it."

"I like thinking big. If you're going to be thinking anything, you might as well think big."

"I'm a bit of P.T. Barnum. I make stars out of everyone."

"Every time you walk down the street people are screaming, 'You're fired.'"

Narcissism Analysis

Donald Trump is considered so narcissistic by so many people, that you will often see or hear his name used as standard of comparison for narcissism, just as the Empire State Building has become a standard of comparison for tallness. The statement he makes about himself in reference to his seminars suggests narcissism. Even if a publicist wrote the opener, it was most likely approved by Trump.

Often the references to Trump's narcissistic tendencies are negative. For example, one interviewer complained about how often his interview with Trump was interrupted by Trump taking phone calls.

Despite the negativity about Trump, he has parlayed his narcissism into becoming one of the world's most successful real estate developers and businesspeople. He has leveraged his success in construction and development into other fields such as writing books, merchandising an assortment of products, and establishing a for-profit university. Driven by ambition and self-adoration, Trump became an enormously successful brand before the personal branding movement became popular. Trump is so ostentatiously successful that he has captured millions of fans.

Trump's boastfulness certainly irritates many people, including business writers and researchers. Yet he is able to combine this outward display of narcissism with a human touch that is well liked by his vendors and employees. Trump's linguistic style (which you can hear on television and radio regularly) adds to his likeability for many people. Trump has a tough-guy New Yorker style of speaking that many people find refreshing and natural.

Source: Most of the facts and observations for this case are gathered from the following: Gittlesohn, John and Nadja Brandt (2011), "Trump Test His Brand on the Golf Links," *Bloomberg Business Week*, January 3–9, pp. 40–41; Kelley, Raina (2009), "Generation Me," *Newsweek* (www.newsweek.com), April 18; ; Kimes, Mina (2009), "Will Donald Get Trumped?" *Fortune*, August 31, p. 16; Wood, Gaby (2007), "Donald Trump: the Interview," *The Observer* (www.guardian.co.uk), January 7, 2007; "Trump Estate," *Rochester Democrat and Chronicle: Real Estate and Rental*, November 20, 2010, p. 1; Parmley, Suzette (2010), "What's In a Name? A Lot When the Name is Trump," *Philly.com*, April 15; DeStefano, Joseph N. (2010), "Can Golf Save Trump as Brand Fades on TV, Schools, Condos?" *Philly.com*, December 30; Flora, Carlin (2004), "Big Egos in Business," *Psychology Today* (www.psychologytoday.com), January 13; Roth, Daniel (2004), "The Trophy Life," *Fortune*, April 19, pp. 70–83; Useem, Jerry (2000), "What Does Donald Trump® Really Want?" *Fortune*, April 3, pp. 188–200; "Donald Trump Biography," *Search Biography.com*, www. biography.com (accessed January 18, 2011); Kohlatkar, Sheelah (2011). "I'm Very Serious," *Bloomberg Business Week*, May 2–8, pp. 42–8.

REFERENCES

1. Freud, Sigmund (1957), "On Narcissism." In J. Strachey (Editor), *The Standard Edition of the Complete Works of Sigmund Freud.* vol. 144, pp. 69–102, London: Hogarth Press. Original work published in 1914.
2. Thoresen, Carl J., Jill C. Bradley, Paul D. Bliese, and Joseph D. Thoresen (2004), "The Big Five Personality Traits and Individual Job Performance Growth Trajectories in Maintenance and Transitional Job Stages," *Journal of Applied Psychology*, **89** (4), 835–53.
3. Emmons, R.A. (1984), "Factor Analysis and Construct Validity of the Narcissistic Personality Inventory," *Journal of Personality Assessment*, **48** (3), 291–305.
4. Rose, Paul and W. Keith Campbell (2004), "Greatness Feels Good: A Telic Model of Narcissism and Subjective Well-being." In Serge P. Shohov (ed.), *Advances in Psychology Research*, vol. 31, New York: Hauppauge, pp. 3–23.
5. Rose and Campbell (2004), pp. 291–305.
6. "Better Self-Esteem," available at www.utexas.edu/student/cmhc/booklets/selfesteem/selfest.html (accessed February 1, 2006).
7. Cited in Edwards, Randall (1995), "Is Self-Esteem Really All That Important?" *The APA Monitor*, May, p. 43.
8. David De Cremer *et al.* (2005), "Rewarding Leadership and Fair Procedures as Determinants of Self-Esteem," *Journal of Applied Psychology*, **90** (1), 3–12.
9. Research mentioned in Snyder, E.R. (1998), book review, *Contemporary Psychology*, **31** (July), 482.
10. "Leo Buscaglia," www.selfgrowth.com/experts/leo_buscaglia.html (accessed January 20, 2011).
11. Cited in "Self-Esteem: You'll Need It to Succeed," *Executive Strategies*, September 1993, p. 12.
12. Flora, Carlin (2007), "The Decline and Fall of the Private Self," *Psychology Today*, May/June, pp. 82–7.
13. Eugene Raudsepp (2004), "Strong Self-Esteem Can Help You Advance," *The Wall Street Journal*, www.careerjournal.com, August 10.
14. Goncalo, Jack, Francis J. Flynn, and Sharon H. Kim (2010), "From a Mirage to an Oasis: Narcissism, Perceived Creativity, and Creative Performance," *Personality and Social Psychology Bulletin,* November. Also available in *Articles & Chapters.* Paper 309, http://digitalcommons.ilr.cornell.edu/articles/309, pp. 1–39.
15. Adapted from Behary, Wendy T. (2008), *Disarming the Narcissist: Surviving & Thriving with the Self-Absorbed*, Oakland, CA: New Harbinger Publications, pp. 28–9. The bracketed information is original, and not from Behary.
16. This section of the chapter about creativity and narcissism is based on Goncalo *et al.* (2010).
17. Rose and Campbell (2004), pp. 291–305.
18. Sheldon, K. and A. Elliot (1999), "Goal Striving, Needs Satisfaction, and Longitudinal Well-Being: The Self-Concordance Model," *Journal of Personality and Social Psychology*, **76**, 482–97.
19. Analysis reported in Wilson, Sara (2008), "Branson," *Entrepreneur*, November, p. 62.
20. Sedikides, Constantine, Eric A. Rudlich, Aiden P. Gregg, Madoka Kumashiro, and Caryl Rusbult (2004), "Are Normal Narcissists Psychologically Healthy?: Self-Esteem Matters," *Journal of Personality and Social Psychology*, **87** (3), 400–416.

5.   Narcissism and leadership effectiveness

To better understand narcissism in the workplace it is essential to delve into the potential benefits of narcissism despite the many problems this personality trait and its associated behavior create. An analogy can be drawn to the potential advantages of red wine. The problems associated with drinking too much wine are well known. Yet many studies have emerged suggesting that moderate intake of red wine has many health benefits including warding off cardiac disease, lowering cholesterol levels, and even living longer. Similarly the right amount and type of narcissism can contribute to leadership effectiveness as will be described in this chapter.

The idea that narcissists can be effective in leadership positions was proposed a while back by Manfred F.R. Kets de Vries and Danny Miller. They differentiated among three types of narcissistic leaders: reactive; self-deceptive; and constructive. The authors contended that the reactive narcissist does not listen to advisors or subordinates, whereas the self-deceptive narcissist will try to make a show of appearing interested in or sympathetic to the opinion of subordinates. Leaders who are constructive narcissists will listen more carefully to group members, partly because they know intuitively that listening to others often results in being liked.[1]

Two scholars at the Center for Public Leadership at Harvard University, Seth A. Rosenthal and Todd L. Pittinsky, reason that the prevalence of narcissistic leaders in all sectors of society suggests that there must be some positive aspects to narcissistic leaders. The air of total confidence and dominance so characteristic of narcissism quite often inspires followers. During a crisis, for example, followers might want a narcissistic leader who believes he or she is talented enough to get through the crisis.[2]

To describe how narcissism can enhance leadership effectiveness, in this chapter we explore the strengths of narcissistic leaders, the links between charisma and narcissism, the self-perceptions of narcissistic leaders, and how narcissism can impact organizational performance.

THE STRENGTHS OF NARCISSISTIC LEADERS

People with narcissistic tendencies often have personal strengths that contribute to their leadership effectiveness, as evidenced by the fact that many people holding leadership positions in business, government, and not-for-profit organizations are narcissistic. Personality psychologist Scott Barry Kaufman reports that narcissism and leadership go hand in hand. The fun-loving narcissist often enjoys widespread networking and being dominant in a group, not solely for the purpose of wanting to exploit as many people as possible. The narcissist's real motive is to receive positive reinforcement from many people.[3] In this section we describe some of the empirical evidence and opinion about the strengths of narcissistic leaders.

A Psychoanalytic Perspective on the Strengths of Narcissistic CEOs

As we entered the new millennium, anthropologist and psychoanalyst Michael Maccoby observed that many CEOs were becoming more narcissistic. Among their narcissistic behaviors were hiring their own publicists, writing books about their approach to management, granting spontaneous interviews, and actively promoting their personal philosophies. Among these CEO superstars still active in running companies is Jeff Bezos of Amazon.com. Narcissists can be grandiose egoists who are on a mission to save humanity – even if they can be rude and insensitive to people around them.

Macobby proposed two major reasons that narcissists come the closest to our collective image of great leaders: they formulate great visions for companies, and they have an ability to attract followers, as described next.[4]

Great visions

The ability to formulate effective visions is a major part of strong leadership. Productive narcissists fully comprehend the importance of being visionary because by nature they are people who see the big picture. They tend not to be analyzers who can divide big problems into smaller, manageable problems. Also they tend not be number crunchers. Instead of attempting to extrapolate to understand the future, they prefer to create the future. A narcissist as a high-level leader will see things that never were, and ask why not. After Amazon.com became entrenched as a seller of books and music, founder Jeff Bezos reformulated his vision into a website that, by linking to other vendors, could sell almost any product to online purchasers.

Maccoby believes that narcissists have opportunities in the modern era they would not have had in the past. They want to leave behind a legacy – and the opportunities are ripe, such as in helping to decrease pollution of the atmosphere, and increasing literacy, numeracy, and graduation rates among children.[5]

Recent research supports the idea that the personality trait of narcissism contributes to the formation of bold visions.[6] Data for the study were collected from a sample of 55 senior business and/or community leaders mostly in the US. The sample was comprised exclusively of individuals with extensive experience in a variety of disciplines and organizational settings. Narcissism was measured by the Narcissistic Personality Inventory, and charisma was measured through a variety of assessments from workers who had first-hand knowledge of the leaders. Visions were measured through simulated interviews of a newspaper reporter questioning the executives about their visions. The expressed vision statements were coded on a continuum of 1 to 3, with 1 = *nonsocialized (personalized) vision*, and 3 = *socialized vision*.

Vision statements receiving a score of 1 tended to focus on dominance, exploiting others, beating the competition, and financial results. These personalized visions usually failed to acknowledge the roles of the team, employees, or other stakeholders. An example of this type of personalized vision is: "My vision is to be the number one supplier of essential office products and services, regardless of what that product line is within the markets that I serve."

In contrast, vision statements rated a 3 (socialized vision) were focused on the collective "we," empowerment, values, the team's contribution to future success, positive outcomes for all stakeholders, and positive contributions to the community and the environment. An excerpt from a socialized vision is "We will operate within an umbrella of a vibrant and productive environment that promotes the best possible working conditions for our workforce and to give them the best possible development opportunities."

The boldness of the expressed vision statements was measured on a scale of 1 (*nonbold*) to 3 (*bold*). Vision statements that scored 1 tended to focus on passive, incremental change, and a desire to maintain the status quo. An excerpt from a vision rated 1 for boldness was "We are trying to focus on old-fashioned American values." In contrast, vision statements that were rated a 3 (bold vision) were focused on passion, daring, risk taking, and a lack of hesitancy. An excerpt from a bold vision is "We want to make a giant impact that creates a revolution in business."

A major result of the study was that a significant negative relationship was found between leader narcissism and socialized vision – narcissistic leaders tend to have personalized visions. Furthermore, narcissistic leaders tended to have bolder visions than less narcissistic leaders. (A study reported below supports the link between narcissism and boldness in formulating strategy.)

Large numbers of followers
A *follower* might be technically defined as a subordinate in a hierarchy. With this definition even a bland, ineffective CEO would still have a large number of followers. A follower in a more psychological sense is a person who believes in

the leader and his or her ideas, and gladly expends effort to help accomplish the leader's goals. Narcissistic leaders are especially gifted in attracting followers. The mechanism for attracting these followers is effective use of language. Narcissists believe that words motivate people and that inspiring speeches can get them to move in a productive direction. Narcissistic leaders are often quite adept at giving speeches, as well as making presentations during a meeting. The personal magnetism of a narcissistic leader helps stir enthusiasm among his or her audience. (Later in the chapter we examine the link between charisma and narcissism.)

The charismatic gift of being able to attract followers involves reciprocity. Although not always obvious, narcissistic leader are dependent on their followers for affirmation and adulation. A narcissist who does not receive fresh supplies of affirmation, adulation, recognition, and compliments is strongly disappointed. The adulation that stems from an effective speech or presentation during a meeting bolsters the self-confidence and conviction of the speaker. If no one responds, the narcissist may become insecure and perhaps angry. During a presentation a narcissistic leader will often make limited use of PowerPoint slides because he or she wants more of the focus on the leader, not the glitz of the computer graphics.

As the narcissistic leader accumulates people who respond positively to his or her thinking, he or she becomes more spontaneous and self-assured. The accompanying energy and confidence further inspire followers.

Narcissism as a Facilitator of Being Promoted

An analysis by Christian J. Resick, a management professor, and his colleagues at the Drexel University suggests that certain qualities of a narcissistic individual often help him or her to be promoted through the management ranks or hired into a high-level leadership position. These qualities focus on presenting a positive, assertive image of the self. The implication is not that all top-level leaders exhibit these tendencies, but that in some leadership situations these tendencies are an advantage, such as being the leader of a professional sports organization.

The leaders studied by Resick were 75 CEOs of Major League Baseball Organizations over a 100-year period. An analysis of the narcissistic tendencies and leadership effectiveness of the subjects was done through carefully examining written biographical information about the baseball team owners. For example, a CEO who appeared to be arrogant and self-centered would receive a high narcissism score. Among these behaviors and traits that facilitate promotion are forming grandiose ideas and exhibiting tendencies to be boastful, aggressive, and elitist.[7]

The focus on positive qualities does not imply that narcissistic characteristics do not often lead to dysfunctional leadership behavior, as will be described in Chapter 6. Part of the problem is that narcissistic leaders may spend significant time and energy enhancing their public image instead of developing subordinates, achieving operational effectiveness, or improving relationships with customers.

A Study of Narcissism, Personality Traits, and Leadership Ratings

Three management professors at the University of Florida, Timothy A, Judge, Jeffery A. LePine, and Bruce L. Rich, conducted a study that provides some insight into how narcissism might contribute to some aspects of leadership effectiveness.[8] The part of this study that relates to leadership effectiveness is reported here. The major part of the study, along with a companion study, that relates to negative leadership outcomes is reported in Chapter 6 about narcissism and dysfunctional leadership. Our major focus for now is how narcissism relates to ratings of leadership.

Relationship of narcissism to self vs. other ratings

In recognition of the link between narcissism and self-enhancement, a worthwhile research question is whether narcissists have enhanced views of their abilities and competence in comparison to those who score lower on the trait. The workplace is a natural environment for studying self-enhancement because work environments are so feedback focused.

Previous research had suggested that people with a strong narcissistic tendency have an inflated view of their traits that reflect an agentic orientation, with cognitive skills being one example. (*Agentic* refers to the view that people are proactive, self-reflecting, and self-regulating, not just reactive organisms who are shaped by environmental forces and inner impulses.) The narcissist reflects, "I am capable. I can do it." In contrast, narcissists do not have an inflated view of their traits reflecting a *communal* orientation, such as caring for others. Narcissists typically see themselves as superior to others which helps them to build the positive self-mage they crave.

The authors of the study wanted to understand how the self-enhancement tendencies of narcissists influence their self-ratings of leadership effectiveness as well as how others rate them. For example, does being narcissistic facilitate getting positive leadership ratings from others? While studying how narcissism might affect leadership, it is also useful to investigate its relationship to performance. In addition to the general idea of inspiring workers, leaders have many tasks to perform, such as budgeting and conducting performance evaluations. The three study hypotheses most relevant to the present discussion are as follows:

1. Narcissism will be positively related to self-ratings of leadership.
2. Narcissism will be positively related to self-ratings of contextual performance. (*Contextual performance* refers to those behaviors that contribute to the organization by fostering a positive social and psychological climate or atmosphere.)
3. Narcissism will be positively related to self-ratings of task performance. (*Task performance* includes those behaviors that are generally perceived to be part of the job and directly contribute to the organization's technical core.)

The study also looked at how narcissism might be related to the Big Five personality traits that previous research has shown to have some relationship with both narcissism and leadership. In review, the Big Five traits are neuroticism, extraversion, openness to experience (much like intellectual curiosity), agreeableness, and conscientiousness. The participants in the study were master's degree candidates in the Master of Business Administration (MBA), or the Master of Science in Management (MSM) program. Participants were administered a personality test that measured the Big Five traits, along with the Narcissistic Personality Inventory. Participants also self-reported their leadership behaviors. The leadership behaviors of participants were also rated by 3–6 other raters with whom they worked most closely – supervisors, coworkers, or fellow students with whom they had worked on team projects. Leadership was measured with the Leadership Practices Inventory that contains the five subscales (challenging, inspiring, enabling, modeling, and encouraging).

As indicated by the results of the study as reported in Exhibit 5.1, the researchers were able to support their hypotheses. Study participants with high

Exhibit 5.1   Relationship of narcissism to several personality traits and leadership

Trait	Correlation with narcissism	Strength of relationship
1. Neuroticism	0.11	Not significant
2. Extraversion	0.36	Moderately positive
3. Openness to experience	−0.01	Not significant
4. Agreeableness	−0.24	Moderately negative
5. Conscientiousness	−0.10	Not significant
6. Leadership-self ratings	0.35	Moderately positive
7. Leadership-ratings by peers	0.20	Weakly positive

Source: Based on data presented in Timothy A. Judge, Jeffery A. LePine, and Bruce L. Rich (2006), "Loving Yourself Abundantly: Relationship of the Narcissistic Personality to Self- and Other Perceptions of Workplace Deviance, Leadership, and Task and Contextual Performance," *Journal of Applied Psychology*, **91** (4), 767.

scores on narcissism tended to rate their own leadership as fairly strong (second line from bottom). A slight positive relationship was found between tendencies toward narcissism and leadership as rated by others. Leadership as rated by others included both contextual and task performance. Another notable finding shown in Exhibit 5.1 is that extraversion is the personality trait with the strongest relationship to narcissism. (You need a little extraversion to brag about yourself to others!) As also suggested by previous research, the traits of narcissism and agreeableness are negatively related.

Egotism and Self-Esteem

Two other notable characteristics of narcissists that facilitate their success as leaders are egotism and high self-esteem. We have already mentioned extensively how self-esteem is a key component of narcissism. In this section we look at some research documenting its contribution to leadership effectiveness as perceived by peers.

The setting for the study in question was the military officer training program at the National Defense College in Helsinki, Finland. The participants were 199 male cadets, all of whom completed a variety of personality measures including the Big Five factors, and a measure of impression management (IM). Unlike most studies of narcissism, the trait was not measured directly. Instead, traits associated with narcissism, such as egotism, were measured. The impression management scale measures the conscious act of attempting to act in a socially desirable manner. Respondents with high scores on the IM scale tend to engage deliberately in impression management intended to convey a positive image to others.[9]

Each cadet in the study received a peer rating questionnaire that instructed him to rate each of his platoon members on the following five items, including the brief definitions: (a) leadership ("is a natural leader"); (b) social popularity ("is a person with whom you would like to spend time"); (c) benevolence ("is helpful, friendly, and trustworthy"); (d) aggression ("angers easily and is destructive to his surroundings"); (e) honesty ("tells the truth at all costs"). Cadets were asked to indicate their peer ratings by making a notation on a 100 millimeter line. The midpoint of the scale (50) was labeled with the verbal anchor, "Average for the group." The left side of the scale was labeled "Below the group average," and the right side of the scale was labeled "Above the group average."

The results showed that the cadets who received the highest rating of perceived leadership from their peers were those who had a certain personality profile. (Perceived leadership is often referred to as *emergent* leadership because the person does not hold a formal leadership position, such as being the captain of a military unit.) The profile included having a strong sense of ego and a high level of self-esteem, fitting into the stereotype of a classic narcissist. A key point of the study was that these characteristics only led to high leadership evaluations if they were present in the absence of manipulative behaviors and impression management tendencies.

The researchers concluded that a strong sense of competency and self-worth might have projected an aura of leadership ability to fellow cadets. But this image of being a leader was undermined if there was a perception that the person was trying to take advantage of others and was consciously managing the impression that he attempted to convey publicly. Another conclusion reached was that narcissism that reflects a strong ego and high self-esteem is usually a sign of good psychological health. As a result, these aspects of narcissism are positively correlated with ratings of emerging leadership. In contrast, narcissism that includes manipulation and impression management tendencies represents a dark side to personality which could lower the perception of leadership effectiveness.

THE LINK BETWEEN CHARISMA AND NARCISSISM

Charismatic leadership and narcissism are linked because many narcissists have an element of charisma in their personality. Many narcissistic leaders have an element of charisma, and many charismatic leaders have an element of narcissism – even if charisma and narcissism are far from synonymous. Here we approach the link between charisma and narcissism by first examining the meaning of charisma, then looking at the vision component of charisma, followed by an analysis of CEO language that reflects charisma and narcissism.

The Meaning of Charisma

The term charisma is so widely used that it has many meanings. In general use, the term *charismatic* means to have a charming and colorful personality, such as shown by many celebrities in sports and popular culture. As defined here, *charisma* is a special quality of leaders whose purposes, powers, and extraordinary determination differentiate them from others.[10] The narcissistic leader is likely to be charming except when engaging in excessive self-puffery and blaming others for mistakes.

Charisma is a positive and compelling quality that makes many others want to be led by that person. Not everybody will respond to a person's charisma, but many will. Donald Trump is a sterling example. Lots of people find the Donald to be a compelling individual and want to work for him or with him. Trump receives untold thousands of unsolicited e-mails, social networking messages, and letters from people who offer to partner with him in a business deal. (Money adds to charisma.) Yet some people are less attracted to Trump because they perceive him to be arrogant and overbearing.

To personalize the meaning of charisma, go through the charisma checklist presented in Exhibit 5.2. If you can respond to the checklist with a reasonable degree of objectivity, the checklist should enhance your understanding of how you might or might not be perceived as charismatic.

Exhibit 5.2 The charisma checklist

Item	Statement related to charisma	Mostly true	Mostly false
1.	I have set visions for my group, organization, or club.		
2.	People often describe me as boring.		
3.	I often use metaphors in my conversations with work associates or fellow students.		
4.	I often use analogies in my conversations with work associates or fellow students.		
5.	Relatively few people trust me.		
6.	I'm known as a high-energy person.		
7	Most work days, I am fatigued much of the day.		
8.	People often say I look tired.		
9.	I have received a lot of compliments about my warm smile.		
10.	I typically speak in a monotone.		
11.	I am effective at expressing my feelings to others.		
12.	I am emotionally expressive.		
13.	Other people rarely know what I am feeling		
14.	I tell other people at work true stories to get them interested in what I am talking about.		
15.	I tend to avoid telling stories to make a point. Instead, I am much more direct.		
16.	I am candid without being tactless.		
17.	When I need help I am more likely to say to a coworker "Are you busy?" rather than "Can you help me with a problem right now?"		
18.	I like to make other people feel that they are important.		
19.	I dislike feeding the egos of other people by attempting to make them feel important.		
20.	I stand up straight both while walking and at meetings. (Or, I sit up straight in my wheelchair.)		

Item	Statement related to charisma	Mostly true	Mostly false
21.	I shake hands firmly but not to the point of bringing pain to the person I am greeting.		
22.	I am a risk taker in terms of making suggestions on the job.		
23.	I prefer to avoid making a suggestion that has even a slight chance of failing.		
24.	People have told me that I am charismatic.		
25.	Taking this quiz makes me feel uncomfortable.		

Scoring and interpretation

Give yourself a plus one for each item you answered in the direction of being charismatic, as follows:

1. Mostly true	6. Mostly true	11. Mostly true	16. Mostly true	21. Mostly true
2. Mostly false	7. Mostly false	12. Mostly true	17. Mostly false	22. Mostly true
3. Mostly true	8. Mostly false	13. Mostly false	18. Mostly true	23. Mostly false
4. Mostly true	9. Mostly true	14. Mostly true	19. Mostly false	24. Mostly true
5. Mostly false	10. Mostly false	15. Mostly false	20. Mostly true	25. Mostly false

20–25: If you responded in the charismatic direction to 20 or more of the above statements, and your answers reflect reality, most people probably perceive you to be charismatic.

6–19: If you responded to between 6 and 19 of the statements in the charismatic direction, approximately and equal number of people perceive you to be charismatic or non-charismatic.

0–5: Very few people most likely perceive you to be charismatic.

Another recommended approach to this checklist is to have two people who have observed you in many situations answer the checklist for you. Compare the score you receive from their responses to the score you attained on your own.

The Vision Component of Charismatic and Narcissistic Leadership

A major buzzword in leadership and management is *vision*, the ability to imagine different and better future conditions and ways to achieve them. A vision is a lofty, long-term goal. An effective leader is supposed to have a vision, whereas an ineffective leader either lacks a vision or has an unclear one. Being a visionary is far from an ordinary task, and recent research in neuroscience suggests that visionary leaders use their brain differently than others.

Studies conducted at Arizona State University by Pierre Balthazard required participants to think about the future. Brain activity was measured through EEG technology. A key finding was that levels of brain activity differed significantly between those participants considered visionaries versus non-visionaries. Classifying a business, academic, or political leader as "visionary" was based on interview observations. Visionaries showed much higher levels of brain activity in the areas of the brain associated with visual processing and the organization of information. For example, visionaries showed higher activity in the occipital lobe that is associated with visual processing and procedural memory.[11]

Creating a vision is one of the major tasks of top management, yet quite often vision statements fail to inspire constituents. According to leadership expert Jim Collins, a vision statement is likely to be more inspirational when it combines three elements:

1. a reason for being beyond making money;
2. timeless, unchanging core values;
3. ambitious but achievable goals.[12]

Here are several examples of vision statements, all of which are supposed to inspire large number of company employees:

- *Google:* To make nearly all information accessible to everyone all the time.
- *Microsoft Corporation:* To enable people throughout the word to realize their potential.
- *Avon:* To be the company that best understands and satisfies the product, service and self-fulfillment needs of women – globally.
- *Estée Lauder Companies:* Bringing the best to everyone we touch.
- *Caterpillar:* Be the global leader in customer value.
- *Ken Blanchard Companies:* To be the number one advocate in the world for human worth in organizations.
- *Kraft Foods:* Helping People Around the World Eat and Live Better.

   Our vision creates the essence of who we are. Everything we do flows from our vision. We just don't happen to be a business that sells food – it's what we're about. Our vision is about meeting consumer's needs and making an easier, healthier, more enjoyable part of life.

   Our vision tells the world – our employees, customers, consumers and the communities where we make and sell our products – what we care about. It captures the importance of health and wellness, but it also embodies all the ways we can eat and live better, such as the enjoyment of a dessert, the conveniences of a microwave meal, the safety and value of our products, and the services and solutions we provide.

So how do these examples of visions relate to narcissism? Vision formulation is an essential component of behaving charismatically, especially for leaders. At the same time a healthy degree of narcissism helps the leader formulate a vision. The example of the Google vision is an extreme example of narcissism by the Google founders as well as the organization itself. How could one website give you nearly all the information in the world? Among the types of information you cannot find on Google would be stories in your local newspaper, articles published in many professional articles, and the profit and loss statement of a neighborhood restaurant. The statement "nearly all information" is a wild, narcissistic boast.

The Microsoft vision also has a preposterous narcissistic tinge. You need to do more than use Microsoft software or play Microsoft video games to be enabled to reach your potential. How about learning math? How about doing physical exercise? How about having a nice family and romantic life? How about loving a pet animal?

Another example, of narcissistic, exaggerated thinking is the vision of Caterpillar: "To be the leader in customer value." Indeed, Caterpillar has been a great company and provides equipment the world needs to construct buildings and roads. The vision of Caterpillar, however, is not limited to its field or even several fields. It includes every type of company. Someone said that visions and hallucinations are quite close, and he or she might be right.

At their best, narcissistic leaders are visionary. According to Maccoby, the narcissistic leader thinks with boldness, creativity, a love of freedom, a willingness to get past conventional thinking. The productive narcissistic leader also invests passionate energy into his or her thinking, such as the entrepreneur who thinks his or her product or service will revolutionize the industry.[13]

The Language of Charismatic and Narcissistic Leadership

Charisma is reflected in part in a leader's language. Accounting professors Joel Amernic and Russell J. Craig analyzed CEO-speak to gain insight into their narcissistic tendencies, as well as other aspects of their language. A major point they make is that many companies are led successfully by CEOs who exhibit narcissist-like language and actions. The same leaders are often charismatic.

According to their analysis, the narcissistic CEO is likely to be more constructive when economic conditions are within the bounds of his or her experience. However, when economic conditions become unfavorable, organizational decline seems likely to be accelerated by a CEO with extreme narcissistic tendencies. He or she may be more likely to minimize the problems associated with the company's deteriorating financial position, and to shun remediation strategies. Equally bad, the narcissistic CEO might live in a delusional state about the company's financial strength.

When expressed in the extreme, narcissistic-like language is dysfunctional because it glosses over real problems. For example, a CEO might speak about how warmly she was greeted and entertained when visiting a large overseas customer, but fail to mention that the customer is actively searching for a lower-priced supplier.

The following four signs in CEO-speak are indicative of narcissism. If carried to the extreme, all of them are dysfunctional because they distort reality. However, in the right doses, this type of narcissistic speech can add to charisma and be inspirational.

1. *Hyperbole.* A narcissistic CEO may use hyperbole to portray the company (and by inference himself or herself) as special, dynamic, growing rapidly, and invincible. Carried to extreme this type of hyperbole stretches credibility. Yet, in limited doses, hyperbole can inspire employees because they like the idea of working for a winning organization.
2. *Self-styling as an archetypal company.* A narcissistic CEO will use language to portray the company (and by inference himself or herself) as a success story to be followed, and a model for emulation. Proud CEOs can be inspirational, yet they have to be on guard that the hype does not depart too far from reality, such as suggesting that a small enterprise software firm will overtake Oracle Corp. within five years.
3. *Language of war, sport, and extremism.* The blatant self-touting of "conquering," "dominating," and "establishing a record," is sometimes a characteristic of charismatic and narcissistic speech. A phrase such as "We have conquered the enemy" symbolically places the CEO in the position of battlefield commander. The functional narcissist is more likely to say "We have conquered the competition." Sports analogies are popular in business, and they can be inspiring if not used repeatedly. One phrase that seems to inspire people is "business is a team sport." Many people can identify with the idea of cooperating with coworkers as if they were members of the same athletic team.
4. *Excessive self-attribution.* The highly narcissistic CEO will extensively use self-serving attributions in his or her speech. When profits are down, the narcissistic CEO will usually attribute the problem to the economy including the idea that difficulties in obtaining credit have discouraged customers. When profits are up, the narcissistic CEO is likely to attribute the good news to his or her excellent management and leadership. Self-attributions contribute to constructive leadership when they suggest pride in taking some credit for having moved the organization in the right direction. Yet, used too frequently, self-serving attributions make it appear that the CEO is attempting to rationalize away setbacks.[14]

An implication of the perspective on CEO-speak just presented is that there is often a fine line between narcissistic behavior that contributes to leadership effectiveness and behavior that represents dysfunctional leadership.

SELF-PERCEPTIONS OF NARCISSISTIC LEADERS

By definition, narcissistic leaders have positive self-perceptions. These positive self-perceptions can contribute to leadership effectiveness to the extent that they contribute to high self-esteem and high self-confidence. Should the self-perceptions become too grandiose, they can become dysfunctional because the leader will often deny criticisms and ignore problems. Here we report on research findings that provide insight into self-perceptions of narcissistic leaders that contribute to leadership effectiveness, or at least do not create problems.

Management consultant Benjamin Dattner studied how the trait of narcissism among leaders influenced self-perceptions of fairness and fairness as perceived by others. A major issue explored was the extent to which narcissism influenced how fair leaders think they are in dealing with subordinates. The study also investigated the impact of narcissism on the accuracy of self-perceptions of how the leader is viewed by others.[15]

The study participants were 92 Executive MBA students throughout the US, with all of them being working adults in professional and managerial positions. Each participant was administered both the Narcissistic Personality Inventory and the narcissism items from the California Psychological Inventory, and had at least three staff members rate them on fairness. The concept of *fairness* was divided into nine categories: (1) consistency; (2) decision making; (3) empathy; (4) equality; (5) relative fairness in comparison to other managers; (6) support-iveness; (7) transactional fairness; (8) treatment of others; and (9) voice (open to advice and feedback from staff). Among the major findings were as follows:

1. The mean self-rating for fairness was higher than fairness as perceived by others. (This fits the observation that managers tend to think they are fairer than they really are, whether or not they are narcissistic.)
2. More narcissistic managers rated themselves as more fair to a slight extent. (At least in this study, narcissistic managers were barely more unrealistic than other managers about their degree of fairness.)
3. More narcissistic managers were not rated as less fair by their staff. (No significant relationships were found between the composite narcissism score and any of the nine fairness items. So, at least in this study, narcissistic managers were not perceived to be unfair.)
4. The discrepancies between self and staff ratings of fairness were about the same for more narcissistic and less narcissistic managers.

An interpretation of this study linked to the subject of the positive aspects of leaders with narcissistic tendencies is that narcissistic leaders are likely to be as fair as those who are less narcissistic. Also, managers with narcissistic tendencies are not more likely to have inflated perceptions of their fairness than managers who are less narcissistic. Perhaps the more narcissistic managers in this study were healthy narcissists who did not go overboard on how fair they perceived themselves to be. A more remote interpretation of this study is that, for managers, being a narcissist is not a disadvantage with respect to self-perceptions of fairness, as well as perceptions by others.

NARCISSISM, STRATEGY, PERFORMANCE, AND CRISIS MANAGEMENT

Another way of understanding the potential link between narcissism and leadership effectiveness is to examine some research and opinion about how a leader being narcissistic might have an impact on certain key outcomes. Three illustrative outcomes examined here are strategy, organizational performance, and the management of a crisis.

Strategy and Performance

Management professors Arjijit Chatterjee and Donald C. Hambrick investigated how the narcissism of CEOs could be used as a variable to explain company strategy and performance.[16] You will recall from Chapter 2 that narcissism in this study was measured through five unobtrusive indicators, such as how frequently the executive used the word "I" or "me" in company reports, and the frequency of his or her photo in the company annual report.

As background to their study, the researchers pointed out that the personality of executives can influence organizational outcomes. For example, John Chambers, CEO of Cisco Systems, apparently has high but prudent risk-taking tendencies. Therefore he has spearheaded Cisco toward a long series of acquisitions of other companies. The acquisition strategy worked well for many years until Cisco became too diversified and complicated, particularly in the area of consumer products.

Another background factor of relevance is that narcissism may help the CEO to have enough self-esteem to advance successfully and feel up to the job of taking on so much responsibility. Two components of narcissism that most likely are related to strategy and performance are (a) a belief in one's superior abilities, and (b) an intense, continuous need for affirmation.

The narcissistic executive's elevated self-image will result in high optimism and confidence about positive outcomes, shifting estimates of payoffs for all alternatives in a positive direction. Calvin Klein might therefore be optimistic about putting the Calvin Klein label on a wide variety of products. Also, a narcissistic executive is likely to pursue alternatives that have the potential for the greatest *narcissistic supply*, or potential for attention. For example, a narcissistic executive might opt for purchasing the naming rights to an athletic stadium rather than purchasing newspaper ads. The study hypotheses were as follows:

- *Hypothesis 1:* The greater the narcissistic tendencies of a CEO, the greater the dynamism of the company's strategy. (Through new strategic initiatives, or taking new directions, narcissistic executives can engage in exhibitionism that will capture an attentive audience.)
- *Hypothesis 2:* The greater the narcissistic tendencies of a CEO, the greater the number and size of acquisitions made by the company. (A bold acquisition can capture a lot of attention.)
- *Hypothesis 3:* The greater the narcissistic tendencies of a CEO, the more extreme the company's performance. (The grandiose and frequently shifting strategic actions taken by the narcissistic CEO will cause extreme performance.)
- *Hypothesis 4:* The greater the narcissistic tendencies of a CEO, the greater the fluctuation in the company's performance. (Following from hypothesis 3, grandiose and frequently shifting strategic actions may lead to more variability in performance even if net performance is not affected.)

The performance was studied of 111 CEOs in the computer and software industry, with their narcissistic tendencies being measured by unobtrusive observation of their behavior. All the CEOs studied have four or more years of experience with their firm. Two measures of *strategic dynamism* were used. One measure was changes in key resource allocation indicators – the reasoning behind this is that change in allocating resources is a strong indicator of changes in strategy. The four resource allocation indicators were: (1) advertising intensity; (2) research and development intensity; (3) selling, general and administrative expenses in relation to sales; and (4) financial leverage expressed by debt in relation to equity. The second indicator of strategic dynamism measure was the extent to which a firm changes its portfolio of businesses from year to year. Making an acquisition is a major method of changing a portfolio, as is selling an acquired company. The size of the acquisition was also taken into consideration.

Performance extremeness was measured in two ways: (1) total shareholder returns; and (2) return on assets. Both of these measures are widely used indicators of company operations. *Performance fluctuation* was also calculated using total shareholder returns and return on assets.

The study found substantial support for the hypotheses. Strategic dynamism in terms of changes in the deployment of resources was related to the extent of CEO narcissism. Narcissism was positively related to strategic grandiosity, as indicated by the number and size of acquisitions. Narcissism was also found to be positively associated with extreme performance, both in terms of return on investment and total shareholder performance. Furthermore, narcissism was also related to the return on asset measure of performance fluctuation.

The researchers concluded that CEO narcissism, as measured early in the CEO's tenure, was predictive of three company outcomes a few years later. The outcomes were strategic dynamism, strategic grandiosity (as indicated by number and size of acquisitions), and fluctuation of performance. A key interpretation of the findings was that less narcissistic CEOs may be inclined to pursue incremental strategies that involve refining and elaborating on the status quo. In contrast, more narcissistic CEOs gravitate to bold and highly visible choices. For example, a narcissistic CEO of a company that manufactured traditional vehicles might opt to acquire a company that manufactured high-performance sports cars. Narcissism could therefore be conceived as an ingredient that stimulates distinctive, extreme managerial actions.

In short, the Chatterjee and Hambrick study demonstrated that CEO narcissism is related to extreme and irregular performance. Narcissistic CEOs may generate bigger wins and losses than their less narcissistic counterparts. However, an additional analysis focused on return on assets and total stockholder return gets to the punchline of the study. It was found that narcissistic CEOs do not generate statistically better or worse performance. Narcissistic CEOs therefore take stockholders and other observers for a wilder ride, even if they do not deliver better or worse performance than their less narcissistic counterparts.

Crisis Management

Organizations face crises regularly, such as product recalls, weather-related catastrophes, dire financial problems, and criminal charges levied against company executives. Granville King III, a professor of organizational communications at Indiana University Southeast, has observed that narcissistic managers often have difficulty in leading an organization successfully through a crisis. Narcissists prefer to involve themselves in tasks that satisfy their ego concerns, and at the same time have a positive experience while doing those tasks. Yet with respect to some aspects of a crisis, a narcissistic leader might perform well. Narcissists are more likely to have a positive experience in completing a task when it gives them the opportunity to display their ability, and demonstrate their superiority over others.[17]

The narcissistic leader is most likely to rise to the occasion and help resolve a major crisis when such actions will be highly visible, and will lead to positive feedback. King observes that, during a crisis, a narcissistic leader may be more disposed to control and eliminate a crisis when his or her ability is perceived as exceptional by others inside and outside the organization. In the case history presented at the end of the chapter, John Thain, Merrill Lynch CEO at the time – a person with strong narcissistic tendencies – rescued the brokerage firm by facilitating its sale to Bank of America. His act was heroic and highly visible, even though his heroism was short lived.

One of the leadership attributes associated with effective crisis management is to display optimism.[18] Pessimists abound in every crisis, so an optimistic leader can help energize group members to overcome the bad times. Narcissists often put on a grand display of optimism so they are well suited to this role. The effective crisis leader draws action plans that give people hope for a better future. Barbara Baker Clark contends that the role of a leader during a crisis is to encourage hopefulness. She states:

> I'm not saying that you have to plaster a stupid grin on your face even if the bottom line is tanking or people are dying in battle. I am saying don't wallow in pessimism. Believe it or not, it matters to your employees that you remain reasonably optimistic. It will reduce anxiety and keep everybody motivated. That's the power of leadership.[19]

GUIDELINES FOR APPLICATION AND PRACTICE

1. Although being an extreme narcissist can often be a career retardant, integrating some aspects of narcissism into your personal behavior can facilitate career acceleration. Displaying high levels of self-esteem is a career asset. Moderate doses of boastfulness and aggressiveness might also be helpful.

2. Behaving narcissistically is most likely to help your career if it is not combined with attempts to manipulate or exploit others and create a false, positive impression. However, honest attempts at impression management, such as being courteous, polite, and speaking well, will be a career asset in a wide variety of positions.

3. A successful narcissist usually has a reasonable amount of charisma. Although charisma is a part of personality that develops over a long period of time, there are actions to take that can help a person appear more charismatic. Consider the following:[20]

   - Communicate a vision.
   - Make frequent use of metaphors and analogies. To inspire people, the charismatic leader uses colorful language and exciting metaphors and analogies.
   - Inspire trust and confidence. Make your deeds consistent with your promises.
   - Be highly energetic and goal oriented. Impress others with your energy and resourcefulness.

- Be emotionally expressive and warm. A key characteristic of charismatic leaders is the ability to express feelings openly.
- Make ample use of true stories. An excellent way of building rapport is to tell stories that deliver a message. (But avoid the narcissistic tendencies to make all the stories about yourself.)
- Be candid. Practice saying directly what you want rather than being indirect and evasive.
- Make everybody you meet feel that he or she is quite important. Here is an opportunity to appeal to the narcissism in others!
- Stand up straight and use other nonverbal signals of self-confidence, such as shaking hands firmly without creating pain.
- Be willing to take risks. Charismatic leaders are typically risk takers, and taking risks adds to their charisma.

4. Although many vision statements appear as if they could be formulated in 15 minutes, managers invest considerable time in their preparation and often use many sources of data. To create a vision, obtain as much information from as many of the following sources as necessary:[21]

- your own intuition about developments in your field, the market you serve, demographic trends in your region, and the preferences of your constituents – think through what are the top industry standards;
- the work of futurists (specialists in making predictions about the future) as it relates to your type of work;
- a group discussion of what it takes to delight the people your group serves – analyze carefully what your customers and organization need the most;
- annual reports, management books, and business magazines to uncover the type of vision statements formulated by others;
- group members and friends – speak to them individually and collectively to learn of their hopes and dreams for the future;
- for a vision for an organizational unit, study the organization's vision – you might get some ideas for matching your unit's vision with that of the organization.

SUMMARY

It has long been known that narcissists can be effective in leadership positions, as reflected in three types of narcissistic leaders: reactive; self-deceptive; and constructive. Also, the prevalence of narcissistic leaders in all sectors of society suggests that there must be some positive aspects to narcissistic leaders.

People with narcissistic tendencies often have personal strengths that contribute to their leadership effectiveness. Macobby proposed two major reasons that narcissists come the closest to our collective image of great leaders: they formulate great visions for companies; and they have an ability to attract followers. A study with high-level leaders showed that there was a significant negative relationship between leader narcissism and socialized vision – narcissistic leaders tend to have personalized visions.

Wanting to create a future helps with vision formulation, and followers are attracted through effective use of language. Narcissistic leaders are dependent on their followers for affirmation and adulation.

Certain qualities of a narcissistic individual help him or her be promoted through the management ranks or hired into a high-level leadership position. These qualities would include forming grandiose ideas and exhibiting tendencies of boastfulness, aggressiveness, and elitism.

People with narcissistic tendencies have an inflated view of their traits that reflect an agentic orientation, with cognitive skills being one example. In contrast, narcissists do not have an inflated view of their traits reflecting a communal orientation, such as caring for others. A study of narcissism and self-ratings of leadership found that narcissism is positively related to self-ratings of leadership, contextual performance, and task performance. The same study found that extraversion was the personality trait with the strongest relationship to narcissism.

Two other notable characteristics of narcissists that facilitate their success as leaders are egotism and self-esteem. A study showed that military cadets who received the highest rating of perceived (or emergent) leadership from their peers were those who had a certain personality profile. The profile included having a strong sense of ego and a high level of self-esteem, fitting the stereotype of a classic narcissist.

A strong sense of ego and high self-esteem only led to high leadership evaluations if they were present in the absence of manipulative behaviors and impression management tendencies. The study suggested that narcissism that reflects a strong ego and high self-esteem is usually a sign of good psychological health. In contrast, narcissism that includes manipulation and impression management tendencies represents a dark side to personality which could lower the perception of leadership effectiveness.

Charismatic leadership and narcissism are linked because many narcissists have an element of charisma in their personality. As defined here, charisma is a special quality of leaders whose purposes, powers, and extraordinary determination differentiate them from others. Charisma is a positive and compelling quality that makes many others want to be led by that person.

A vision is a lofty, long-term goal, with effective leaders having a vision. A study found that levels of brain activity differed significantly between those participants considered visionaries versus non-visionaries. A vision statement is likely to be more inspirational when it includes the following: a reason for being beyond making money; timeless, unchanging core values; and ambitious but achievable goals. Being narcissistic to a healthy extent helps the leader formulate a vision. At their best, narcissistic leaders are visionary. A narcissistic leader can think with boldness, creativity, a love of freedom, and a willingness to get past conventional thinking. The productive narcissistic leader also invests passionate energy into his or her thinking.

Charisma is reflected in part in a leader's language. Many companies are led successfully by CEOs who exhibit narcissist-like language and actions. Yet when expressed in the extreme, narcissist-like language is dysfunctional because it glosses over real problems. Four signs of CEO-speak are indicative of narcissism: hyperbole; self-styling as an archetypal company; language of war, sport, and extremism; and excessive self-attribution.

The positive self-perceptions of narcissistic leaders can enhance leadership effectiveness to the extent that they contribute to high self-esteem and self-confidence. Should the self-perceptions become too grandiose, they can become dysfunctional because the leader will often deny criticisms and ignore problems. A study investigated the self-perceptions of fairness and their link to narcissism among a sample of Executive MBA students. It was found that narcissistic leaders are likely to be as fair as those who are less narcissistic. Also, managers with narcissistic tendencies were only slightly more likely to have inflated perceptions of their fairness than managers who are less narcissistic.

Two components of narcissism that are most likely related to strategy and performance are: (a) a belief in one's superior abilities; and (b) an intense, continuous need for affirmation. A study about narcissism (as measured by observing behavior unobtrusively), strategy, and organizational performance found the following: strategic dynamism in terms of changes in deployment of resources was related to the extent of CEO narcissism; narcissism was positively related to strategic grandiosity as indicated by the size and number of acquisitions; narcissism was also found to be positively associated with extreme performance, both in terms of return on investment and total shareholder performance; narcissism was also related to the return on asset measure of performance fluctuation. Overall, the study demonstrated that CEO narcissism was related to extreme and irregular performance. However, narcissistic CEOs do not generate statistically better or worse performance.

Narcissistic managers often have difficulty leading an organization successfully through a crisis. Yet, with respect to some aspects of a crisis, a narcissistic leader might perform well. Narcissists are more likely to have a positive experience in completing a task when it gives them the opportunity to display their ability and demonstrate their superiority over others. The narcissistic leader is most likely to rise to the occasion and help resolve a major crisis when such actions will be highly visible and will lead to positive feedback. The tendency of narcissists to be optimists can be an asset during an organizational crisis.

CASE HISTORY OF A WORKPLACE NARCISSIST

The following case history is about a financial executive who has held a series of key positions. Based on his many successes he could be considered an effective leader, yet several of his decisions have engendered controversy.

John Thain, the Broadly Experienced Financial Executive

John Thain was appointed as chairman and chief executive of the lending institution CIT Group in February 2010. (This company is not the giant Citigroup.) The company specializes in lending money to small and medium-sized businesses, yet had trouble managing its own finances. CIT resurfaced from Chapter 11 bankruptcy protection after an unsuccessful attempt to restructure its debt and large numbers of loan write-offs as customers increasingly defaulted on repaying loans during the recession.

Upon joining CIT, Thain said, "Much has been accomplished in recent months to position CIT for renewed success. We will build upon this progress and work even harder to support small and mid-market businesses. CIT can and will serve an important role in the recovery of the US economy and the creation of jobs."

Several reporters have assigned the nickname Superman to Thain, based on his close resemblance to Clark Kent, Superman's alter ego. The fact that Thain built a reputation for being mild mannered was another source for the nickname. Also, his career accomplishments may also have contributed to his being nicknamed Superman.

In December 2007, Merrill Lynch & Co. hired John Thain, the CEO of the New York Stock Exchange, as its new CEO. It appeared that Merrill Lynch wanted a pair of steady hands at the helm to stabilize a company that had experienced inner turmoil and rapid expansion. Thain's financial expertise was also a major factor influencing his appointment.

Thain is an electrical engineering graduate of Massachusetts Institute of Technology and received an MBA from Harvard. He has typically delved into the details of any business he has run.

Thain spent 24 years at Goldman, holding various jobs from mortgage-bond trader to chief financial officer before rising to president in 1999. He took the NYSE job for the opportunity to be a CEO and work to transform an important financial institution facing governance and technological challenges. Thain said he accepted the offer from Merrill Lynch because it was a great brand name with strong positions in such areas as wealth management, investment banking, and sales and trading. He thought he had the technical expertise to help Merrill Lynch recover from its substantial losses.

At the NYSE, Thain also stayed close to technical aspects of the operation. At a meeting with a consultant at the stock exchange on its lower trading floor, Thain posed questions about what color the prices and data on the screen should be to make the job easier for traders. Two years earlier, a visit to the Chicago Board Options Exchange ran overtime when Thain asked a series of questions about how the floor-traders on that exchange used information technology to their advantage.

When Thain joined Merrill Lynch, a reporter expressed concern that he did not have enough charisma to inspire a firm that included 16000 brokers. He responded, "I think I have better interpersonal skills than people give me credit for." He added that he had taken a lot of time to get to know the Big Board's floor traders, a task somewhat akin to one challenge at Merrill Lynch: winning the support of its army of stockbrokers.

Another selling point for the Merrill Lynch board was that Thain was known to be a consensus builder, and has the ability to attract and retain talent. A few former Merrill Lynch finance professionals expressed surprise that their former employer would turn to an outsider and an ex-rival. "It's shocking they picked someone from a Goldman Sachs background," said former Merrill Lynch CEO Dan Tully. He added that Thain seemed to lack the folksy touch to fit the culture of Merrill Lynch. "I understand he's very cerebral," Tully said.

Thain at times grew frustrated with parts of the job at the NYSE, especially the ceremonial ones. Early on, he preferred to stay away from twice-a-day bell-ringing on the balcony above the trading floor. Later he showed up at bell-ringing more often, using it as an opportunity to show CEOs and other business leaders in person what actually happened on the trading floor.

"He's a detail person and understands the inner workings, but he also appreciates the big picture and is well connected," says Amy Butte, a former NYSE finance executive.

Adding to the board's confidence when Thain was hired by Merrill Lynch was his extensive experience in one of the very areas bedeviling the company: mortgage trading. Thain is also known to be willing to take bold action when necessary.

Shortly after Thain joined Merrill Lynch, he navigated the sale of the company to Bank of America. Plans were laid for Thain to become the president of global banking, securities and wealth management. Rumors suggested that Thain would eventually become CEO of the combined companies. In helping to negotiate the deal with Bank of America, Thain was able to get Merrill Lynch shareholders a high price for their stock. However, his tenure at Merrill Lynch lasted only 13 months. In January 2009, Bank of America announced that Merrill Lynch had an unexpected loss of $15 billion for the fourth quarter of 2008. Just three weeks after completing the Merrill Lynch acquisition, Bank of America Chairman and CEO Kenneth Lewis asked Thain to resign. Lewis was upset with how Thain handled unexpectedly large fourth-quarter losses at Merrill Lynch.

Thain had left for vacation in Vail, Colorado after the big losses surfaced. Thain also scheduled a trip to attend the World Economic Forum in Davos, Switzerland, even though Bank of America disliked the idea. The New York Attorney General at the time, Andrew Cuomo, investigated the bonus payments.

Thain also faced two other embarrassing problems. He was criticized for having paid $3.6 billion in bonuses to Merrill Lynch employees just before the company was acquired by Bank of America. Also, it was revealed that he spent more than $1.22 million to renovate his office and two conference rooms at Merrill Lynch despite the company's mammoth losses. Specific expenses included $131 000 for area rugs, a $68 000 antique credenza, guest chairs for $87 000, a $35 000 commode, and a $1400 wastebasket. Later, Thain apologized for his poor judgment, and reimbursed the company in full for the costs of the renovation.

During his tenure at Merrill Lynch, Thain became so frustrated with the mounting losses that he lost his mild-mannered veneer. Angry about another losing quarter for the firm, he once stopped a meeting with his chief financial officer and hurled a chair against the wall. Allegedly, he shattered a nearby glass panel.

On January 23, 2009, President Barack Obama made indirect reference to Thain in these words: "The reports that we've seen over the last couple of days about companies that have received taxpayer assistance and then going out and renovating bathrooms or offices or in other ways not managing these dollars appropriately."

Financial compensation for Thain

As he began his role at CIT, Thain was assigned a $500 000 annual cash salary, plus $5.5 million in stock annually. He was also eligible for $1.5 million in performance bonuses. Thain received a $15 million signing bonus when he joined Merrill Lynch, and plans were to pay him $50 million per year. In 2007, the Associated Press reported that Thain earned over $83 million in total compensation at the New York Stock Exchange.

He was criticized both inside and outside Merrill Lynch for suggesting to the board in October 2008 that he should be paid an annual bonus somewhere between $30 million and $40 million. Thain justified the bonus because he salvaged Merrill Lynch by selling the investment firm to Bank of America. By December, Thain allegedly reduced his demand to $10 million. Thain never received the performance bonus, and later denied asking for one.

Narcissism Analysis

The evidence is not so clear that Thain is highly narcissistic, but he demonstrates a few tendencies in that direction. It requires some strong narcissistic tendencies to expect such a high bonus, and to pay an outlandish sum to decorate your office and its surroundings when your firm is losing billions of dollars. Going on a vacation and attending an economic conference in Switzerland as his company was sinking could be characterized as insensitive and self-centered. Also, a top-level executive digging so deeply into technical details reflects a degree of inflated self-importance.

Source: The facts and some of the observations in this case are based on the following: Joe Weisenthal (2010), "He's Back: John Thain Gets Top Job at CIT," *Business Insider* (www.businessinsider. com), February 7, pp. 1–4; Stephen Bernard (2010), "John Thain to Lead CIT," *Huffington Post* (www.huffingtonpost.com), February 8, pp. 1–2; Jack Willoughby (2010), "On the Road to Redemption,"

Barrons (http://online.barrons.com), October 11; Julie Cresswell and Louise Story (2009), "Thain Resigns Amid Losses at Bank of America," *The New York* Times, January 23; Dan Fitzpatrick, Susanne Craig, and Carrick Mollenkamp (2009), "Thain Ousted in Clash at Bank of America," *The Wall Street Journal*, January 23, pp. A1, A2; Miriam Marcus (2010), "Thain Tapped for Top Spot at CIT," *Forbes.com*, February 8; Randall Smith and Aaron Lucchetti (2007), "Merrill Taps NYSE's Thain as CEO," *The Wall Street Journal*, November 15, pp. A1, A21. Daniel Fisher (2008), "No Thain, No Gain," *Forbes*, April 7, pp. 76–82.

REFERENCES

1. Kets de Vries, Manfred F.R. and Danny Miller (1985), "Narcissism and Leadership: An Object Relations Perspective," *Human Relations*, **38** (6), 583–601.
2. Rosenthal, Seth A. and Todd L. Pittinsky (2006), "Narcissistic Leadership," *The Leadership Quarterly*, **17**, 617–33.
3. Kaufman, Scott Barry (2011), "The Paradox Peacock," *Psychology Today*, **44** (4), 60.
4. Maccoby, Michael (2000), "Narcissistic Leaders: The Incredible Pros, the Inevitable Cons," *Harvard Business Review*, January–February, pp. 68–77.
5. Anonymous (2003), "Michael Maccoby Wants to Know Your Type," *Across the Board*, May/June, pp. 13–14.
6. Benjamin M. Galvin, David A. Waldman, and Pierre Balthazard (2010), "Visionary Communication Qualities as Mediators of the Relationship between Narcissism and Attributions of Leader Charisma," *Personnel Psychology*, **63** (3), 509–37.
7. Resick, Christian J., Daniel S. Whitman, Steven M. Weingarden, and Nathan J. Hiller (2009), "The Bright-Side and the Dark-Side of CEO Personality: Examining Core Self-Evaluation, Narcissism, Transformational Leadership, and Strategic Influence," *Journal of Applied Psychology*, **94** (6), 1365–81.
8. Judge, Timothy A., Jeffery A. LePine, and Bruce L. Rich (2006), "Loving Yourself Abundantly: Relationship of the Narcissistic Personality to Self- and Other Perceptions of Workplace Deviance, Leadership, and Task and Contextual Performance," *Journal of Applied Psychology*, **91** (4), 762–76.
9. Paunonen, Sampo V., Jan-Erik Lönnqvist, Markku Verkasalo, Sointu Leikas, and Vesa Nissinen (2006), "Narcissism and Emergent Leadership in Military Cadets," *The Leadership Quarterly*, **17**, 475–86.
10. Conger, Jay A. and Rabindra N. Kanungo (1998), *Charismatic Leadership in Organizations*, Thousand Oaks, California: Sage Publications).
11. Research reported in Dvorak, Phred, and Jaclyne Badal (2007), "This Is Your Brain on the Job," *The Wall Street Journal*, September 20, pp. B1, B6,
12. Collins, Jim (2004), "Aligning Actions and Values," "Leader to Leader Institute, as reported in "Actions: Louder than Vision Statements," *Executive Leadership*, May, p. 8.
13. Lister, Eric D., Book Review of Michael Maccoby (2003), *The Productive Narcissist: The Promise and Peril of Visionary Leadership*, New York: Broadway Books.
14. Amenic, Joel H. and Russell J. Craig (2007), "Guidelines for CEO-Speak: Editing the Language of Corporate Leadership," *Strategy & Leadership*, **25** (3), 25–31.
15. Dattner, Benjamin (1999), "Who's the Fairest of Them All? The Impact of Narcissism on Self- and Other-Rated Fairness in the Workplace," Doctoral Dissertation, Department of Psychology, New York University, pp. 1–82.

16. Chatterjee, Arijit and Donald C. Hambrick (2007), "It's All About Me: Narcissistic CEOs and Their Effects on Company Strategy and Performance," *Administrative Science Quarterly*, **32**, 351–86.
17. King, Granville III (2005), "Narcissistic Leaders & Effective Crisis Management: A Review of Potential Problems and Pitfalls," *Midwest Academy of Management Proceedings*.
18. DuBrin, Andrew J. (2010), *Leadership: Research Findings, Practice, and Skills*, 6th edition, Mason, Ohio: South-Western/Cengage, p. 158.
19. Baker Clark, Barbra (2001), "Leadership During a Crisis," *Executive Leadership*, December, p. 8.
20. DuBrin, Andrew J. (2012), *Human Relations: Interpersonal, Job-Oriented Skills*, 11th edition, Columbus, Ohio: Pearson/Prentice Hall, pp. 216–18.
21. A couple of ideas on the list are from "Nailing Down Your Vision: 8 Steps," *Executive Leadership*, May 2004, p. 8.

6. Narcissism and dysfunctional leadership

Few people who become leaders in organizations begin their career as dysfunctional narcissists and, despite their behavior, receive a series of promotions until they occupy an executive position. The situation of a dysfunctional narcissist in a high-level leadership position is more likely that of a productive narcissist whose narcissism later intensified when given considerable power. The opportunity suddenly to have control over others and spend large sums of money without being closely scrutinized, triggers the person into such behaviors as sexually harassing subordinates and vendors, and purchasing an elaborate residence used more for personal than business purposes.

As analyzed by Seth A. Rosenthal and Todd L. Pittinsky, dysfunctional narcissistic leadership occurs when leaders' actions are principally motivated by their own egomaniacal needs and beliefs. Furthermore, these needs and beliefs supersede the needs and interests of the constituents and institutions they lead.[1]

When narcissism is carried to its pathological extreme, narcissistic leaders can do a lot of damage. They might leave damaged systems and relationships in their wake, and spearhead activities that bring them glory but damage the organization. An example would be a narcissistic leader of an industrial products company encouraging the investment in a consumer products company for the real purpose of extending his power and scope. The charm and other persuasive skills of the narcissist convince the board that the thrust into consumer products is a good idea. The expansion into consumer products proves to be a dud, draining off precious resources.

In this chapter we describe various aspects of dysfunctional narcissistic leadership including the characteristics and behaviors of destructive narcissists, the abuse of power, the enablers of narcissism, and the prevention of problems created by extreme narcissistic leaders.

CHARACTERISTICS AND BEHAVIORS OF DESTRUCTIVE NARCISSISTIC LEADERS

The negative actions of leaders with strong narcissistic tendencies stem from their narcissistic traits, many of which have already been described in previous chapters. Assume that Anna was a highly narcissistic child, teenager, and young adult, and that arrogance was one of her most pronounced traits. When somebody disagreed with her, she would swear at the person and demean him or her in other ways also. As a leader, Anna will most likely continue her arrogance, such as saying to a subordinate who makes a mistake, "Are you going to be stupid for the rest of your life?"

In this section we describe many characteristics and behaviors of destructive narcissistic leaders, but attempt to avoid repeating all the negative traits associated with narcissism described in previous chapters. Exhibit 6.1 provides an overview of how various negative elements of narcissism link to leadership behavior. The exhibit can be used as a checklist of attributes of the potential negative aspects of narcissistic leaders. You will find some overlap between this list and the description of traits and behaviors that follows.[2]

1. *Arrogance.* The archetypal narcissistic trait is arrogance, and as exhibited by leaders it is the most evident to subordinates. It may take considerable arrogance to formulate a grand vision, but it can be an impediment to the interpersonal aspects of leadership. Many group members rebel against being insulted and laughed at when they offer constructive criticism to the leader. Arrogant complacency can also lead an executive or executive team to dismiss the relevance of competition, such as not taking seriously the loss of potential sales of PCs to people who prefer to do all their written communication on a smart phone.

2. *Feelings of inferiority.* Despite the outward arrogance, some theory and research suggests that their grandiose ideas and behavior may really be a defense against deep-seated feelings of inferiority. The leader who feels inferior may engage in actions to make him or her feel superior, such as lavishly decorating an office. One business leader has a five-inch platform on the floor beneath her desk chair, so she can look down at visitors thereby feeling more powerful.

   A leader experiencing feelings of inferiority might also engage in the self-attribution bias of taking too much credit for success and blaming others for failures. Another manifestation of feeling inferior could be taking bold action to appear strong, such as a retaining executive arbitrarily closing a number of stores. Another possible exaggerated action to ward off feelings of inferiority might be downsizing a company even when it is doing well. The executive in question might say the action was taken to increase profits and stay competitive.

3. *Insatiable need for recognition and superiority.* Another narcissistic behavior to help cope with feelings of inferiority is a continuing quest to gain recognition and prove superiority. Narcissists in positions of major power have a diverse assortment of means by which they can demonstrate their potency. One narcissistic leader arbitrarily changed the company's insurance agent for no reason other than to exert power. A narcissistic leader might engage in conspicuous consumption such as throwing an elaborate party at company expense even though the business justification for the party is quite indirect. Another aspect of craving recognition and superiority is to demand unquestioning devotion and loyalty from subordinates, such as forbidding them from talking to executive recruiters. The leader might also insist that nobody question his or her ideas during a meeting.

4. *An intense desire to compete.* A spirit of competitiveness is essential for advancement to a leadership position in most organizations. People who on the surface are good team players yet want to advance will do what they can to ensure that higher-level management is aware that they are thoughtful, independent thinkers despite being team players. Dysfunctional narcissistic leaders take competitiveness to the extreme, even to the point of unethical behavior. For example, several of the key people at Lehman Brothers colluded with their accountants to find ways to hide losses from investors. The basic technique was to move debt off the balance sheet, in a technique known as Repo 105 transactions. The New York State Attorney General, at the time, said, "This practice was a house-of-cards business model designed to hide billions in liabilities in the years before Lehman collapsed." This practice was carried out for more than seven years before Lehman declared bankruptcy in 2008.[3]

5. *Excessive desire for power, wealth, and admiration.* The narcissistic pursuit of power, wealth, and admiration becomes dysfunctional when it becomes so intense that ethics, and perhaps the law, are violated. It is well known that the agents of professional athletes demand incredible payouts for their clients, such as a baseball player signing a $100 million contract. Some executives now have agents to handle their salary negotiations and find them lucrative employment. It could be argued that even the act of a business leader being represented by an agent is a bold expression of narcissism in the form of wanting to be regarded as a celebrity.

Part of the desire for power among dysfunctional narcissistic leaders is to structure an external world that supports their grandiose needs and visions. With enough power it is possible to make a vision come true, such as an automobile executive believing that by creating a world-wide

Exhibit 6.1   Negative elements of narcissism and examples of corresponding leadership behavior

Element	Example of corresponding leadership behavior
Grandiosity of personal belief system	Claims to be one of the true rising stars in the industry.
Arrogance	Refers to staff member who mildly criticizes his or her plan as a "dumb little creep."
Self-absorption	Spends first five minute of staff meeting talking about his or her recent vacation including flight delays, and the virus he or she caught.
Sense of entitlement	Demands to stay at $1000-per-night hotels during a business trip because of the importance of his or her position.
Fragile self-esteem	Regularly fishes for compliments about accomplishments and appearance, so as to feel good. Asks, for example, "What did you think of my suggestion for cost cutting in the meeting this morning?"
Hostility to negative feedback	Says to administrative assistant who points to errors in his or her proposed budget, "What makes you think you are qualified to judge me?"
Inflated self-view	Claims to have performed nearly flawlessly during the past year despite financial losses and high turnover.
Intense need for positive reinforcement	Frequently asks people, "Pretty good, don't you think?" expecting a positive response.
Attention seeking	Frequently interrupts others in a meeting to make a humorous comment. Also, will let others know whenever not feeling well.
Exploitive attitude/ entitlement	Attempts to squeeze every possible executive perk from company including two personal assistants and concierge service.
Self-admiration	Has trade magazine article, in which he or she was quoted, laminated and framed, and placed prominently in office. Also has two mirrors in office to facilitate looking at self.
No room for self-improvement	Declines offer to attend seminar on marketing use of social networking with comment, "It would be a waste of time. I would most likely know more than the instructor."
Over-confidence in abilities	Quite confident of negotiating skills, yet in reality is a poor negotiator who is usually perceived by other side as not negotiating in good faith.

Element	Example of corresponding leadership behavior
Hubris	Demands a $2 million bonus even though company lost money the previous year and went through heavy downsizing.
Excessive need for power	Requests that two new acquired companies report to him even though the product lines are not in his or her field of expertise.
Excessive need for achievement	Takes on new projects although already overloaded with responsibility. Justifies the project acquisition by saying, "I love new challenges."
Dominance	Insists on sitting at head of table during a meeting even when another staff member will be presenting.
Intolerant of criticism	When told by staff member that his or her suggestion for renovating the lobby might be too expensive, he or she says, "What gives you the right to judge my proposal? If you don't like my suggestion, just quit."
Unwilling to compromise	Informs the director of human resources, "We are going to cut our pension benefits by 25 percent. There is no need to discuss the matter further."
Lack of empathy	When told by a subordinate that a report will be late because the company servers were down for 24 hours, he or she replies, "I don't want to hear any excuses. I want those figures by four this afternoon."
Intense need for admiration	Arranges a dinner meeting so he or she can present the positive business results attained by the division in the recent quarter. Hints to administrative assistant that she should start the applause right after the presentation.
Hypersensitivity	When staff member suggests to executive that his or her sales forecasts are wildly optimistic, the executive replies, "Are you telling me I don't know a ******* thing about making sales forecasts?"
Poor listener	Often rambles in conversation during one-on-one meetings; will consult smart phone periodically when other person talks.
Inflexibility	As director of engineering, establishes goal of hiring five Latino micro-electronic engineers by end of year. The manager delegated the responsibility says, "We need to lower the goal to two Latino micro-electronic engineers. There are just not enough of these people available." The director of engineering replies, "Five is your number. Get the job done."

Source: The elements presented in the left column are adapted from Higgs, Malcolm (2009), "The Good, the Bad and the Ugly: Leadership and Narcissism," *Journal of Change Management,* **9** (2), 171. As observed by Higgs, several of these elements overlap such as "inflated self-view" and "over-confidence in abilities."

distributorship for one or two models, he or she can become a world-recognized figure in the industry.

6. *Hypersensitivity and anger.* Narcissists often draw on feelings of superiority to overcome a sense of inferiority. As a result, in situations where the feeling of grandiosity is threatened, they are likely to react with extreme hypersensitivity and anger. A real estate development executive, known for his pomposity, was edged out in a vote for "Developer of the Year" awarded by a trade association. The executive wrote a series of angry e-mail messages to the trade association explaining why he should have been chosen as Developer of the Year. The executive also became sullen and touchy in his dealings with subordinates. He consumed ten minutes in one meeting outlining why his accomplishments during the past year warranted his winning the coveted award.

   Hypersensitivity can also take the form of high sensitivity to criticism. The narcissist who often erects an emotional wall becomes uncomfortable when criticized. Part of the problem could be that the narcissistic leader behaves with bravado but in reality is not so supremely confident. A marketing executive was presenting a plan to use pyramid sales to help sell a line of inexpensive smart phones. When a member of the marketing team mentioned that multi-level marketing (pyramid selling) might damage the image of the company, the executive blurted out, "Get out of this conference room right now. I don't want any negative thinkers around me."

7. *Poor listening skill.* Listening is a major leadership skill, so being a poor listener detracts from leadership effectiveness. A fundamental reason that many narcissists are poor listeners is that they believe they have all the answers. Why listen to suggestions when you do not need input? Instead of asking the team, "Do you have any other suggestions for reducing costs this quarter?" the narcissistic leader will say, "Here are the ideas I have developed for reducing costs. Now I need you to implement them."

   Poor listening is also linked to hypersensitivity to criticism. Narcissistic leaders listen poorly when they feel threatened or attacked, and will sometimes completely shut out the criticism. A widely used way of denying criticism is not to react at all, including the non-response of a blank expression.

8. *Lack of empathy.* A lack of empathy, or even limited empathy, is another characteristic associated with narcissism that lends itself to dysfunctional leadership. Emotional intelligence is regarded as a primary leadership trait, with empathy being one of its main components. Both theory and research suggest that empathy is an essential trait for leaders. Empathy may be even more important than cognitive skills in some situations because without empathy it is difficult to process input from others.

Given that narcissistic leaders lack or have limited empathy, they are more likely to make decisions guided by a self-centered view of the world and to dismiss advice that conflicts with this view. A chief operating officer, for example, might think that low-cost manufacturing is the best possible way for the company to earn a better profit. The COO is advised by several staff members that two of the low-cost suppliers have unsafe working conditions and use underpaid child labor. Lacking empathy, the COO dismisses the concerns as being illogical. Eventually the company's outsourcing practices are exposed and its products are boycotted by several human rights group leading to very unfavorable publicity for the company.

9. *Amorality.* An extreme narcissistic leadership behavior would be to act amorally, showing no concern for the potential negative consequences of one's behavior. The narcissistic workplace leader might turn on supporters as well as the competition to exact revenge or simply to display power. An example of behavior that could be interpreted as amoral is how one retail store executive, aided by his team, reacted to the threat of unionization. The branch store in question was located in a rural area, and the workers started a union drive, led by a union leader. Up to that time no other stores in the retail store chain were unionized. The home office executive recognized that he could not prohibit a union drive from a legal standpoint. Yet he did mention that he wanted the employees to show appreciation for company management. When the store employees voted in favor of the union, the company announced that the branch would be closed in 30 days because of "underperformance." Over 250 jobs were lost immediately in a poor community.

10. *Irrationality and inflexibility.* At its extreme, narcissism is an enduringly inflexible pattern of thinking and behavior. Typically a person who is irrational and inflexible is screened out early in his or her career before obtaining a high-level leadership position. A small example of remaining irrational and inflexible was a steakhouse restaurant owner in San Francisco. She persisted with the idea that there was a permanent market for a steakhouse despite the "lunatic fringe" who wanted a vegetarian or poultry choice on the menu. As the number of customers gradually declined, the owner insisted that the crazy trend toward not eating red meat would soon be over. Her eponymous restaurant would again prosper. After three years of hanging on to her irrational and inflexible thinking, the restaurant closed. A sushi bar has taken over the premises.

11. *Inability to follow a consistent path.* A person with a high level of narcissism will often lack a clear set of values, will be easily bored, and therefore often changes course. It might not be easy for such a person to get promoted into a leadership position. However, when one does slip through, the result can be a person who keeps changing plans, leading to ambiguity and frustration

for subordinates. A germane example is the narcissistic manager who instructs a subordinate to prepare a report on a subject such as potential markets for a particular product. Ten days later the subordinate says she is about ready with the report, and the manager replies, "Oh forget that report. I'm on to something else now."

12. *Distaste for mentoring.* The limited empathy and strong independence of narcissistic leaders make it difficult for them to mentor or be mentored. Being hesitant to mentor is dysfunctional because mentoring has become an essential leadership role. Narcissistic leaders seldom mentor others, and when they do they ordinarily expect their protégés to be reflections of themselves. When narcissists do have mentors, they prefer mentors whom the can control. A 32-year old marketing vice president – a narcissist with CEO potential – told psychoanalyst Michael Maccoby that she had declined her manager's offer to be her mentor. As she put it, "First of all, I want to keep the relationship at a distance. I don't want to be influenced by emotions. Second, there are things I don't want him to know. I'd rather hire an outside consultant to be my coach."[4]

13. *Paranoid thinking.* Perhaps the most extreme trait of a narcissistic dysfunctional leader is paranoid thinking. The extreme egomaniac might create enemies where there are none, and suspects the motives behind most behavior. Although the paranoid narcissistic leader by definition thrives on compliments and accolades from sycophants, he or she will often be wary of their true intentions. If the paranoid thinker receives compliments from five different staff members on the quality of his vision, he might reflect, "I think the first four people meant it, but I question Sara's intentions."

Many leaders who might be described as destructive narcissists also have a positive side because they have contributed to the growth of an enterprise. Angelo Mozilo, founder and former chief executive of Countrywide Financial (now part of Bank of America) appears to fit the category of a destructive narcissist who built a company that was at one time quite successful.

We tentatively classify Mozilo as a narcissist based on his appearance, and the amount of money he took from his company. About his appearance, it was written, "Central casting would be hard-pressed to produce a CEO with a more luxurious tan, shinier teeth or louder pinstripes." He was paid about $400 million dollars during a six-year period of housing boom and bust. After Countrywide was acquired by Bank of America, he was paid about $100 million plus country club fees.[5] The Securities and Exchange Commission charged that Mozilo and two colleagues did not tell investors the truth about Countrywide's exposure to risky mortgages. On the eve of the trial, the two sides settled, with Mozilo agreeing to pay a penalty of $67.5 million and reparations to investors.

Mozilo also accepted a permanent ban from serving as an officer or director of a public company.

On the positive side, just before the troubled Countrywide Financial was acquired, Mozilo told investors, "I believe very strongly that no entity in this nation has done more to help American homeowners achieve and maintain the dream of homeownership than Countryside."[6]

THE LEADER'S NARCISSISTIC SUPPLY

An occasional narcissist living alone in the woods can be self-sufficient, providing there is at least one mirror in the cabin. The person can engage in self-admiration most of the day and night, perhaps even sending e-mails to himself or herself with lavish compliments. The typical organizational narcissist, however, cannot operate independently. As with narcissists in personal life, the individual needs sources of compliments and other forms of positive feedback. The *narcissistic supply* is what nourishes the narcissist. The supply usually takes the form of the people who provide positive statements about the narcissist to furnish evidence of his or her exceptional worth. The dysfunctional narcissistic leader needs a bigger and more intense narcissistic supply than does a less extreme narcissist.

The narcissistic supply is often classified as being primary or secondary. The *primary narcissistic supply* provides all the attention the narcissist craves. Such attention can be gained in a public form, such as fame and celebrity, or in a private form, such as admiration and flattery. The attention can be positive or negative, as long as the narcissist is the center of attention.

The *secondary narcissistic supply* refers to those people or things that provide supply on a regular basis, including work associates, family members and friends. This form of supply encourages the narcissist living a normal existence, providing him or her with pride, financial safety, and alliances.

The narcissistic supply is not restricted to people, because inanimate objects serving as status symbols that attract attention and admiration to the narcissist can feed the narcissist. Nonhuman sources of narcissistic supply would include a flashy vehicle, an expensive condo, an office overlooking an ocean or the Eiffel Tower, and a sports trophy in the cubicle.[7]

Enablers are the primary source of narcissistic supply for the dysfunctional narcissistic leader. The enablers are those people who surround the narcissistic manager and work beyond healthy limits to satisfy his or her narcissistic demands. Management psychologist Alan Downs notes that, because narcissists crave power and enablers crave security, they are attracted to one another. This symbiosis perpetuates narcissistic behavior in organizations. However, the perpetuation is not healthy because the enablers eventually resent having to supply the narcissist, and may suffer from exhaustion.[8] The enabler may eventually mutter, "How much do I have to keep complimenting this egomaniac?"

Life coach Chandra Alexander offers insight into the characteristics narcissists typically seek in their enablers. Narcissists typically want someone they perceive to be inferior to themselves. At the same time an enabler is sought who is reasonably intelligent, but not more intelligent than the narcissist. Gullibility is also a useful characteristic in an enabler because the narcissist often exaggerates the truth. Submissiveness and availability are other desired characteristics that the narcissist seeks in his or her supply.[9]

Having difficulty in finding ideal sources of supply, the narcissist will supplement the sources of supply with whoever is available. For example, a narcissist might be seated in an airplane busily engaged in a document on his laptop computer. Needing a quick boost to the ego, the narcissist gently bumps his elbow against the person seated next to him and asks, "How do you like this photo of me surfing? I'm going to use it to open a marketing presentation."

Although many narcissists have a healthy level of self-esteem, some dysfunctional narcissists have a fragile ego. The narcissistic supplies are used to feed the fragile ego.[10] Assume that Ashley, a dysfunctional narcissistic executive, has an administrative assistant named Bruce who is an enabler. Bruce knows to make frequent comments such as, "You look sharp and refreshed today, Ashley. I know the budget meeting will go well." Ashley needs frequent compliments like these to bolster her ego, much like many people need coffee in the morning to feel mentally and physically alert.

A narcissist such as Ashley is likely to gather multiple sources of narcissistic supply. She is wise enough to know that one person cannot provide all the ego-building she needs. Perhaps Ashley has a husband who regularly tells her how smart and beautiful she is; as well as other staff members who feed her steady doses of flattery.

Business consultant and narcissism writer Sam Vaknin reminds us that we all search for positive cues from people around us, but there are two major differences between the dysfunctional narcissist and the less narcissistic counterpart. Most people welcome a moderate amount of attention in the form of affirmation, approval, or admiration. The attention can be in words, or expressed nonverbally, such as smiling and nodding. A wink and a smile directed at one's presentation in a meeting can be a more powerful form of affirmation than saying, "Nice job." Too much attention, however, might be perceived as onerous and would therefore be avoided.

According to Vaknin, the narcissist is the emotional equivalent of an alcoholic, because of his or her insatiable need for attention and affirmation. Highly narcissistic managers, and other narcissists as well, direct much of their behavior towards gathering these pleasurable tidbits of attention. The narcissist embeds the affirming comments into a coherent, biased self-image. The comments are used to construct a fluctuating sense of self-worth and self-esteem.[11]

The dysfunctional narcissist will sometimes distort his or her image in a positive direction in order to elicit the needed supplies. He or she might exaggerate the number of powerful people in his network, allude to accomplishments not really achieved, and pump up his or her appearance by working with a personal trainer. All these forms of positive impression management can be effective in receiving more positive comments.

Another method of obtaining narcissistic supplies is quite similar to the one politicians regularly use during public appearances. The audience is sprinkled with a few people who are supplied in advance with questions to ask the politician. The politician has prepared a constructive answer for the questions, and appears intelligent and well-informed when responding. The smiles and cheers that emanate from members of the audience make the politician feel good. Three examples of these questions follow:

- How true is it that you have been working on a program to increase safety in our coal mines?
- What state-level program do you have in mind to reduce the drop-out rate in our high schools?
- What will be done to help balance our state budget without raising property taxes?

Similarly, the dysfunctional narcissistic leader will arrange in advance for a few staff members in a small-group meeting, a town-hall meeting, or a video conference, to ask certain questions at the meeting. As with the political meetings, the "plant" will ask the question with a serious, inquisitive facial expression. Three examples follow:

- How will we be able to hold on to our market share with all the new competitors in the field?
- What new social responsibility initiatives do we have planned for next year?
- To what extent is the rumor true that our profit picture for the year is quite positive?

A caution about enablers is that they are sometimes perceived to be co-dependents who facilitate the narcissist acting so vainly. They play a role similar to the co-dependent of the alcoholic who feels useful as long as the alcoholic needs help. The enabler feels he or she has a useful role in bolstering the ego of the narcissistic leader.

THE ABUSE OF POWER

A major dysfunction of narcissistic leaders is that they may abuse power by enticing subordinates into engaging in activities that work against their best interests, including unethical and illegal acts. A major illustration is that narcissistic and charismatic leaders have been behind some of the major financial scandals of our time. Some of these scandals have been of such grand magnitude that they required key subordinates to work with the leader. A case in point is Bernard Madoff whose Ponzi scheme has been classified as one of the greatest financial scandals of all time. We regard Madoff as highly narcissistic based on his grandiosity and limited empathy for his thousands of investors. Madoff's charisma added to his ability to abuse power.

Despite his financial brilliance, Madoff apparently was not acting alone: he brought a few close associates into his web of fraud and wrongdoing. Madoff abused his power by enticing subordinates who trusted him into supporting his nefarious activities. A total of eight Madoff employees were charged in the case. Many of the Madoff affiliates around the world who steered investors in his direction probably also facilitated his abuse of power. Specific examples of associates who facilitated his abuse of power are Annette Bongiorno and JoAnn Crupi, who were eventually indicted on frauds and conspiracy charges related to Madoff's multibillion-dollar Ponzi scheme. Both long-term Madoff employees, the women were accused of earning millions from the fraud. David Friehling, a CPA for Madoff, was another key associate charged with securities fraud by the FBI. Authorities said that when Bernard Madoff lied, Friehling swore to it – for 17 years and $65 billion in swindled funds.[12]

Preet Bhara, a US attorney in Manhattan, reinforces the idea that Madoff was assisted in his large-scale power abuse. "Bernard Madoff perpetrated the largest financial fraud in history, but as we allege again today, others criminally assisted his epic crime," said Bhara. "A house of cards is almost never built by one lone architect."[13]

Psychoanalyst Manfred Kets de Vries believes that narcissism played a key role in the major financial scandals that surfaced in 2008. Such misdeeds are obviously ethical and legal violations, but they also represent power abuse because financial executives are trusted with the power of guarding other people's money. Kets de Vries says that part of the problem is that we reward our executives for short-term results (a pronouncement made by many other observers). Relatively few executives look at the long run, and this can be attributed to greed. As Kets de Vries sees it, when you earn something like $35 million per year it is totally obscene.

When people are at the top of the organization they tend to behave in peculiar ways. Company outsiders and insiders often project unrealistic expectations and unrealistic results on powerful figures. Powerful figures start to get stripped of reality, and no longer get the information they need. A narcissistic executive might feel, "If I get $30 million this year, that's fine. I deserve it." He or she begins to believe, "Rules aren't for me. I am beyond the rules."[14] Executives who believe they are beyond the rules are abusing power because rules are supposed to apply to them as well as others.

The Combination of Charisma and Narcissism

According to Daniel Sankowsky, professor emeritus of management at Suffolk University, a major potential for power abuse exists among charismatic narcissistic leaders because they combine the power of charisma with the pathology of the narcissistic personality. Such leaders are particularly likely to promote visions that reflect their own sense of grandiosity and sweep followers into their fold. Often they are more confident of their own abilities than of the details of what they are doing.[15] However, intimate knowledge of the transactions is helpful, as in Madoff's in-depth knowledge of financial manipulations.

The combination of charisma and narcissism is formidable because narcissistic charismatic leaders can exploit the conscious and pre-conscious feelings of their followers. Exploitation is facilitated because charismatic leaders often have symbolic value, such as symbolizing an adored parent or other family member. Many of the people who contributed to the financial scams such as securities based on high-risk mortgages really wanted to believe that they could contribute to creating wealth for themselves based on nothing of real value. In short, followers might go along with a scam because they believe in the personal strengths of the leader who is both charismatic and narcissistic.

Eight Power-Abusing Behaviors of Narcissists in Power

Another way of understanding how leaders with strong narcissistic tendencies might abuse power is to review the eight behaviors of the narcissist in power observed by psychotherapist Sandy Hotchkiss.[16]

1. *Poor interpersonal boundaries.* Equilibrium for narcissists is a state of fusion with other people who have something they need. Narcissists expect others to know what they want and to want it themselves. If the narcissist wants you for something, you become an extension of her, like an extra arm on her body. She may flatter her target and offer him or her rewards, to get the target into her web. As part of not understanding boundaries, narcissistic leaders will often confuse roles and expect subordinates to run personal errands or become sex objects.

2. *Scapegoating.* The narcissistic leader will sometimes abuse power by blaming a subordinate for his wrongdoing. A telecommunication executive was accused of reporting outlandish sums on travel and expense reports, including a few receipts for $2000-per-night hotel rooms where he allegedly entertained sexual escorts. When confronted with this extreme rule violation, the executive blamed the bookkeeper, who he claimed had the responsibility for filing his expense reports.

3. *The grand vision.* The grand vision of a power-abusing leader will sometimes represent his or her personal ambition to make fantasies of perfection a reality by goading subordinates into a frenzy of productivity. Employees become caught up in "working for the cause," such as getting a large acquisition accomplished before the end of the year. (The purpose of the acquisition might be more to satisfy the narcissist's power needs than to increase company profits.) Working 70 hours in one week is not too much because the grand vision becomes all-consuming. Employees who do not invest extraordinary effort into the cause are made to feel ashamed.

4. *The idealization of the useful.* A subtle form of power abuse is for the dysfunctional narcissistic leader to promote an ordinary person into a key position who makes the boss feel good or pumps his or her ego. Placing someone in a good position just to make you feel good is an abuse of power because a more capable person merited the promotion. The person plucked from the crowd to be close to the executive is often someone with the same weight/height ratio and hairstyle as the executive. Perhaps in this way the narcissistic executive does not feel shown up by somebody who stands in physical contrast.

5. *Shameless exploitation.* In some environments headed by a dysfunctional narcissistic leader, a subordinate can expect to be used mercilessly, criticized frequently for whatever disappoints or deflates the leader, and fired when no longer needed. The practice of stretching employees until they snap, and then getting rid of them, has become labeled, "rubber-band management." A narcissistic leader might admit to practicing rubber-band management just to brag about being powerful. An occasional management consulting firm might practice shameless exploitation of staff professionals, including heavy travel and 70-hour work weeks.

6. *Mood swings from elation to rage.* The more powerful the narcissistic leader the more he or she can get away with mood swings. Power abuse is present because the expression of so much mood variability is unacceptable for workers of lesser rank. An infamous dysfunctional executive known for his mood swings was Jeffrey Skilling, the former Enron CEO executive. He was sent to prison for over 24 years, based on convictions of conspiracy, insider trading, and lying to auditors. Skilling claimed to be innocent,

and in June 2010, the US Supreme Court vacated (removed) part of the conviction.

7. *Envy.* Narcissists commonly experience envy because they are keenly sensitive to potential shifts in the balance of power within the organization. Envy is frequently expressed through contempt, trying to outdo others, or by excessive praise. Contempt helps the dysfunctional leader demean what makes him or her feel diminished, such as a colleague who has an excellent idea for a work process. Competing, or outdoing others, helps narcissists get what they want while moving themselves forward at the expense of others. Insincere praise helps the narcissist deny contemptuous feelings about others. Praise can also be a way for the narcissist to preempt another person from attacking him or her.

8. *Admiration seeking.* At the opposite end of the continuum from envy is the narcissistic leader's strong motive to feel admired, or to crave narcissistic supplies. Politically astute subordinates know when the narcissistic leader needs a dose of admiration or flattery. Wanting to be flattered is certainly not a strong abuse of power, but using subordinates for continual ego boosting is abusive – particularly when the subordinates do not feel that flattery is warranted.

Additional Abusive Behaviors toward Coworkers and Staff

A few additional examples of how a dysfunctional narcissistic leader abuses power will be helpful in understanding how pervasive the power abuse can be. As observed by Jean Ritala and Gerald Falkowski, here is a list of abusive behaviors toward coworkers and staff:[17]

*   Emotionally abusive talk and actions as a way to exert power and control over others. (The leader might tell an accountant that he was not good with numbers, or tell a staff member to leave a meeting because she was making a zero contribution.)
*   Giving the silent treatment to those who have slighted or corrected the leader. (Not looking at person when they meet in the hall and not acknowledging the person's comment during a meeting exemplify this abusive behavior.)
*   Establishing unrealistic rules. (Staffers are asked to prove that they have tried three different websites before booking a flight for business purposes.)
*   Prohibiting personal objects in the workplace, such as photos of family or household pets. (Even if the case can be made for creating a polished, professional environment, many workers regard personal objects as a way of literally personalizing the workplace.)

- Unrealistic job expectations for others. (As mentioned above, the dysfunctional leader might expect salaried staffers to work 60 hours or more per week.)
- Setting up management peers or employees for failure so they can belittle them later for their inabilities. (A sales manager might be ordered to increase sales by 10 percent during a major downturn in the industry. When the sales manager does not make the target he is belittled for making excuses rather than finding a way for the sales staff to meet customer needs.)
- Shouting at or picking on people in front of others. (Somehow dysfunctional narcissistic leaders frequently violate the most basic human relations principle of all – criticize in private, praise in public.)

Although the list just presented does not include abuses of power on a grand scale, these small behaviors on the part of the narcissistic leader can be humiliating and damage morale.

THE IMPACT ON PERFORMANCE AND MORALE

A major concern about highly narcissistic leaders is that they can become dysfunctional enough to damage performance and morale in the organizational units under their control. We have already mentioned that research has shown how even a functional narcissist CEO can create considerable variability in performance, including extreme losses and gains.[18] A negative narcissist in a position of power can create more substantial problems. According to Malcolm Higgs, the study of CEO failures has sparked an interest in narcissistic leadership as a possible explanation for these failures.[19] The extreme case is the dysfunctional narcissist Bernard Madoff, who destroyed his organization, as well as severely damaging the welfare of many of his staff and thousands of customers. Several suicides and deaths among the victims of the fraud appear to have been triggered by Madoff's quest for more power and glory.

Here we look at some research and opinion about how highly narcissistic leaders can negatively impact performance and morale. The term *dysfunctional* used throughout the chapter refers to the idea that the leader is damaging the smooth functioning of the system.

The study of major league baseball owners mentioned earlier illustrates how extreme narcissist leadership can lead to less-than-fulfilling exchanges between the leader and group members. It was found that narcissistic dispositions detract from a CEO's use of contingent reward leadership, or rewarding subordinates when they do something right. Because high narcissists have little concern for others, they are unlikely to worry about developing equitable exchange relationships with organizational members. The study also found that narcissistic CEOs are also less likely to give special recognition to others for their efforts or accomplishments.[20] The link to performance and morale of these results is that contingent reward leadership is useful in boosting both performance and morale. When contingent rewards are lacking, organizational performance and employee morale might decline.

As observed in the case studies of Ritala and Falkowski, extremely narcissistic leaders can be dangerous in the workplace. The costs attributed to highly narcissistic leaders include higher insurance premiums due to more clinic visits, and more prescription drugs by workers trying to cope with narcissists and the toxic workplace they create.[21]

During an interview with an information technology reporter, Ritala said, "The cost to the organization from narcissism in the workplace is staggering, as the narcissist's coworkers become ill with stress, teamwork deteriorates, projects fail, and turnover rises. Up to one-third of a narcissist's victims in the workplace will quit the company or transfer to a different department if nothing is done."[22]

Executive coach and psychiatrist Roy Lubit systematically gathered evidence on the potential negative impact of destructive narcissistic leaders. He found that their grandiosity, devaluation of subordinates, sense of entitlement, negative values, and excitement seeking can significantly damage an organization. Dysfunctional narcissistic leaders can compromise their business unit's long-term performance by driving away highly talented workers. Furthermore, they divert workers' energies away from their real work, foster a negative corporate culture, and sometimes make reckless business decisions. An example of a reckless business decision by a narcissist would be Jeffery Skilling's maneuver, of hiding losses by passing off debts to a subsidiary created for the purpose of absorbing Enron's losses.

Destructive narcissism, according to Lubit, limits the ability of managers to work effectively with colleagues and subordinates. A major problem is that their arrogance, sense of entitlement, lack of concern for the feelings of others, devaluation of other's abilities, and desire for the spotlight, makes them poor team players. Obsequious direct reports of destructive narcissistic leaders are likely to be promoted, a situation that prompts capable people to find employment elsewhere. Another morale problem is that good ideas of subordinates are likely to be ridiculed because they might draw attention away from the narcissistic manager. In sum, dysfunctional narcissistic leaders work ineffectively with peers and subordinates.[23]

AVOIDING THE NEGATIVE IMPACT OF DYSFUNCTIONAL NARCISSISTIC LEADERS

Two major thrusts in avoiding the negative impact of dysfunctional narcissistic leaders would be, first, to attempt to block dysfunctional narcissists from holding a key leadership position and, second, to help them overcome their problems if already holding the position. Here we look briefly at both the selection of leaders to prevent the problem, and the development of leaders whose narcissism is creating dysfunctional leadership.

Selection of Leaders without Dysfunctional Leadership Tendencies

Many effective leaders have at least a tinge of narcissism to their persona, so it would be counterproductive to exclude all people from leadership positions who have previously exhibited narcissistic tendencies. However, it does make sense to attempt to avoid selecting candidates for leadership positions who demonstrate strongly negative narcissistic tendencies. The screening process begins with sensitivity to the possibility that extreme narcissism could be detrimental in most leadership positions.

Here is not the place to review the basics of executive selection, except to highlight a few points. The candidate assessment would have three major components. First would be individual and group interviews by company managers and human resource professionals. A major screening question would be, "How self-centered and egotistical is this candidate?" No one sign is an absolute knockout factor, but should be considered in relation to other data about the candidate. Among the potential indicators of extreme self-centeredness and arrogance would be:

- Does the candidate take credit for all past successes, or does the candidate share some of the credit with present or past teammates?
- Does the candidate talk only about himself or herself, or does the candidate also ask a reasonable number of questions about the company and the interviewers?
- Does the candidate make several phone calls during the interview, as well as sending and receiving text messages during the selection interview?
- To what extent does the candidate describe the kind of contribution he or she would like to make for the company, or does the candidate focus mostly on wanting to know what the company can do for him or her?

The second component to the candidate assessment would be a comprehensive psychological evaluation by an outside assessment firm. The screening devices might include a personality test such as the Narcissistic Personality Inventory. Yet such a test would be used primarily to provide clues for digging further into the candidate's personality via interviews and other tests. Although the NPI is widely used in research, it would be just one contributor to diagnosing the extent to which a person is a narcissist. Psychological assessment for high-level candidates is more in vogue than ever because so many executive failures and financial scandals have been linked to personality problems.

The third component to the selection procedure would be an extensive background check. This would include reference checks that include input from superiors, subordinates, and coworkers. Some assessment firms include a background check in their investigation. The interviews conducted by company personnel will often provide areas of concern for investigation in background checks. For example, the interviews might suggest that the candidate takes too much credit for success yet readily blames others for any lack of success. This would be a matter worth investigating during the reference checks.

Assistance to Dysfunctional Narcissistic Leaders

Better selection may help prevent the problem of the dysfunctional narcissistic leader. For those dysfunctional leaders already working for the organization, development or some other modification of behavior is required. Michael Maccoby has suggested three basic ways in which productive narcissists can avoid the traps of their own personality.[24] If these steps are followed, the productive narcissist can avoid becoming a dysfunctional leader.

Finding a trusted colleague or coach

Many narcissistic leaders develop a close relationship with a trusted colleague, or sidekick, who acts as an anchor, keeping the narcissist on track. The colleague really has to understand the leader and what he or she is attempting to achieve. It is best if the narcissistic leader feels that the trusted colleague is an extension of himself. Effective sidekicks are able to point to the operational requirements of the narcissistic position, such as what goals he or she must achieve. A chief operating officer (COO) will often help the grandiose narcissistic leader to stay on track in such matters as converting visions into reality.

Since the writings of Maccoby, executive or leadership coaches have become more ingrained into executive life. The coach may serve as a trusted colleague and help the narcissistic executive know when his or her behavior has gone over the edge. Some coaches regularly solicit feedback from work associates to help guide the executive. Furthermore, the coach might meet with several subordinates and the leader at the same time to have a productive feedback session. The coach might say to the group, "This morning let's talk about whether Jack has become so self-centered lately that he won't even listen to you." Because the group activity has a spirit of development rather than revenge, the feedback can be helpful. Repeated sessions are necessary because behavior as ingrained and complex as narcissistic leadership rarely changes after one feedback session.

Another developmental approach a leadership coach might take is to sit in on meetings and observe the leader in action. The focus is on the leader's interaction with others at the meeting, and whether his or her narcissistic tendencies are creating a problem. Here is an example of the possible feedback by the coach: "Jack your behavior at this afternoon's meeting could use improvement. You spent most of the time talking about your vision, your plans, your goals, and your recent vacation. You talked and talked but didn't listen carefully enough for what others were thinking. Also, you neglected to ask for constructive criticism and feedback."

Indoctrinate the organization

Another approach to making the dysfunctional narcissistic leader functional is to indoctrinate the organization into his or her way of thinking. In this way people are not working at cross purposes with the leader so he or she becomes productive. The co-founders of Google Inc., Sergey Brin and Larry Page, are productive by almost any definition of productivity. Also, their grandiosity suggests a tinge of narcissism. These two industrialists, however, might become dysfunctional if thousands of "Googlers" did not buy into the culture of continuous, mammoth expansion. Among its other forays, Google has become (a) a verb, (b) a smart phone, (c) a photo map of the world, and (d) a type of television emission.

Get into psychotherapy

Maccoby explains that narcissists are often more interested in controlling others than in knowing and disciplining themselves. From this standpoint, most narcissistic leaders would resist psychotherapy that forces such self-examination. (Another viewpoint is that most narcissists would like psychotherapy because they can spend 50 consecutive minutes each time talking about themselves and their feelings. The therapist is often a non-judgmental listener.) Macobby believes that some forms of psychoanalysis (an intensive form of psychotherapy) can help narcissists work through their rage, alienation, and grandiosity. An example of a dysfunctional narcissist being helped in therapy would be to understand why he became so furious when he did not receive enough praise from subordinates.

Whether or not it is advisable, many executives use coaches to take over the role of a psychotherapist. It is also ethically questionable whether executive coaches who are not certified mental health specialists should be probing into the personalities of leaders of any kind.

Of the several approaches to lessening the impact of dysfunctional narcissistic leadership, Malcolm Higgs, Professor of Organisation Behaviour and Change, at the University of Southampton School of Management, prefers better selection. His analysis suggests that a more systemic approach to reducing the emergence of destructive senior level leadership entails reviewing the selection methods and criteria for choosing leaders and potential leaders. More fundamentally in terms of both selection and development, there should be a change in thinking about which leadership model is best. The shift should be from a "heroic" leadership model that is leader-centric to a more "relational" model.[25] The focus should be on the leader collaborating and partnering with group members rather than being an inspirational figure who creates all the visions.

GUIDELINES FOR APPLICATION AND PRACTICE

1. A wide variety of narcissistic characteristics and behaviors described in this and other chapters could interfere with your leadership effectiveness, even if a tinge of the characteristics and behaviors could be an asset. For example, a narcissistic leader is usually grandiose, but so are leaders such as the founders of Apple Inc., Microsoft, Google, and Martha Stewart Living Omnimedia. Yet if a person is consistently too grandiose, followers might be turned away.

2. Next we will list 50 characteristics and behaviors observed among dysfunctional narcissistic leaders. Similar to calcium in the blood stream, the right amount can help you. With respect to calcium, the right dose might give you strong bones, yet too much calcium might create kidney stones as well as other dysfunctions. Reflect on each characteristic and behavior, and visualize whether you might have just the right amount. Respond yes or no, with respect to your having the right amount of the characteristic or behavior. It will be instructive and amusing to get input from a couple of close members in your network as to whether you have the characteristic or behavior in the right amount. Self-development might be possible in terms of increasing or decreasing the characteristic or behavior.

No.	Characteristic or behavior	Yes or no
1.	Motivated by egomaniacal needs or beliefs	
2.	Grandiose personal belief system	
3.	Arrogant	
4.	Self-absorbed	
5.	Sense of entitlement	
6.	Self-esteem	
7.	Hostility to negative feedback	
8.	Inflated self-view	
9.	Intense need for positive reinforcement	
10.	Attention seeking	
11.	Exploit others	
12.	Feeling of entitlement, including being overpaid	
13.	Feel I have no room for self-improvement	
14.	Overconfident of abilities	
15.	Hubris	
16.	Excessive need for power, wealth, and admiration	
17.	Excessive need for achievement/intense desire to compete	
18.	Dominance	
19.	Intolerant of criticism	
20.	Unwilling to compromise	
21.	Lack of empathy	
22.	Intense need for admiration	
23.	Hypersensitivity	
24.	Poor listener	
25.	Inflexible	
26.	Feelings of inferiority	
27.	Insatiable need for recognition and superiority	
28.	Hypersensitivity and anger	
29.	Poor listening skills	
30.	Amorality (no ethics)	
31.	Irrationality and inflexibility	
32.	Inability to follow a consistent path	
33.	Distaste for mentoring	
34.	Paranoid thinking	
35.	Strong need for daily narcissistic supply	
36.	Will distort image in positive direction to get supplies	

No.	Characteristic or behavior	Yes or no
37.	Abuse power by enticing others into unethical and illegal activities	
38.	Maintain poor interpersonal boundaries in terms of roles others play on the job	
39.	Scapegoating (blaming someone else for my wrongdoing)	
40.	Grandiose vision	
41.	Would be willing to promote someone just because person made me feel good	
42.	Shameless exploitation of others	
43.	Mood swings from elation to rage	
44.	Envy toward people who gain power in organization	
45.	Admiration seeking	
46.	Emotionally abusive talk and actions	
47.	Silent treatment toward person who has slighted me	
48.	Set up other people to fail	
49.	Unrealistic expectations of others	
50.	Shout at or pick on others in public	

3. Leadership professor and psychoanalyst Manfred F.R. Kets de Vries says that self-awareness can break the destructive pattern of narcissism with a leader. He recommends that the leader celebrate the fun and meaning in the work itself. In this way the leader takes away some of the self-focus.[26]

SUMMARY

Dysfunctional narcissistic leadership occurs when leaders' actions are principally motivated by their own egomaniacal needs and beliefs. When narcissism is carried to its pathological extreme, narcissistic leaders can do a lot of damage. The negative actions of leaders with strong narcissistic tendencies stem from their narcissistic traits. Thirteen characteristics and behaviors of narcissistic leaders described here are as follows: (1) arrogance; (2) feelings of inferiority; (3) insatiable need for recognition and superiority; (4) an intense desire to compete; (5) excessive desire for power, wealth, and admiration; (6) hypersensitivity and anger; (7) poor listening skills; (8) lack of empathy; (9) amorality; (10) irrationality and inflexibility; (11) inability to follow a consistent path; (12) dislike for mentoring; and (13) paranoid thinking.

As in personal life, the organizational narcissist needs sources of compliments and other forms of positive feedback, or a narcissistic supply. The primary narcissistic supply provides all the attention the narcissist craves. The secondary narcissistic supply is people or things that furnish the supply on a regular basis, including work associates and family members. Inanimate objects, such as a flashy vehicle, can also be a narcissistic supply. Enablers are the primary source of narcissistic supply for the dysfunctional narcissistic leader. Narcissists crave power and enablers crave security, and are therefore attracted to each other. The narcissist typically wants an enabler he or she perceives to be inferior to him or her, but still reasonably intelligent.

Narcissistic supplies are used to feed the fragile ego of the narcissist. We all search for positive cues from people around us, but the highly narcissistic person has an insatiable need for attention and affirmation. The dysfunctional narcissist will sometimes distort his or her image in a positive direction in order to elicit the needed supplies, such as exaggerating the number of important people in his or her network. Enablers are sometimes perceived to be co-dependents who facilitate the narcissist acting so vainly.

A major dysfunction of narcissistic leaders is that they may abuse power by enticing subordinates into engaging in activities that work against their best interests, including unethical and illegal acts. Narcissism appears to have played a key role in the major financial scandals that surfaced in 2008. Such misdeeds are power abuse because financial executives are trusted with the power of guarding other people's money.

A major potential for power abuse exists among charismatic narcissistic leaders because they combine the power of charisma with the pathology of the narcissistic personality. Such leaders are particularly likely to promote visions that reflect their own sense of grandiosity and sweep followers into their fold. The combination of charisma and narcissism is formidable because charismatic narcissistic leaders can exploit the conscious and pre-conscious feelings of their followers.

Eight power-abusing behaviors of narcissist in power are as follows: (1) poor interpersonal boundaries; (2) scapegoating; (3) the grand vision; (4) the idealization of the useful subordinate; (5) shameless exploitation; (6) mood swings from elation to rage; (7) envy; (8) admiration seeking. Additional abusive behaviors toward coworkers and staff include the following: emotionally abusive talk; the silent treatment; unrealistic rules; prohibiting personal objects in the workplace; unrealistic job expectations for others; setting up others for failure; shouting at or picking on people in front of others.

Highly narcissistic leaders can become dysfunctional enough to damage performance and morale. A study of major league baseball owners illustrates how narcissistic leadership can detract from a CEO's use of contingent reward leadership. The same leaders are less likely to give special recognition for efforts and accomplishments.

Costs attributed to highly narcissistic leaders include higher heath insurance costs for employees. Also, the narcissist's coworkers become ill with stress, teamwork deteriorates, projects fail, and turnover rises. Destructive narcissistic leaders can damage the organization through their grandiosity, devaluation of subordinates, sense of entitlement, negative values, excitement-seeking, and driving away talented workers. Destructive narcissism limits the ability of managers to work effectively with colleagues and subordinates, making them poor team players.

A major thrust in avoiding the negative impact of dysfunctional narcissistic leaders would be, first, to attempt to block dysfunctional narcissists from holding a key leadership position and, second, to help them overcome their problems if they already hold the position. The candidate assessment to screen out excessive narcissism would include interviews by company personnel, outside psychological evaluation, and a thorough background check.

Three basic ways in which productive narcissists can avoid the traps of their own personality are as follows: (1) find a trusted colleague or coach to provide feedback; (2) indoctrinate the organization into his or her way of thinking; and (3) get into psychotherapy. Another approach to circumventing the potential problems of dysfunctional narcissistic leadership is selection in terms of shifting from a "heroic" leadership model which is leader-centric to a more "relational" or collaborative model.

CASE HISTORY OF A WORKPLACE NARCISSIST

The following case history presents the story of the director of marketing for one of the largest luxury vehicle dealerships in the region in which the company is located. Although the dealership remains successful, many people at the dealership believe that Lola creates too many problems for staff members, and sometimes customers.

Lola, the Luxurious Marketer of Luxury Vehicles

"Why, why, why are only three sports cars on the floor decorated with gift ribbons this week?" shouted Lola, the director of marketing and sales at a luxury vehicle dealership in New Jersey. "Don't you know that at holiday time, big bold ribbons draped around a car help sell that vehicle? This is the time of the year when rich people buy their spouses, lovers, or children a fun car as a wild indulgence. We are here to sell an exotic lifestyle, not just vehicles."

Rick, the floor manager reacted quickly to Lola's request by going to the back of the showroom to fetch two more giant decorative ribbons to drape on cars. On the way to the back of the showroom, he muttered to a credit specialist seated in a cubicle, "There goes Lola again on one of her rants about creating the right image. Right now she's not creating a good image for me."

Lola began her way into the world of luxury as a high school student. Her enthusiasm and striking appearance as a boy's basketball team cheerleader led to a modeling assignment for a store. Soon thereafter she received an invitation to work as a fashion photographer's model. Her modeling activities continued while she studied at a community college, with a major in business and marketing. Lola's work as a model took considerable time, so she took three and one-half years to graduate from community college. As Lola approached getting her associate's degree, she decided that she wanted a more durable career than modeling.

Lola worked with the career center at the community college to find a suitable position. She landed a position quickly as an assistant store manager at a branch of a national clothing store. Lola enjoyed working with both customers and store associates and proved to be a strong performer. A side feature to the job that Lola particularly appreciated was the opportunity to wear fashionable clothing to work, as well as receive so many compliments about her appearance from customers and store associates.

After two years of good performance as an assistant manager, Lola was promoted to store manager. She enjoyed being the center of attention, but soon became dissatisfied with her earnings at the store. Lola reasoned, "Unless I become a home-office executive, I'll never make the big bucks. I'm too talented to suffer along with a store manager's pay. Maybe I could use my sales talent elsewhere."

In her search for a position with greater earning potential, Lola quickly found a job as a sales consultant at the luxury car dealer where she is now the director of sales and marketing. Lola was a quick study about the luxury vehicles because of both her good cognitive skills and her fascination with aesthetic goods. Lola enjoyed the opportunity to wear stunning outfits to work, interact with customers and potential customers, and comment on the technical features of the vehicles. Every working day Lola received compliments on her appearance and smile.

After two years of well above average sales, Lola faced an interesting opportunity. The director of marketing and sales left the company to work in California. The owners of the dealership were so impressed with Lola's sales performance and personal demeanor that they thought she would be an effective head of marketing and sales. Lola was assured that her high earnings would continue because she would receive a reasonable salary plus a year-end performance bonus. Lola thought, "Why not take this position? I have been great in any other job I have attempted."

One of Lola's first initiatives as the director of marketing and sales was to place more fresh flowers around the dealership and on her desk as well. A few sales associates and office personnel thought the expense was unjustified, but they did not complain out of concern of being perceived as petty. An initiative Lola instigated about four months into her job did cause some concern for the sales consultants. The sales staff were instructed to mention Lola's name and title as soon as it appeared that a customer was ready to negotiate a sale. She told the staff, "It gives more status to a sale when you mention that Lola Argent, the Director of Marketing and Sales, will personally help negotiate the deal. Whenever I am available, I want to meet the customer before he or she signs a deal. Our customers are buying luxury, and when they are personally introduced to me it will add to the status of their purchase."

A few of the sales consultants thought that Lola intervening in sales would add a layer of bureaucracy to the sales process, and perhaps add an element of confusion. As the months passed, most of the sales consultants disliked Lola getting so much credit for their sales. She would often make a comment to the effect, "I am so glad that I can help so many of you close a sale. After all, a person with my experience and high-level position can make a difference in closing a sale. I am helping you earn a big commission every time I get involved with your customer."

Greg is one of the sales consultants who think that Lola goes too far in getting involved in the sales, as well as taking credit for closing the deal. A few weeks ago he was about to close a deal on a top-of-the line SUV. The customers were a couple who made what they considered to be a final offer of $75 500. Greg showed the deal to Lola for her approval. Lola then accompanied Greg to sit down with the couple. Part of her pitch to the couple was, "I know that you have made your final offer to our sales consultant Greg, who is certainly in charge of this sale. But you are now dealing with Lola. I am the director of marketing and sales, and I give final approval on most deals. Please recognize that if we sell you this SUV for $75 500, the dealership will be making only $1150 in profit. I need you to pay at least $77 500 for this SUV."

Within a few minutes after Lola returned to her office, the wife in the couple said to Greg "We're leaving. We thought you could make the deal. My husband and I made our best offer."

A couple of months later, an outstanding sales consultant, Wendy, quit the dealership to join a competitor. When asked by Lola how she could be so unfaithful by joining a rival, Wendy explained, "You don't treat me like a professional. You expect me to tell you how great you were in closing a deal for me. But you really make me feel like a trainee. I can understand bringing a deal back to you for approval. That's standard stuff. What I can't take is your jumping in to close a deal that I have already closed."

Lola thought to herself that although Wendy is a good sales representative she is a poor team player. Her problem is that she does not want to work cooperatively with management in closing sales.

Lola once decided to run a few newspaper adds with a different twist than the usual ads for the dealership. The owners of the dealership were a little hesitant but they deferred to Lola's expertise. She decided that the traditional ads for the dealership lacked a human touch; that they focused too much on vehicles rather than the people selling and servicing them. Lola's idea was to feature photos of the entire sales and service staff with their names attached. Each photo would be about 2¼ square inches, with one exception. The photo of Lola would be 5 by 7 inches in size. It appeared to the owners of the dealership that the ad attracted many fewer inquiries than most of their newspaper ad campaigns.

Narcissism Analysis

Lola first displayed perhaps a healthy degree of narcissism as a model, and then as an assistant store manager who liked to be complimented by customers. The pride she took in her appearance and her winning smile seemed to reflect narcissism to a healthy extent. Lola was effective as a sales consultant, a type of work in which a moderate degree of narcissism is an asset provided the sales consultant is careful to empathize with the customer.

The emphasis on luxury in the dealership, such as more red ribbons on the vehicles and the fresh flowers, were positive, or at least neutral, consequences of her narcissism. Lola's narcissism slipped into the dysfunctional leadership mode when she began to micromanage closing deals made by sales consultants. Her approval on deals is standard practice, but her insistence on being physically present to close deals takes away authority from the sales consultants. Wendy's departure exemplifies this problem. It appears that Lola uses the word "I" too often for a leader who wants to develop teamwork.

Lola's idea for a newspaper ad campaign also illustrates the potential dysfunctional impact of her narcissistic leadership. She wanted to use company money to promote herself conspicuously.

REFERENCES

1. Rosenthal, Seth A. and Todd L. Pittinsky (2006), "Narcissistic Leadership," *Leadership Quarterly*, **26** (4), 638.
2. Rosenthal and Pittinsky (2006), pp. 620–622; Maccoby, Michael (2004), "Narcissistic Leaders: The Incredible Pros, the Inevitable Cons," *Harvard Business Review*, **81** (1), pp. 103–4; Downs, Alan (1997), *Beyond the Looking Glass: Overcoming the Seductive Culture of Corporate Narcissism*, New York: AMACOM; Lubit, Roy (2002), "The Long-Term Organizational Impact of Destructively Narcissistic Managers," *Academy of Management Executive*, **16** (1), 127–38.
3. Freifeld, Karen (2010), "Cuomo Sues Lehman Accountant," Bloomberg News, December 22.
4. Maccoby (2004), p. 98.
5. Farzard, Roben (2008), "In Search of a Subprime Villain," *Business Week*, February 4, p. 077.
6. McClean, Bethany (2010) "How the Roof Fell In On Countrywide," *Fortune*, November 15, pp. 90, 98. Excerpt from McLean, Bethany and Joe Nocera (2010), *All the Devils Are Here: The Hidden History of the Financial Crisis*, New York: Portfolio.
7. "Understanding the Phenomenon of Narcissistic Supply," *The Roadshow for Therapists*, http://narcissisticbehavior.net, August 12, 2010.
8. Downs (1997).
9. Alexander, Chandra (2011), "What Is Narcissistic Supply?" *Coachgirl.com*, http://coachgirl.com (accessed January 4, 2011).
10. Hotchkiss, Sandy (2002), *Why Is It Always about You? The Seven Deadly Sins of Narcissism*, New York: The Free Press, p. 133.
11. Vaknin, Sam (2007), *Malignant Self-Love: Narcissism Revisited*, 8th edition, Republic of Macedonia: Lidiza Rangelovska Vaknin, 2007); "Narcissists, Narcissistic Supply, and Sources of Supply," http://samvak.tripod.com (accessed January 25, 2011).
12. *Daily News* staff writers (2009), "David Friehling, a CPA for Bernard Madoff, Charged with Securities Fraud, Surrenders to FBI," *Daily News* (NYDailyNews.com), March 18.
13. Quoted in Peter Lattman (2010), "2 Former Aides Indicted in Madoff Scheme," *The New York Times Deal Book* (http://dealbooknytimes.com), November 18. The facts about the two women Madoff associates are from the same source.
14. Kets de Vries, Manfred (2008), "Narcissism in the C-Suite," *Workforce Management*, December 15, p. 8.
15. Sankowsky, Daniel (1995), "The Charismatic Leader as Narcissistic: Understanding the Abuse of Power," *Organizational Dynamics*, **24** (2), 57–71.
16. Hotchkiss (2002), pp. 141–50.

17. Ritala, Jean and Gerald Falkowski (2007), *Narcissism in the Workplace*, US: Red Swan Publishing for IT Service Management Institute, p. 1.
18. Chatterjee, Arijit and Donald C. Hambrick (2007), "It's All about Me: Narcissistic CEOs and Their Effects on Company Strategy and Performance," *Administrative Science Quarterly*, **52** (3), 351–86.
19. Higgs, Malcolm (2009), "The Good, the Bad and the Ugly: Leadership and Narcissism," *Journal of Change Management*, **9** (2), 170.
20. Resick, Christian J., Daniel S. Whitman, Steven M. Weingarden, and Nathan J. Hiller (2009), "The Bright-Side and the Dark-Side of CEO Personality: Examining Core Self-Evaluation, Narcissism, Transformational Leadership, and Strategic Influence," *Journal of Applied Psychology*, **94** (6), 1365–81.
21. Ritala and Falkowski (2007), p. 7.
22. Hoffman, Thomas (2009) "The 'It's All About Me' Syndrome," *Computer World,* August 4, p. 32.
23. Lubit (2002), pp. 127, 130.
24. Maccoby (2004), pp. 98–100.
25. Higgs (2009), p. 174.
26. Cited in "Nip Narcissism Before It Nips You," *Executive Leadership*, December 2010, p. 2.

7. Dealing with the narcissistic coworker

Highly narcissistic coworkers represent yet another problem for people who want their workdays to run smoothly without having to resolve complex interpersonal problems. Narcissists are part of a category of workers classified as *difficult people*. A coworker is difficult when he or she is uncooperative, disrespectful, touchy, defensive, hostile, or even unfriendly.[1] Difficult people include many different subtypes, such as high-maintenance workers, and lone wolves who do not want to be part of any team.

About ten percent of the workforce might be classified as difficult, and perhaps one-tenth of these people could be classified as narcissists. Yet other types of difficult people have an element of narcissism, such as the yes-person who readily agrees to assume responsibility for a project yet often fails to follow through. As a result, the percentage of the workforce that creates problems for others based on narcissistic tendencies is probably much higher than one percent.

Nina Brown, counseling professor at Old Dominion University, reminds us that we are not helpless in dealing with destructive narcissist coworkers. People can develop and use strategies and tactics that will help them cope with negative narcissistic behavior as well as dealing with their own feelings.[2] In this chapter we include some of Brown's ideas in our approach to dealing with narcissistic coworkers. We begin by describing some of the problems created by narcissistic coworkers. We then describe a study about coping with workplace narcissists, followed by advice about taking care of oneself when dealing with narcissists. Other major topics include providing feedback to the narcissistic coworker, defending against a controlling narcissist, and avoiding codependence with the office narcissist.

POTENTIAL PROBLEMS CREATED BY NARCISSISTIC COWORKERS

As with the dysfunctional narcissistic leaders described in Chapter 6, intensely narcissistic coworkers can create problems in the workplace. Many, if not most, types of work are accomplished through collaborative effort. If the narcissist believes that he or she is much superior to coworkers, cooperating with him or her and sharing ideas will be limited. Here we describe some of the problems created by narcissistic coworkers, classified as average intensity versus high intensity or destructive. The categories may overlap, but the dichotomy is useful because some narcissistic behaviors are annoying to coworkers, whereas others can be destructive. Here is an example of the distinction: It might be annoying that a narcissist named Bart takes time from a meeting to show photos of himself participating in a fencing exhibition. In contrast, it is destructive if Bart is such a thrill seeker that he uses his company credit card to engage in high-stakes gambling and loses heavily.

Narcissistic Behavior of Average Intensity

Specifics about the myriad of annoyances and problems created by narcissistic coworkers are found in a checklist presented in Exhibit 7.1. The checklist reflects many of the better recognized symptoms, or behaviors, of narcissists. When these symptoms are displayed on the job, they can be irritating and stressful to the person on the receiving end.

Exhibit 7.1   A checklist of narcissistic tendencies with the potential to annoy coworkers
Directions: The checklist below lists 25 potentially annoying behavior of coworkers with a high standing on the trait of narcissism. To help you personalize the information in this chapter, as well as others, indicate which one of these behaviors you have observed personally.

Item	Narcissistic tendency or behavior	Observed personally
1.	Talks a lot about visions instead of concentrating on work.	
2.	Is a control freak.	
3.	Frequently exaggerates achievements and accomplishments.	
4.	Demands a lot of credit for things he or she really has not accomplished.	
5.	Asks leading questions, such as "Don't you think this is great?"	
6.	Expects others to comply right away with personal requests.	
7.	Corrects coworkers' mistakes in an arrogant way, such as saying, "Don't you know the first thing about social networking?"	
8.	Gives very little weight to the opinion of others.	
9.	Often explains own viewpoint in elaborate detail.	
10.	Becomes impatient when somebody else wants to express his or her opinion.	

Item	Narcissistic tendency or behavior	Observed personally
11.	Becomes verbally aggressive when criticized by somebody else.	
12.	Blames somebody else when he or she makes a mistake.	
13.	At times unapproachable and difficult to talk with even when his or her input is needed.	
14.	Doesn't "get it" when somebody else attempts to explain a problem he or she is facing.	
15.	Frequently preens self, including combing the hair, putting on makeup, or adjusting a belt.	
16.	Stays angry at anyone who disagreed with him or her.	
17.	Wants the group to set goals so high that failure to reach the goals is almost inevitable.	
18	Acts like a workaholic, making the person who wants to lead a balanced life look bad.	
19.	Frequently wants praise, such as asking a coworker, "How do you like the change I made on our website yesterday?"	
20.	Will do whatever it takes to be the center of attention, including disrupting a conversation with a joke.	
21.	Sulks when other people don't get excited about his or her ideas.	
22.	Acts as if he or she has the authority and power to tell coworkers what to do.	
23.	Almost never recognizes the contribution of other worker's ideas.	
24.	When another worker makes a suggestion, he or she quite often says something to the effect, "I think I have a better idea."	
25.	When another worker describes an accomplishment, describes how he or she accomplished something equally good or better.	

Scoring and interpretation: Another way of using the checklist just presented is for diagnostic purposes. Visualize the behavior of a specific work associate, and apply the checklist to that person. If that person has exhibited 15 or more of these behaviors, he or she is probably a narcissistic personality. You may need to use some of the techniques described in this chapter to avoid being stressed by your narcissistic coworker.

Source: The literature review appearing in pages 5–16 of the master's thesis listed as follows was helpful in preparing this checklist: Wesner, Bradley S. (2007), *Responding to the Workplace Narcissist*, Bloomington, Indiana: IUPUI Scholar Works (http://idea. iupui.edu).

An important implication from this checklist is that the highly narcissistic worker is capable of creating a wide variety of problems that might hamper morale and productivity. Statement 8 is but one example. If Sherry, a direct marketing specialist, gives very little weight to the opinion of others then she might not be willing to modify a marketing plan of hers as suggested by coworkers. Her direct marketing of a company product fails to meet its expectation, and considerable company money is lost.

As implied at many places in our exploration of workplace narcissism, people with strong narcissistic tendencies are poor team players. In general, their self-centeredness places more emphasis on individual achievement than collaboration. Limited empathy can be a deterrent to teamwork because team members may not care about insulting or hurting the feelings of other members. For example, high narcissist Connie might say this about Max during a meeting: "Of course, we can't take Max's optimistic projections too seriously. He's from marketing."

High-Intensity Narcissistic Behavior

The analysis of the long-term organizational impact of destructively narcissistic managers prepared by Roy Lubit also provides insight into how high-intensity narcissistic behavior by coworkers can create problems for others.[3] Here we make note of five of Lubit's observations most relevant to coworkers, along with two contributed by Vaknin.

1. *Defining characteristics of destructive narcissists.* High-intensity narcissism is characterized by three sets of behavior: (a) grandiosity, arrogance, preoccupation with power and wealth, and excessive admiration seeking; (b) a sense of being entitled to whatever they want, including a readiness to exploit others in their quest; and (c) a lack of concern for and devaluation of others. Attitudes and behaviors like these make it difficult to develop a cooperative relationship with a coworker. One example is that an effective coworker focuses on the task at hand rather than ruminating about getting promoted and occupying a powerful position. At the same time, the coworker who doesn't care about the welfare of team members has a destructive impact on morale, such as the team member who so frequently finds an excuse for not being able to work on weekends, and expects others to cover for him or her.

2. *Limited concern for others as humans with rights and needs.* Working with someone who has an extreme lack of empathy can be a highly negative experience. High-intensity narcissists are concerned only with how others serve their own needs for admiration and support. Field tech support specialist Peggy went on a three-day business trip with Kristen to troubleshoot a failed, large-size scanning machine at a customer site. Peggy came back emotionally depleted. In her words, "Kristen is an energy vampire. Any time we were not with the customer or working on the equipment, she talked nonstop about herself, her plans, her skills, and her boyfriend. She never once asked a question about me. She didn't show

too much concern for the customer's technical problem either, but at least she got the job done."

3. *Constantly envious.* The extreme narcissist is so envious of any advantage gained by a coworker that coworkers become uncomfortable in his or her presence. Extreme narcissists seek what is not theirs, simply because another person has it rather than because it has intrinsic value for them. Seth, a logistics specialist, mentioned to high-intensity narcissist Ted that the company was granting him a day of personal leave to visit a cousin who was seriously injured in an automobile accident. Ted proceeded to ask their manager why he had denied a day of personal leave for a similar reason the previous year. The manager then reprimanded Seth for having created a problem for him with Ted. (If Ted had been less self-centered and concerned about squeezing out every little advantage that others gained he would not have placed Seth in an embarrassing predicament.)

4. *Preoccupation with reinforcing self-esteem.* As a result of this preoccupation the high-intensity narcissist will greedily extract admiration from others. As already mentioned several times because it is a key symptom of narcissism, the narcissist wants to be admired. Asking occasionally, "How do I look?" or "What do you think of my new smart phone?" can be annoying. However, continually being asked to flatter and praise a coworker can become highly stressful.

Preoccupation with self-esteem also makes it difficult to form true caring bonds with coworkers. As a result, coworkers feel a void in terms of having a satisfying relationship with the destructive narcissist. A coworker who wants a strictly task-oriented relationship with coworkers does not suffer. But the coworker who wants work as a way of satisfying social needs will be strongly dissatisfied by his or her interactions with the intensely narcissistic coworker.

5. *Strong paranoid streak.* Destructive narcissists sometimes engage in paranoid thinking. To lessen their sense of shame, they devalue coworkers and project their bad self-image onto them. Extremely negative narcissists will sometimes be preoccupied with hidden motives of others and exaggerate threats. They look for faults in others in order to support their projection of their own shameful self-image onto others.

Assume that Laura, a destructive narcissist, recognizes that she wants others to fail so she can look good in comparison. Feeling ashamed about having these feelings, she deals with her anxiety by thinking that others also want coworkers to fail. As a result she looks for any sign of rivalry by coworkers as confirmations of her suspicions. One day Maurice asks Laura, "Were you able to load all the software you need into our Android?" Laura interprets this simple inquiry as an attempt by Maurice to uncover information technology skills she might lack. Laura now mistrusts Maurice, thinking that he is trying to make her look to be deficient in an important job skill.

6. *Thrill seeking and constant stimulation.* Another problem sometimes created by narcissistic coworkers is that they constantly seek new thrills and stimulation.[4] For some positions, such behavior could be an asset, such as an investment banking associate who is frequently assigned to work on new deals that bring him or her excitement. However, a reliable coworker often has to stay interested in more mundane, repetitive work. The highly narcissistic worker has a low threshold of resistance to boredom.

    Visualize Trevor, a narcissist who is assigned to a team attempting to track down lost customers and to look for trends as to why some customers do not return. The team works for a large downtown hotel. Trevor's assignment, as decided by the team leader, is to collect data to enter into a spreadsheet analysis for groups who previously stayed at the hotel, or used its banquet facilities. Being a thrill-seeker, Trevor thinks his assignment is too dull. As a result he falls behind in collecting data that needs to be entered into the spreadsheet, and the deadline for the report passes. Top management at the hotel then becomes skeptical about the team's ability to deliver the analysis.

7. *Creating post-traumatic stress disorder for others.* The extreme point of view of the negative consequences of working with or under a narcissist is expressed by Vaknin. He claims that a person will never forget the experience. It is traumatic and may lead to actual bullying and stalking behaviors. Many people in close work contact with narcissists develop post-traumatic stress disorders. Others quit and even relocate.[5] Only the extreme narcissists are likely to create problems of such a magnitude for other workers. Furthermore, the worker who suffered post-traumatic stress disorder from interacting with a narcissistic coworker probably was previously in fragile emotional condition.

A STUDY ABOUT RESPONDING TO THE WORKPLACE NARCISSIST

Dealing effectively with narcissistic coworkers is such a widespread problem that a study was conducted to uncover which methods might actually be effective. Bradley S. Wesner, a graduate student in communication studies at the time, reasoned that people with strong narcissistic tendencies are disruptive to the productivity and morale of the organization as a whole. Wesner wanted to address two major issues: First, how does one cope with an individual who exhibits narcissistic tendencies when forced to work with him or her every day?

Second, how is the coping process impacted when the narcissist is not in a position at higher levels in the corporate structure?

The Wesner study examined how individuals with narcissistic tendencies are perceived by their coworkers at the lower and mid-levels of organizations. Of particular interest was the experience of those who interact with narcissists in their daily work lives. Which methods were used to cope with narcissistic coworkers? At the same time, the study wanted to investigate the relative effectiveness of these coping methods.[6]

Narcissistic tendencies were defined in terms of how narcissism is understood in the definition of the Narcissistic Personality Disorder presented in the DSM-IV. As part of the perspective on narcissism presented in the study, it was recognized that narcissists frequently assume that other people are highly concerned with their welfare and point of view. An example would be a narcissistic worker assuming that coworkers are strongly interested in whether he or she was assigned a smart phone that had a defect, and what he or she thinks of an IT department that could commit such a flagrant error.

As a result of this perception of others being highly interested in them, office narcissists often discuss their ideas in self-important ways while being indifferent to the ideas of others. When coworkers attempt to express their views, the narcissist will frequently become impatient with the conversation, and oblivious to pain that their lack of concern causes the coworker. Another idiosyncrasy of narcissists is that when they do recognize the feelings of others, they tend to regard those feelings as a sign of weakness of the person who expressed the feelings.

Based on the many symptoms that a strongly narcissistic person exhibits, Wesner reasoned that the narcissist would have substantial problems functioning in the team environment so typical in the modern organization.

The Method Used to Study Ways of Coping with the Narcissistic Coworker

Both graduate and undergraduate students were enlisted to make observations about past and present narcissistic coworkers. The volunteers all had work experience, and were taking courses in interpersonal communication, public speaking, and research methods. Study participants had to identify critical incidents they had faced at some point in their career in dealing with a coworker with strong narcissistic tendencies. It was also required that the respondent would have attempted to cope with the narcissist.

(A *critical incident* refers to a live situation in which the respondent played an active role in dealing with the situation. The critical incident involves direct observations of human behavior that are critically important to the situation. A critical incident in dealing with an office narcissist might be as follows: "I told this woman that I was two hours late for work because my car slid off the road and was totaled. She said, 'So what. Your car is insured.' Her lack of empathy for me brought me to tears.")

The primary goal of research using the critical incident technique had three components: First, identify which coping strategies are used when people are dealing with coworkers with strong narcissistic tendencies. Second, determine if one such method is preferred over another. Third, assess the respondents' perception of the effectiveness of these coping methods.

Participants were given a list of symptoms of narcissism from the DSM to determine if they had to work in the past with an individual displaying strong narcissistic characteristics. The respondent was asked to describe a memorable experience or encounter they had had with their narcissistic coworker, and how the respondent worked through the experience. Participants also rated the effectiveness of each coping technique on such dimensions as (a) satisfaction with how the situation worked out, (b) belief that the tactic prevented further conflict, and (c) whether the respondent would use the same technique again.

Effectiveness of the Five Techniques for Responding to the Narcissistic Coworker

The surveys submitted by the study participants were analyzed to determine that the persons described by respondents exhibited at least five of the criteria of narcissism as described by the American Psychiatric Association. In this way the coworkers being reported met the criterion of having strong narcissistic tendencies. Five categories of dealing with narcissistic coworkers were identified:

1. *Non-responding (ignoring the person)*. A coping method was classified as "non-responding" when a study participant indicated that he or she simply put up with the behavior of the narcissist and did nothing about the situation. For example, one respondent noted, "I just went on with my day and put up with it because it didn't bother me to the point of trying to get even or anything."
2. *Confronting*. A coping method was defined as "confronting" when a respondent indicated that he or she initiated a one-on-one interaction with the person to describe frustration with the narcissistic behavior. An example of confrontation would be saying to a narcissistic coworker, "I am tired of you telling me about all the details of your work and your social life. How about sometimes asking me how I am doing?" (Confrontation is such an important technique in dealing with workplace associates who have narcissistic tendencies that the technique will be described separately later in the chapter.)

3. *Informing management.* Coping methods were labeled "informing management" when a respondent indicated that he or she spoke to management concerning the behavior of the person with annoying narcissistic tendencies with the expectation that management would intervene and solve the problem. One respondent noted in the survey, "He wouldn't listen so we all got fed up and went to management. Our manager did the best he could, and things began to change for the better."
4. *Befriending.* Coping methods were labeled "befriending" when a respondent indicated an attempt to befriend the annoying narcissist in some way. One respondent who used the befriending tactic stated, "He offered me a spot in his clique and I took it. It wasn't as great as I thought, but there were privileges beyond what I imagined."
5. *Quitting.* The coping method of "quitting" refers to voluntarily leaving the place of employment to avoid further contact with the narcissistic person creating the problem. For example, one study participant said, "Two weeks after the incident I walked out because I was fed up. I never talked to or saw him (the person with the narcissistic tendencies) again."

Respondents were asked if one of the identified coping strategies was preferred. Among the 55 respondents, the breakdown was as follows: 20 chose non-responding; 12 chose confrontation; 13 chose informing management; 2 chose befriending; and 3 chose quitting. Two coping methods, informing management and quitting, were perceived to be relatively effective. The other three methods (non-responding, confronting, and befriending) were not perceived to be effective.

One of the conclusions reached in the study is that some respondents feel that the only way out of the negative situation in dealing with narcissists is to quit the job or not respond to the situation and simply be miserable. An implication of this conclusion is that some workers may need to learn more effective methods of dealing with workplace narcissists so that they – the recipients of narcissistic behavior – do not have to be grossly inconvenienced or suffer.

TAKING CARE OF YOUR OWN NEEDS FIRST

A key strategy for dealing with destructively narcissistic coworkers is to recognize that your mental and physical health should receive paramount importance. You might not be able to change the narcissist with whom you are dealing, so there is a limit to the time and energy you should invest in attempting to change that person into a more flexible, caring person. As Nina Brown observes, the negative effects on you are gradual and cumulative and may have adversely affected your life in ways you have not recognized.

There are some adjustments and minor changes that you can make to improve your working relationship with an intense narcissist, as to be explained later. Yet changing that individual's personality is unlikely.

Assume that you continue to engage the self-absorbed coworker in conversation even though you usually come away feeling angry, frustrated, and incompetent. Brown admonishes that if you take the initiative for the conversation, your feelings are your responsibility. If you are the initiator, you are helping to keep yourself in a negative emotional state. Brown suggests several ways to take better care of yourself.[7]

1. *Do not respond.* When criticized or blamed, people generally respond with some kind of explanation, denial, or excuse. You will be better off emotionally if you can condition yourself not to react to any blame or criticism given you by the destructive narcissistic coworker. Most responses will result in negative feelings for you, and being defensive will disturb you even more. (The present author recognizes that for many assertive and self-confident people, remaining silent when blamed or criticized will be unnatural. Communicating about the problem, as described later, will be more effective than not responding for some people.)

2. *Overcome irrational thinking about being perfect.* Distress is often caused by irrational thinking and beliefs, particularly the belief that we need to be perfect. A destructive narcissist is free with criticism, prompting his or her coworkers to think that they are flawed. To overcome this irrational thought that you must be perfect, you are advised to give yourself permission (a) to make mistakes, (b) to be wrong, (c) to be good enough, and (d) not to feel guilty about not being perfect. Suppose a perfectionist, destructive narcissist criticizes you for having spelled Botox with a small "b" in an email. He wants you to feel stupid, and he thinks he has found an opening. An effective thought for you would be, "So what. I made a mistake thousands of people make everyday, and I did not make a major spelling error."

3. *Don't pursue their approval.* Attempt to develop the attitude that you do not need the highly narcissistic coworker's approval to feel competent, worthwhile, or well accepted. If the self-absorbed coworker approves of you, it can add to your positive emotional state. If he or she rejects you, attempt to shrug off the negativity. This tactic is important because the destructive narcissist often disapproves of the actions of coworkers.

4. *Do not try to empathize.* Empathizing with the destructive narcissist is often frustrating because you will most likely receive no empathy in return. When you empathize with another person, you become aware of their experiences and feelings. The openness will sometimes lead to the narcissist using you as a target for projection of his or her uncomfortable thoughts onto you.

For example, if you empathize with an angry narcissist you may wind up being tricked into feeling angry because the narcissist will act as if you are angry. One such tactic is to ask you "Why are you angry with me?" when you were not angry in the first place.

Another reason that empathizing with the highly narcissistic coworker may backfire is that he or she may not appreciate your efforts. The narcissist focuses on being admired, and does not care if he or she is understood. Instead of expressing appreciation for being understood, the strongly self-absorbed person may instead look for more compliments from you.

FEEDBACK AND CONFRONTATION FOR DEALING WITH THE SELF-ABSORBED COWORKER

As mentioned above, there may be times when not responding to a destructive narcissist will be an effective tactic of self-preservation. In general, it is much more productive to communicate with an intensely narcissistic coworker who is creating problems for you, especially when you desire and need a reasonable working relationship with that person. Here we describe several tactics related to communicating with the self-absorbed worker.

Give Ample Feedback and Confront When Necessary

The primary technique for dealing with counterproductive behavior of the narcissist is to feed back to that person how his or her behavior affects you. As in other forms of feedback, be clear about what you want. Focus on the person's behavior rather than on characteristics or values. If in your opinion the self-absorbed person spends too much time talking about his or her personal life instead of the problem at hand, say something to this effect: "I have difficulty getting my work done when you talk so much about yourself." Such a statement will engender less resentment than saying, "I find you to be a narcissist, and it annoys me." It is better to avoid *should* statements because they often create defensiveness instead of triggering positive behavior. Instead of saying "You shouldn't be talking about your personal life when we are working," you might try, "Could you perhaps bring up your social life when we are on break?"

Feedback will sometimes take the form of confrontation, and it is important not to lose emotional control during the confrontation. If you perceive that a narcissistic coworker has criticized you unjustly, attempt not to be defensive. Ask the narcissist exactly what he or she is upset about rather than argue. In this way the burden of responsibility is now back on the antagonist. For example, if a narcissist was insulting your PowerPoint presentation during a meeting, later ask for the reason behind the insult. You might agree with at least one of the narcissist's points to help establish rapport. An example: "Yes, I should have asked for your input before preparing my slides. I apologize for the oversight."

Based on her clinical experience, Wendy T. Behary recommends *empathic confrontation* for dealing with the highly self-absorbed coworker. You confront the bothersome narcissist with empathy. Many people will decide that empathizing with a narcissist is a waste of time. In contrast, Behary thinks that showing empathy and compassion may improve communication between you and your difficult coworker. The empathy and compassion you express does not mean letting the narcissist treat you in any way he or she wants. It is important to hold the narcissist accountable when he or she acts arrogant, selfish, controlling, or nasty. You confront, but with some empathy.[8] An example would be saying to the narcissist who was critical of you during the meeting, "You were obviously upset with my presentation today. Perhaps you were facing some problems of your own. But I still thought your tone was too harsh, and that you were trying to embarrass me."

An important element of empathic confrontation is to *establish the rules of reciprocity*. With respect to the narcissist the reciprocity rule means that the self-absorbed behavior is a little more acceptable if you have a chance to counter. You explain that you are willing to listen to your narcissistic coworker's problems and work routine, if you too get a chance to discuss your own problems and routines occasionally. A sample statement would be, "Jason, I do like to hear about how well your performance evaluation went. But for me to listen attentively to you, I also want you to listen attentively to me."

Empathic confrontation is also strengthened when you offer *warranted positive feedback*. Even the most hard-core narcissist will sometimes engage in behavior that is more constructive than usual. When such behavior surfaces, it should be rewarded with positive feedback to increase the probability that it will occur again.

Suppose a coworker of yours, Claudine, is a disruptive narcissist who freely takes credit for other people's ideas in order to be impressive. Today she mentions that somebody in another department gave her a suggestion about making internet searches more precise. She said, "Ron in purchasing showed me that I was not putting the keyword first, but preceding my keyword with less relevant words." You respond to Claudine in this manner: "Hey Claudine, I like the way you credited Ron with that search technique. He would be happy to hear that." You have helped Claudine be aware of the importance of giving due credit for ideas.

Criticize Constructively

Feedback sets the stage for criticism. Although you do not have formal authority over a coworker, you still have the right to criticize the person when he or she does something you perceive to be way out of line. It is best to criticize in private and to begin with mild criticism. Base your criticism on objective facts rather than subjective impressions. Point out, for example, that the narcissist's lack of follow-through resulted in the loss of a $10 000 sale for you. Express your criticism in terms of a common goal. For example, "We can get the report done quickly if you'll firm up the statistical data while I edit the text." When you criticize a coworker, avoid acting as if you have formal authority over the person.

Constructive criticism is often helpful because it encourages less retaliation than does destructive or hostile criticism. If you defame the narcissist's character or diagnose his or her problem the person will most likely become defensive. Assume that you say, "You neglected to get me the data I needed. As a result, I lost out on that $10 000 order." Your coworker might think through the importance of following through. Assume instead that you say, "Being the self-centered person that you are, you screwed up once again. As a result I lost the $10 000 sale." In this instance your coworker might become too angry to learn anything.

Help the Narcissistic Coworker Experience a Boost in Self-Esteem

Self-esteem for people on the high end of the narcissism scale is a tricky issue. Although many narcissists have high self-esteem that enables them to be successful, many have fragile self-esteem. Narcissists with fragile self-esteem might be more civil in their behavior if you can bolster their self-esteem occasionally. We are not saying that a person should take on the project of rebuilding the self-esteem of a troublesome coworker, yet a shot of self-confidence building may be helpful. We mention self-confidence because it is a basic component of self-esteem.

Many workplace narcissists are simply low in self-confidence and self-efficacy. (Self-efficacy refers to confidence in performing a particular task.) They use stalling and evasive tactics because they are afraid to fail. Working with your manager or team leader, you might be able to arrange a project or task in which you know the self-absorbed person will succeed. With a small dose of self-confidence and self-efficacy, the person may begin to complain less about other people. With additional successes, the person may soon develop more self-confidence and self-esteem and become less difficult. Self-confidence building takes time. However, self-efficacy can build more quickly as the person learns a new skill.

Communicate Humility toward the Narcissist

Psychotherapist Les Carter suggests that demonstrating humility when working with a narcissist may help make him or her become more cooperative. Being humble does not mean giving in passively to the narcissist's demands. What it does mean is being proactive in seeking reasonable treatment with an attitude of decency and without demeaning the other person. By acting with humility we accept the fact that work relationships are not always exactly what we want. A few of the techniques for being humble with a workplace narcissist are as follows:[9]

1. *Be respectful even when respect is not reciprocated.* Narcissists feel entitled, and crave respect to the extent that they think others are mistaken when they do not give them the highest regard. Treating the narcissist with respect may lessen his or her tendency to become increasingly upset when not treated with respect. An opportunity for remaining respectful (and biting your tongue) would be when a narcissist speaks with sarcasm and condescension toward you. Instead of reciprocating, you decide to remain dignified, and respond with a non-vindictive statement such as, "You are angry with me, and you have made yourself clear."

2. *Refrain from power struggles in communications.* Highly self-absorbed coworkers live with the delusion that others will conform to their standards once they truly understand the facts. The narcissist might become stubborn and aggressive in attempting to get others to agree to their way of thinking. Rather than fight back in a power struggle, simply state your point of view in a firm, relaxed manner. A narcissistic coworker was trying to convince a coworker that in the future there would be almost no face-to-face meetings in business with people from different physical locations. He also argued that in-person sales visits would soon be obsolete. The listener to the message replied a few times patiently, "I think you may be extrapolating a trend toward videoconferences a little too aggressively. But I do respect your opinion." In this way future discussions of the topic were less heated, with the narcissist calming down a little.

3. *Accept the reality that the narcissist might think ill of you.* The narcissist will often express insulting attitudes when in conflict with a coworker, and may often ridicule ideas and preferences that appear quite normal to the other person. Being humble allows you to accept the fact that insults exist, and that you will receive your share. It takes the sting out of insults to know that they are part of the narcissist's took kit. (Yet you might set a limit to the intensity and frequency of insults, with a statement such as, "Now you have gone too far.")

4. *Release your disillusionment and move on.* Repeated negative interactions with a narcissist can leave a person feeling weary and disillusioned. If you have tried some of the techniques for coping with narcissists, and the relationship with a specific narcissist remains a stressor, minimize future contact. Cut your losses and rely more on another coworker for satisfying interactions.

DEFENDING AGAINST THE CONTROLLING NARCISSIST

A behavioral pattern of narcissists that has received less attention than others is the narcissist's need to control. By controlling another person, the narcissist attempts to make that other person conform to his or her perspective on how things should be done. Narcissists are so convinced that they are right that they can barely tolerate anyone with different ideas. At times, the controlling relates to minor, trivial issues.

> Alice, a mature narcissist, was walking in the parking lot on a day when the vehicles stationed outside were covered with snow. On the way to her vehicle, Alice spotted coworker Ned scraping snow and ice from the windshield on his SUV. Alice went over to Ned, took the brush/ice scraper from his hand, and said, "Here is the right way to scrape ice." Ned was mildly irritated, but then reflected that Alice acts the same way in the office.

Being controlled by a narcissist in both major and minor ways is uncomfortable for many people so a defense against the control becomes necessary. Frequent feedback and confrontation about the control attempts is the method of choice. The workplace narcissist needs frequent reminders that he or she is engaging in unwanted controlling techniques. Tact and diplomacy may be helpful in explaining why the attempt at control is being rejected. Information technology is a representative area of control attempts by office narcissists. They enjoy telling others which software and hardware to use for their computers, cell phones, and smart phones, as illustrated next:

> Kevin, the office narcissist and self-designated computer software expert, overheard Cindy saying that she was still using Microsoft Explorer as her browser. Kevin jumped in with the comment. "Cindy, get out of the dark ages. Firefox is the best browser, and you should switch right away. It is far superior to Microsoft Explorer."
> To counter the control attempts by Kevin, Cindy responded: "Thank you for your opinion, Kevin. I know you are a tech expert, but I'm sticking with Explorer. It has served me faithfully for years. Besides, I don't want to face any compatibility issues."

We emphasize again, that one confrontation session is not sufficient to combat the thrusts of a narcissist. Cindy will most likely have to confront Kevin again in the near future about his attempts at control. Carter offers four additional productive ways of responding to a hyper-controlling narcissist:[10]

1. *Choose your own path.* As Cindy did in response to Kevin, it is often best not to be intimidated by a controlling narcissist. Do what you think is best, and do not worry about not accepting the advice or demands of the narcissist. Tact and diplomacy, however, is good in terms of preserving a good working relationship with the hyper-controller.
2. *Maintain self-respect.* Any work associate – coworker, subordinate, manager, and customer included – who continually attempts to control what you do or how you think is nibbling away at your self-respect. To maintain your self-respect it is essential to establish limits, even about mundane activities. Suppose coworker Emma attempts to choose the restaurant whenever you have lunch together. She might say, "Okay, we must go to the Liberty today, I have discount coupons." A reasonable response might be, "No, Emma, you chose the restaurant the last four times. It is my turn to choose." The point being emphasized is that one loses self-respect when the other person always makes the choice.
3. *Establish boundaries and consequences.* A narcissist will often make demands on a coworker that inconvenience the latter, such as insisting that he or she stay late once again to help the narcissist with a work project. The boundaries in this situation refer to the limits to which one coworker should be obliged to help a coworker regularly. A consequence could be linked to the frequent demand to stay late to help the coworker. The coworker subject to the demand might say, "If our good working relationship depends on my helping you after hours so frequently, I will have to back out of the good relationship."
4. *Remove yourself from the person or situation when necessary.* As implied in specifying consequences about a controlling relationship with a coworker, you may need to exit a coworker relationship that smothers you with control. If the manager assigns you to work jointly with a particular coworker, you cannot exit the relationship. Yet you do have a choice with voluntary arrangements, such as having lunch with the person, or listening to his or her advice about work and personal life.

AVOIDING CODEPENDENCE WITH THE NARCISSISTIC COWORKER

A potential problem in working with a narcissist is that you become drawn into a codependent relationship. You enable the narcissist by furnishing the narcissistic supply. In your desire to be helpful and supportive toward the narcissist, you run the risk of creating a dependency. Knowing what the office narcissist craves, you faithfully compliment his or her appearance and the work he or she produces.

Codependency typically refers to enabling people with addictions such as alcohol, tobacco, gambling, and internet use. However, codependence also fits the situation of a coworker who craves a narcissistic supply even if the relationship is not as serious as that between a codependent and a cocaine user. Codependency is also regarded as an emotional and behavioral condition that affects an individual's ability to have a healthy, mutually satisfying relationship. In personal life, as well as on the job, codependence can create unhealthy, dysfunctional relationships. The codependent is mutually dependent because he or she relies on the other person's dependence. The codependent has a tendency to place the needs and wants of others first, to the exclusion of acknowledging one's own needs. For example, the codependent may want compliments also, but defers to the needs of the narcissist.

The codependent will often only feel good when the dependent person feels good, so the codependent tries hard to please the dependent person. As a result the codependent person is extremely dependent and eager to please, and therefore easily submits to the wishes of others. The codependent to an office narcissist would feel best when the narcissist is happy about getting his or her demands satisfied. The codependent has a strong need to rescue or fix another person, so it is easy to fall into the trap of wanting to make the narcissist feel good.

A few suggestions for avoiding a codependent relationship with a workplace narcissist are in order. The codependent must become aware of the problem, and carefully process information about codependency. The codependent must examine thoroughly his or her caretaking. Good questions to ask yourself are: "Is my behavior reinforcing this person's narcissistic tendencies?" "Who appointed me to the role of submitting to the narcissistic demands of _____?"

The codependent person must learn to say "No," perhaps in small steps. For example, he or she might say, "I am busy this morning. Perhaps somebody else has the time to listen to your story about your exploits on the golf course last weekend?"

GUIDELINES FOR APPLICATION AND PRACTICE

1. A realistic point of view about workplace narcissists is that the nature of their personality is likely to breed conflict. Among these characteristics are self-centeredness, arrogance, and a disinclination to accept the advice of others. If you are in close contact with a narcissistic coworker, you should be prepared to resolve conflict with that person from time to time. A useful technique would be to confront the problem by explaining in detail how the narcissist's behavior is adversely affecting you. After the confrontation, it is essential to find a way to resolve the problem, including reaching a compromise.

    Assume that the narcissist in question inevitably criticizes your point of view during a team meeting, often to a disparaging extent. You might confront the person in private about the excessive criticism. A possible compromise would be for the narcissistic critic to soften criticism during a meeting, but to send you an e-mail or text message after the meeting summarizing his or her criticisms.

2. Many narcissism researchers and observers believe that trying to change the behavior of a workplace narcissist is futile, so it is best just to placate him or her. In other words, appease the narcissist and concede to his or her demands.[11] Attempt not to become so upset, and bring problems to the narcissist's attention only when he or she is creating a major problem. Placating a narcissist might be useful when you are too busy or too fatigued to get involved in interpersonal conflict. In the long term, however, it is best to deal more assertively with the narcissistic personality in an attempt to have a more tranquil work environment.

3. A constructive perspective about interacting with negative narcissistic coworkers is that they are simply another type of difficult person. Because negative narcissists are difficult people they must be regarded as yet another workplace challenge. Quitting your job, as is sometimes recommended, is a self-defeating tactic for dealing with a narcissist. This is true particularly because the next workplace will probably have its share of difficult people – including perhaps a workplace narcissist.

SUMMARY

Narcissists are part of a category of workers classified as difficult people, with other types of difficult people having an element of narcissism. People can develop and use strategies and tactics that will help them cope with the negative narcissistic behavior as well as dealing with their own feelings.

Intensely narcissistic workers can create problems in the workplace, such as not cooperating with others. When the symptoms of narcissistic behavior presented in Exhibit 7.1 are displayed on the job, they can be stressful and irritating to the person on the receiving end. The highly narcissistic worker is capable of creating a wide variety of problems that might hamper morale and productivity. People with strong narcissistic tendencies are poor team players because their self-centeredness places more emphasis on individual achievement than collaboration. Limited empathy also hurts teamwork.

High-intensity narcissistic behavior includes the following categories: (1) defining characteristics of destructive narcissists including grandiosity, sense of entitlement, and a lack of concern for and devaluation of others; (2) limited concern for others as humans with rights and needs; (3) constantly hungry and envious; (4) preoccupation with reinforcing self-esteem; (5) strong paranoid streak; (6) thrill seeking and emotional stimulation; and (7) creating post-traumatic stress disorder for others (in some cases).

A study examined how individuals with narcissistic tendencies are perceived by their coworkers at the low and middle levels in organizations. Coping methods were identified, as well as their relative effectiveness. Narcissistic tendencies were indicated as they relate to the formerly labeled Narcissistic Personality Disorder. Students were enlisted in the study to make observations about past and present narcissistic coworkers. Study participants had to identify critical incidents they had faced in dealing with a narcissistic coworker, as well as their coping methods. Participants were given a list of symptoms of narcissism to determine if they had to work in the past with an individual displaying strong narcissistic characteristics.

Five categories of dealing with narcissistic coworkers were identified: (1) non-responding; (2) confronting; (3) informing management; (4) befriending; and (5) quitting. Non-responding was the category most frequently preferred. Informing management and quitting were perceived to be relatively effective; whereas the other three methods were not perceived to be effective.

A key strategy for dealing with destructively narcissistic coworkers is to recognize that your mental and physical health should be of paramount importance. There are some adjustments and minor changes that you can make to improve your working relationship with an intense narcissist, yet changing that individual's personality is unlikely. Four ways of taking better care of yourself in working with the narcissist are as follows: (1) do not respond; (2) overcome traditional thinking about being perfect; (3) do not pursue their approval; and (4) do not try to empathize.

Rather than not responding, it is generally more productive to communicate with an intensely narcissistic coworker who is creating problems for you. Several tactics for communicating with the self-absorbed worker include the following:

(1) Give ample feedback and confront when necessary. This includes empathic confrontation which itself involves establishing the rules of reciprocity, and offering warranted positive feedback. (2) Criticize constructively. (3) Help the narcissistic coworker experience a boost in self-esteem. (4) Communicate humility toward the narcissist. A few techniques for being humble are (a) be respectful even when respect is not reciprocated, (b) refrain from power communications, (c) accept the reality that the narcissist might think ill of you, and (d) release your disillusionment and move on.

Being controlled by a narcissist in both major and minor ways is uncomfortable for many people so a defense against the control becomes necessary. Frequent feedback and confrontation about the control attempts is the method of choice. Four additional productive ways of responding to an overly controlling narcissist are as follows: (1) choose your own path; (2) maintain self-respect; (3) establish boundaries and consequences; and (4) remove yourself from the person or situation when necessary.

A potential problem in working with a narcissist is that you become drawn into a codependent relationship by furnishing the narcissistic supply. The codependent must become aware of the problem, and carefully process information about the codependency. Also, the codependent must examine carefully his or her caretaking, and learn to say, "No."

CASE HISTORY OF A NARCISSIST

The following case history is about a marketing professional who centers his marketing on an activity that brings him considerable personal enjoyment.

Jack Whitman

Jack Whitman is the Director of New Business Development at the Agency for Economic Development in his state. The broad purpose of the Agency is to attract new business to the state, as well as retain existing business firms. One of the many reasons for the existence of the Agency for Economic Development is that most of the other states within the US attempt aggressively to attract new business and retain old business. Most states grant liberal tax concessions to entice new business firms.

A major part of Whitman's responsibility is to meet with rep-resentatives of various business firms around the country, and sell them on the advantages of relocating to his state. Whitman also meets with executives from firms already in the state to help persuade them to expand their facilities and workforce within the state. Whitman's pitch to business executives includes a listing of the many advantages of his state, including: a workforce that is educated, talented, and motivated; an above-average education system; availability of an almost unlimited water supply; a moderate state income tax; and a reasonable regulatory environment.

In describing the justification for his position, Whitman says: "I could cite facts for hours about what a great state we are. But so what? The other states have the same glitzy PowerPoint presentations touting all their advantages. What I must do is to develop a personal relationship with the business executives. They have got to like doing business with yours truly, Jack Whitman. The executives I deal with have to be persuaded by my personality even more so than the tangible advantages of our state.

"The problem with selling on only the tangible advantages of our state is that these advantages have become almost commodities. All the states brag about the talented workforce, the friendly regulatory environment, and the natural beauty of their state. So it's my personality that has a big impact on whether a company decides to relocate, stay, or expand. Entertaining these executives is an extension of my personality."

An audit conducted by another state agency uncovered that Whitman invested heavily in entertainment during a two-year period, including a total of $110 000 spent in restaurants and tickets to professional football, basketball, and hockey. At times the explanation for the purpose of the entertainment was vague, including such terms as "spreading good will," and "developing my network of business contacts."

Whitman's fascination with professional football, basketball, and hockey extended to his home. The entertainment center in his basement resembles a shrine to his favorite players. Athletic jerseys are displayed in cases, and three-dimensional photos of many of Whitman's favorites players are posted on his wall. One wall is decorated with photos of Whitman shaking hands with eleven different professional athletes, including two well-known football quarterbacks.

Many of the entertainment expenses were incurred while business executives from other cities came to town to explore the Agency's city as a potential business site. In one entry, Whitman noted expenses of $1650 to take three people to an NFL game, plus dinner. When asked by an auditor to justify this expense, Whitman explained that he was at his best in a sports venue, and could therefore conduct business more confidently.

Another expense item Whitman submitted to the Agency for Economic Development was $1350 for taking three executives to an NBA game in another city. To justify this expense, Whitman explained that when visiting executives in their town, he likes to create an entertainment environment in which he feels comfortable. He therefore chose a NBA game as the best venue because he would be at his best in such an environment. Whitman explained that he knows so much about the NBA that he would impress the business executives he was entertaining. As a result, they might be more receptive to consider locating at least part of their operations in the city Whitman represents.

When Whitman's lavish entertainment expenses leaked outside the agency, several politicians called for an investigation of the legitimacy of his expenses. A state senator expressed the opinion that business executives can be entertained in a less elaborate way than taking them to professional sports games. A state representative pointed out that the Agency for Economic Development is a non-profit organization and should not entertain so lavishly. She also wondered if Whitman might be using the Agency expense budget to feed his own hobby.

Whitman responded that the investigations were not justified because he was doing such a fine job of producing good results for the Agency. He explained that his way of charming business executives had resulted in 400 new jobs for the city in the last several years.

Narcissism Analysis

Jack Whitman's narcissistic tendencies may be endangering his job, even if he has not committed fraud. As he admits, he enjoys entertaining business executives in an environment that best fits his personal preferences. In this way, he can be at the center of attention because of his expertise. Similarly, Whitman's narcissistic tendencies are reflected in his choosing an entertainment venue that fits his preferences. He appears to be less concerned about the preferences of the executives he is entertaining.

Whitman's ever-so-positive analysis of his personality suggests strong narcissistic tendencies. His casual approach to documenting his business expenses is not unusual for a narcissist because the person believes that he or she is beyond ordinary rules.

The act of spending so much money on entertainment also reflects self-centeredness on Whitman's part. Working for a not-for-profit agency, he should be more concerned about investing money conservatively. Whitman's preference for lavish entertaining reflects the poor team play characteristic of a person with a strong narcissistic trait.

REFERENCES

1. Janove, Jathane (2007), "Jerks at Work," *HR Magazine*, **52** (5), 111.
2. Brown, Nina (2002), *Working with the Self-Absorbed: How to Handle Narcissistic Personalities on the Job*, Oakland, California: New Harbinger, p. 31.
3. The first five on the list are from Lubit, Roy (2002), "The Long-Term Organizational Impact of Destructively Narcissistic Managers," *Academy of Management Executive*, **16** (1), pp. 128–9
4. Cited in Benton, Megan (2007), "Narcissism in the Workplace: How to Spot It and What to Do," December 17, www.mychurch.org/blog.
5. Vaknin, Sam (2009), "Narcissism FAQ # 82: The Narcissist in the Workplace," http://www.mental-health–matters.com, February 16, pp. 1–2.
6. Wesner, Bradley S. (2007), *Responding to the Workplace Narcissist*, Bloomington, Indiana: IUPUI Scholar Works (http://idea.iupui.edu).
7. Brown (2002), p. 35.
8. Behary, Wendy T. (2008), *Disarming the Narcissist: Surviving & Thriving with the Self-Absorbed*, Oakland, California: New Harbinger, pp. 111–30.
9. Carter, Les (2005), *Enough About You, Let's Talk About Me*, San Francisco: Jossey-Bass, pp. 144, 146–54.
10. Carter (2005), p. 47.
11. Research reviewed by Wesner (2007), pp. 17–18.

8. Dealing with the narcissistic manager

A majority of career-minded people face the challenge of developing a good working relationship with their manager. Good superior–subordinate relationships lead to positive outcomes including above-average performance evaluations, salary increases, bonuses, choice work assignments, and recommendations for promotion. In contrast, poor superior–subordinate relationships lead to negative outcomes including below-average performance evaluations, salary increases limited to a cost-of-living adjustment, the absence of performance bonuses, undesirable work assignments, and blocked promotions.

When your immediate manager is strongly narcissistic, developing a positive relationship with him or her is all the more challenging. Despite the advice frequently offered about quitting your job when your boss is a narcissist, such behavior is usually self-defeating. You may not be able to find a better job or even another job in the time frame needed. Also, voluntarily terminating employment in most fields is hardly an asset to your career – especially if you quit without a replacement position.

In this chapter we present information that should prove helpful in doing a professional job of dealing with a narcissistic manager. The topics include how coping tactics might vary in response to different types of narcissistic managers, the importance of using emotional intelligence to cope with the narcissistic boss, and how 360-degree feedback is useful in dealing with narcissistic managers. We also describe a handful of specific tactics for coping with the narcissistic manager.

APPROPRIATE COPING TACTICS FOR DIFFERENT TYPES OF NARCISSISTIC MANAGERS

Throughout this chapter we will describe tactics for dealing with narcissistic managers as if one general type of narcissistic manager existed. With slight modifications, the tactics to be described can be applied to deal reasonably well with most narcissistic managers. On a practical level, it would be difficult to diagnose finely the type of narcissistic manager you are dealing with. Roy

Lubit, however, has observed four different types of narcissistic manager, and he suggests different coping tactics for dealing with each one. Lubit's ideas merit attention because in some instances you will be able to make a fine diagnosis of the type of narcissistic manager you face, and adjust your coping tactics accordingly. The four types and coping tactics are presented next.[1]

1. *Grandiose: psychodynamic.* This type of narcissist has an outward grandiose self-image, and will typically exploit others and devalue them. When this type of grandiose narcissist experiences a threat to the self-esteem, he or she will become enraged. He or she exhibits the typical pattern of a weak conscience and limited ability to empathize with others. Much of his or her behavior is geared toward protecting a fragile self-esteem. The major objective of the "grandiose: psychodynamic" is to be admired.

   A recommended survival tactic is to outwardly display admiration toward this type of narcissistic manager. Criticism should be avoided because retaliation is most likely.

2. *Grandiose: learned.* This type of narcissistic manager has a grandiose self-image, and will exploit others based on a lack of caring, such as forcing subordinates to work so many hours that their work and personal life balance suffers. He or she often treats others inconsiderately due to not receiving negative feedback for such behavior in the past. The major objective of the "grandiose: learned" is to be admired.

   A recommended survival tactic is to show admiration and avoid criticism of this type of narcissistic manager. People with grandiose self-images are typically thin-skinned.

3. *Control freak.* By definition this type of narcissistic manager is a micromanager. He or she seeks total control of every detail and transaction in his or her area of responsibility. The control freak has an inflated self-image and devalues the abilities of others with a strong belief that other people are less capable. Another characteristic is fear of chaos if everything is not tightly managed. The major object of this type of manager is to control others.

   A recommended survival tactic is to avoid direct suggestions. By making suggestions indirectly, the control freak may think that he or she made the suggestion. Criticism should be avoided, but admiration and respect should flow freely. It is best not to perform better than the control freak. Instead, play down your accomplishments and ambition. Document your work so you will have a clear record of your accomplishments. Stay alert to opportunities for getting a transfer to another organizational unit.

4. *Antisocial.* The antisocial type of narcissistic manager will take what he or she wants, and will lie to get ahead. He or she will hurt others who are in his or her way, such as giving an undeserved poor performance evaluation

to a subordinate with high potential to replace him or her. The antisocial narcissist has almost no conscience, and also has limited empathy. A major objective of the antisocial narcissist is to experience the thrills of violating rules. Another objective is to abuse others in the workplace.

A recommended survival tactic is to avoid provoking them. Transferring away from the antisocial narcissist is often the best coping tactic. Avoid getting dragged down into their unethical and illegal activities such as insider trading or expense account abuses. You may need the emotional support of allies in the form of coworkers and mentors.

EMOTIONAL INTELLIGENCE AS A COPING STRATEGY

According to Lubit, an effective strategy for dealing with a narcissistic manager, as well as other difficult people, is to make good use of your emotional intelligence.[2] The reason that emotional intelligence is particularly helpful in dealing with a narcissistic manager is that the problem of narcissism is highly charged emotionally. When you are dealing with a narcissist, you are in an emotionally sensitive situation. For example, suppose you have a boss named George who appears to be heavily narcissistic. He frequently talks about his feelings, his accomplishments, and how he feels physically. Furthermore, he frequently fishes for compliments such as asking you what you thought of his presentation at the Monday morning meeting.

The logical approach in dealing with George would be to follow the advice of people who tell you to communicate your feelings directly in the workplace. Be candid and explicit about how George's behavior annoys you. Say something to the effect, "George, I wish you would stop talking so much about yourself, and fishing for compliments. As the boss, you should be talking about the group members, and complimenting them." The emotionally intelligent person would recognize that such an approach to George is likely to backfire. He will become upset and think that you are insubordinate. You need to use a more emotionally sensitive approach, such as complimenting George when he talks about group members instead of himself.

The Basic Components of Emotional Intelligence

The term *emotional intelligence* has gathered different meanings, all relating to how effectively a person makes constructive use of his or her emotions. John D. Mayer, a professor of psychology at the University of New Hampshire, along with Yale psychology professor Peter Salovey, originated the concept of emotional intelligence. Mayer explains that from a scientific (rather than a popular) viewpoint, *emotional intelligence* is the "ability to accurately perceive your own and others' emotions; to understand the signals that emotions send about relationships; and to manage your own and others' emotions."[3]

A person with high emotional intelligence would be able to engage in such behaviors as sizing up people, pleasing others, influencing them, and not taking narcissistic behaviors by others personally. Four key components or factors included in emotional intelligence are as follows:[4]

1. *Self-awareness* is the ability to understand your moods, emotions, and needs and their impact on others. Self-awareness also includes using intuition to make decisions you can live with happily. (A person with good self-awareness knows whether he or she is pushing other people too far. With self-awareness you would recognize when you are not flattering a narcissistic boss sufficiently to please him or her.)

2. *Self-management* is the ability to control one's emotions and act with honesty and integrity in a consistent and acceptable manner. The right degree of self-management helps prevent a person from throwing temper tantrums when activities do not go as planned. Effective workers do not let their occasional bad moods ruin their day. If they cannot overcome the bad mood, they let coworkers know of their problem and how long it might last. (A person with low self-management would suddenly decide to drop a project because the work was frustrating. Quite often a narcissistic boss does not want to bother dealing with the emotions of a subordinate because he or she is so self-absorbed.)

3. *Social awareness* includes having empathy for others and having intuition about work problems. A team leader with social awareness, or empathy, would be able to assess whether a team member has enough enthusiasm for a project to assign him or her to that project. Another facet of social skill is the ability to interpret nonverbal communication, such as frowns and types of smiles. (A supervisor with social awareness, or empathy, would take into account the most likely reaction of group members before making a decision affecting them. It takes good social awareness to deal well with a narcissistic manager because that manager is likely to regard his or her feelings and mood as so important. For example, it would be helpful to recognize when your manager is sending out signals that he or she needs a compliment.)

4. *Relationship management* includes the interpersonal skills of being able to communicate clearly and convincingly, disarm conflicts, and build strong personal bonds. Effective workers use relationship management skills to spread their enthusiasm and solve disagreements, often with kindness and humor. (A worker with relationship management skill would use a method of persuasion that is likely to work well with a particular group

or individual. In general, it takes above-average interpersonal skills to develop a good working relationship with a narcissistic manager.)

Tests of emotional intelligence typically ask you to respond to questions on a 1–5 scale (never, rarely, sometimes, often, consistently). For example, indicate how frequently you demonstrate the following behaviors:

I can laugh at myself.	1 2 3 4 5
I help others grow and develop.	1 2 3 4 5
I watch carefully the nonverbal communication of others.	1 2 3 4 5

Acquiring and Developing Emotional Intelligence

Many people believe that emotional intelligence can be acquired and developed, much like a person can learn to become more extraverted or learn to control his or her temper. Many consultants offer training programs for helping employees develop emotional intelligence, and school systems throughout North America provide students some training in emotional intelligence. Elkhonon Goldberg, a clinical professor of neurology at New York University School of Medicine, explains that emotional intelligence can be learned to a degree, much like musical talent or numerical ability can be developed. Having the right natural talent, however, is an important starting point. The combination of biological endowment (such as being aware of your emotions) and training will enable most people to enhance their emotional intelligence.[5]

Given that emotional intelligence is composed of different components, to acquire and develop such ability would usually require working on one component at a time. For example, if a person had difficulty in self-management, he or she would study and be coached in an aspect of self-management such as anger control. Training in anger management is widespread today because so many people have difficulty in managing their anger.

According to Lubit, there are four keys to developing your *personal competence* (his term for the combination of self-awareness and self-management), as follows:[6]

1. Pay attention to your emotional reactions to situations, such as reflecting, "How do I feel about my boss suggesting that I should show more willing-ness to come to the office on weekends?"
2. Enhance your understanding of why you react as you do. Self-reflection is also useful here, such as saying, "Why didn't I laugh at Kim's joke this morning when everyone else did?" You might also get the opinion of a confidant, such as asking a coworker why she thought you might not have laughed at Kim's joke.

3. Think of alternate ways to interpret upsetting situations. It is natural to become angered, and even a little bit depressed, when faced with an upsetting situation. Yet you can sometimes learn to give a positive spin to the situation that will reduce some of the emotional sting. Suppose your boss criticizes the depth of an analysis you prepared on a competitive business problem, such as the market for bathing suits in Alaska. The positive spin would be to obtain practice in being more thorough in gathering marketing intelligence.

4. Find constructive ways to deal with whatever emotional stress remains. Most people have developed preferred methods of dealing constructively with negative stress. Many of these approaches relieve symptoms, as well as helping you deal better with frustration. For example, millions of people use some form of the relaxation response, including yoga, deep breathing, taking a warm shower, or napping. Yet stress relief is only temporary if you do not modify the problem that is the true stressor, such as learning to deal more effectively with a narcissistic boss.

The combination of self-reflection (or introspection) and talking with a confidant about how to understand your emotional reactions will help you grow your self-awareness and self-management.

Lubit also gives advice for enhancing *social competence*, his term for the combination of the social awareness and relationship management components of emotional intelligence. Social competence grows through a process similar to the growth of personal competence, as follows:

1. Pay attention to the emotions and behaviors of others, such as observing carefully whether a manager really cares about your opinion when asking you a question. A manager might ask you, "Do you think I was justified in getting rid of that overly-demanding, money-losing customer?" Observe carefully your manager's facial expression. Does she really care what you think, or is she just expecting you to confirm that she showed the right judgment?

2. Seek to understand the behavior of other people through reflection and discussions with individuals whose judgment you trust. For example, you might ask a coworker who you think understands human behavior well, "I notice that Gil (the vice president of engineering) keeps moving his feet back and forth when he talks about technology coming down the pike that could be commercialized. What do you make of his foot shuffling?"

3. Think of various ways to deal with situations. An important part of emotional intelligence is being able to relate effectively to others, and more than one tactic may be required to reach a particular goal. You might find that your manager does not show much interest in what you are proposing,

and therefore is not listening carefully to your proposition. Try framing your suggestion in another way, such as explaining the potential return on investment from your suggestion.

4. Observe the effects of your actions. A key strategy for enhancing emotional intelligence is to observe how people react to your behavior, and then make appropriate adjustments. Assume that Frank thinks an effective way of building a good working relationship with teammate Kenosha is to compliment her frequently on her appearance, such as saying, "What a stunning outfit you are wearing today." If Kenosha simply shrugs her shoulders or does not respond, Frank should recognize that Kenosha does not welcome comments about her appearance. As a result Frank begins to compliment Kenosha about her job-related skills and suggestions. Rapport with Kenosha is now enhanced, and Frank has learned an important lesson about dealing with his teammate.

Lubit also suggests that you can learn from situations without being directly involved in them. Social competence can be enhanced by observing others, thinking about why people react the way they do, and observing what behavior is effective in which situations.

Applying Emotional Intelligence to Dealing with the Narcissistic Manager

Most of the strategies for coping with the narcissistic manager presented later require good emotional intelligence. For example, you need to be able to size up a person's feelings to understand how to compliment him or her effectively. Among the factors you need to observe is how receptive the person might be to a compliment today. Suppose your narcissistic boss José seems to have a negative mood tone today because his favorite team in the World Cup competition was eliminated at 3 this morning (your time). As you detect the frown on José's face, you decide to wait until later to deliver the compliment about his shiny new smart phone because you know he will not be in a mood to receive the compliment at this moment.

Another example of an emotionally intelligent approach to dealing with a narcissistic manager is not to cross or threaten that person. The avoidance of threatening behavior is particularly important if the narcissistic manager has fragile self-esteem because such an individual depends on positive feedback. Research suggests that narcissists become aggressive when they perceive an ego threat. The problem is that the threat confronts the reality that they are not special. Aggressiveness can also be triggered when narcissists feel they are not getting enough respect.[7] Here are several examples of behavior from a direct report that would be perceived as threatening by a narcissistic boss (and perhaps most bosses).

- Stating that you are dissatisfied with your performance evaluation and that you intend to discuss your concerns with your manager's boss.
- Indicating that you disagree on a technical issue with your boss and that you plan to present data to support your position.
- Pointing out that the performance of the organizational unit has not been so good during the previous year, and that you think he or she needs to take action to improve performance.

360-DEGREE FEEDBACK TO IDENTIFY THE PROBLEM

Although this chapter focuses on what the individual can do to deal with a narcissistic manager, the organization also has some responsibility in identifying dysfunctions created by a destructive narcissist. One of the most effective tools for early recognition of dysfunctional narcissism is 360-degree feedback.[8] A key feature of this approach to feedback that makes it helpful in identifying problems is that the input is anonymous. Given that subordinates provide the input to the assessment, 360-degree feedback is a combined venture of the organization and the individual worker. A brief description of the basics of 360-degree feedback follows, with a focus on how the process might relate to dealing with a highly narcissistic manager.

In most large organizations, managers not only provide feedback to group members, but they also receive feedback that gives them insight into the effects of their attitudes and behaviors. The feedback is systematically derived from a full sampling of parties who interact with the manager. Specifically, *360-degree feedback* is a formal method of evaluating managers based on input from those who work for and with them, sometimes including customers and suppliers. The process is also called a 360-degree survey because the input stems from a survey of a handful of people. The multiple inputs become another way of measuring managerial effectiveness.

Specialists in the field view 360-degree feedback as more suited for its original purpose of development for a manager or leader than for administrative purposes such as performance evaluation and salary administration. With respect to a manager whose narcissism is creating problems, he or she could be offered leadership coaching to decrease the problems.

When used for development, 360-degree feedback should emphasize qualitative comments rather than strictly quantitative ratings.[9] For example, being told, "You do not listen to me when I attempt to contribute to a meeting," is more helpful than simply receiving a low rating on listening skill. The feedback is communicated to the manager and interpreted with assistance from a human resource professional or an external consultant.

The data from the survey can be used to help managers fine-tune their attitudes and behaviors. For example, if all interested parties gave the manager low ratings on "empathy toward others," the manager might be prompted to improve his or her ability to empathize. Such approaches would include reading about empathy, attending a seminar, or simply making a conscious attempt to empathize when involved in a conflict of opinion with a subordinate. An executive or leadership coach might also provide assistance in helping the manager learn how to be more effective at empathizing.

Many 360-degree surveys give the manager an opportunity for self-rating, as well as receiving ratings from others. Some managers, including the highly narcissistic, feel crushed when they feel a gap between how they might rate themselves on a dimension of behavior (such as empathy) and the perceptions of the group. When such gaps occur, sometimes professionally trained counselors should be involved in the 360-degree feedback.

A sampling of specific dimensions of behaviors related to narcissism that might be found in a 360-degree feedback form includes the following:

- empathy for others
- listens carefully
- concern for the group welfare
- considerate of people
- gives emotional support
- hostile toward individual group members.

If the 360-degree feedback form allows for qualitative comments, almost any dysfunctional behavior of the highly narcissistic manager might be included. A sampling follows:

"This guy is so stuck on himself, his nickname should be Velcro."

"All she cares about is her and how great she is."

"Just goes through the motions of being interested in the group. Is really just looking for personal glory."

"He is the only person I know who has a bigger ego than Donald Trump or Steve Jobs."

"She makes Martha Stewart look shy about promoting herself in comparison."

"I don't think he ever really listens to a thing I am saying."

"Won't stop babbling about himself and his accomplishments."

Some critics of the 360-degree feedback system are concerned that it is somewhat like posting an anonymous blog on the internet. You can be as nasty and hostile as you want because nobody knows the source of the comment. Also, if you do not take responsibility for a negative comment, it does not have to be carefully reasoned and based on fact. Despite these reservations, in a corporate culture that fosters honesty and constructive behavior 360-degree feedback can provide the narcissistic manager with useful ideas for needed changes in behavior.

A VARIETY OF INDIVIDUAL COPING STRATEGIES

Several tactics for coping with a highly narcissistic manager have already been mentioned in passing, such as not provoking an antisocial narcissist, and showing admiration for a grandiose narcissist. In this section we provide more details about these coping tactics, as well as presenting a few more. Exhibit 8.1 lists the seven tactics to be presented.

Assess the Relationship Realistically

An essential tactic in dealing with a narcissistic boss is to assess your relationship realistically with him or her. Recognize that you will have to proceed with sensitivity and caution in order to develop a good working relationship with that person. Use your understanding of the narcissistic personality to help you overcome frustrating situations, such as the boss wanting to talk about a recently acquired dance trophy while you have an important budget problem to discuss.

Psychotherapist Sandy Hotchkiss recommends that you should know the narcissist's primary weakness – the fragile self-esteem beneath the mask of superiority and power. Develop an awareness of what triggers his or her shame and envy. Be alert to deciphering the meaning behind the grandiosity, arrogance, need for admiration, entitlement, disdain for others, and rage. She

Exhibit 8.1   A variety of strategies for coping with a narcissistic manager

1. Assess the relationship realistically.
2. Maintain your professionalism.
3. Flatter the narcissistic manager.
4. Confront the problem gently and tactfully.
5. Document your accomplishments.
6. Be willing to accept criticism.
7. Over-respond to the manager's pet peeves.
8. Maintain a strong network.

recommends that you then treat the narcissist as you would a young, vulnerable child, but with twice the respect. Another aspect of realism is to not do anything that disturbs the self-absorbed manager's images or illusions.[10]

If you worked for a manager who considered herself to be a finance whiz, would you tell her that you would like to help her learn how to understand annual reports? If you happen to deflate a narcissistic boss, be ready to do damage control. Rework your suggestion from a different perspective. With respect to the example of the annual report, if your boss develops an angry look, rework your suggestion. Explain that you have found a few new financial ratios that you are not certain your boss has seen, and that this is where you wanted to offer assistance.

Another reality of dealing with a highly narcissistic manager is that you should not compete for attention with that person. If your boss mentions that he received an accolade from upper management for the department's performance, do not mention that an executive complimented you for your sterling performance.

Being realistic can also mean being prepared to accept any of the known symptoms of narcissism. For example, a narcissistic manager will sometimes display grandiosity that is unrealistic. Visualize Shirley, a narcissistic manager heading up a small unit of a major conglomerate such as General Electric (GE). At a Monday morning staff meeting she talks about her desire for the unit to become the most outstanding performer in the entire organization by the end of the year. You calculate that sales would have to increase 2000 percent to attain her goal. Instead of confronting your manager with the reality that her vision is grandiose beyond reason, you say, "Shirley, you have given us a great target to shoot for. We will certainly be hunting for new business."

Maintain Your Professionalism

In working with a strongly narcissistic manager, it is important not to become readily upset because you object to his or her decisions or behavior. Do not overreact by fighting back over such matters as not receiving enough recognition or the boss being preoccupied with his or her own achievements. An easy way to lose professionalism is to search for allies in counterattacking the narcissistic boss, or to complain about him or her to other members of the group or others in the company.

An exception to the suggestion for not complaining about the narcissistic boss to anyone outside your unit would be when the narcissistic boss far exceeds his or her legitimate power. Two examples are misappropriating company money or sexually harassing subordinates. In these instances, whistle-blowing is justified.

A useful perspective on maintaining professionalism is to recognize that in most organizations, reporting relationships are only temporary. Eventually your narcissistic boss will move to another unit, quit, or be downsized. As mentioned above, quitting yourself is usually a bad idea. Yet asking for a specific transfer as an opportunity for professional growth can sometimes work. Asking for a specific transfer is preferable to asking for a transfer anywhere out of the department because the latter implies escape motivation.

An aspect of professionalism implied from the examples presented so far is to take most mistreatment from the narcissistic manager professionally, not personally. You may simply represent a stepping stone for the narcissistic manager to get what he or she wants. For example, if the narcissistic manager takes too much credit for an idea that you developed, he or she probably has nothing against you personally. The manager just likes to accumulate as much credit for ideas as possible as part of his or her narcissistic predisposition.

Flatter the Narcissistic Manager

The most direct approach to building an effective relationship with a narcissistic manager, as well as any other narcissist, is to flatter the person sensibly and credibly. Flattery directly feeds the strong need of the narcissist to be admired. Despite the risk of being called obsequious or a cheap office politician, the flatterer wins in relationships with narcissistic managers as well as those less narcissistically inclined.

A study on how to advance in big business pointed out that a company's top employees tend to be equal in performance. Advancing was based on image (30 percent) and contact time with the manager (50 percent). Flattery can play a big role in both.[11] Another study indicated that even at the highest positions in business, flattery helps a person get ahead. Specifically, ingratiating yourself to the CEO, including flattery, was a major factor in receiving an appointment as a board of director at major companies. Not carefully monitoring (carefully scrutinizing) the CEO's activities also worked in a person's favor for obtaining a board appointment.[12] You might interpret not finding fault with a CEO to be a subtle form of flattery.

Flattery is likely to be effective because the narcissistic manager (as well as most people) want to receive accolades, even if they are not completely warranted. The person who pays the narcissistic manager compliments is likely to be treated kindly in turn.[13] An example of an effective compliment to the admiration-hungry manager would be: "Everyone in the meeting was listening so attentively when you gave your report. And the industry statistics you found really drove home the point."

Another way of flattering the narcissistic manager is to listen attentively. If you actively listen to the self-admiring manager, he or she will feel flattered. The manager might think, "What I have to say is valuable. This person really cares about what I have to offer." Flattery can also take the form of quoting the manager, or referring to something he or she said to you earlier. To a narcissist, as well as to many others, hearing or seeing one's thinking repeated is a sound of joy.

Confront the Problem Gently and Tactfully

A general-purpose way of dealing with a problem manager is to confront the problem, then look for a solution. Because your manager has more formal authority than you, the confrontation must be executed with the highest level of tact and sensitivity. Confronting a person with strong narcissistic tendencies requires even more sensitivity because most narcissists dislike criticism intensely. The more fragile the self-esteem, the more discomfort the manager will have with being criticized or corrected.

A beginning point in confronting a narcissistic manager is to ask gently for an explanation of the problem. Suppose, for example, you believe strongly that your team leader snubs you because he or she dislikes you. You might inquire gently, "What might I be doing wrong that is creating a problem between us?"

Another situation calling for confrontation would be outrageous behavior by the manager, such as swearing at and belittling group members. Because narcissists are readily triggered into anger, this problem will surface often. For example, a worker reported that in meetings his manager openly belittles his peers and the people higher in the organization. The worker was concerned that this behavior fosters poor morale and unprofessional attitudes among team members, and hurts productivity.[14] Because several or all group members are involved in the example cited, a group discussion of the problem might be warranted. You and your coworkers might meet as a group to discuss the impact of the manager's style on group morale and productivity. This tactic runs the risk of backfiring if the manager becomes defensive and angry. Yet confrontation is worth the risk because the problem of abuse will not go away without discussion.

Confrontation can also be helpful in dealing with the problem of *micromanagement*, the close monitoring of most aspects of group member activities by the manager. "Looking over your shoulder constantly" is an everyday term for micromanagement. Narcissistic managers are particularly prone to micromanagement because they typically believe they have superior judgment and ability. If you feel that you are being supervised so closely that it is difficult to perform well, confront the situation. Say something of this nature, "I notice that you check almost everything I do lately. Am I making so many errors that you are losing confidence in my work?" As a consequence, the manager might explain why he or she is micromanaging or begin to check on your work less frequently.

Confrontation appears logical, and well suited for an open organizational culture in which people freely criticize each other in order to accomplish goals.

Yet in some instances, confrontation will not work with a narcissistic manager. If the manager is a destructive narcissist who is hypersensitive, confrontation will be interpreted as a personal attack. As a result, the relationship between you and the narcissistic manager will deteriorate.

To test the narcissistic manager's tolerance for being confronted, first try a confrontation about a relatively trivial work issue, such as a small correction. Here is an example of a minor correction and trial balloon. "Ray, you told me that you did not want me to have any errors on our Facebook page. But you also told me not to waste too much time getting the page absolutely correct. Which course of action do you prefer?"

Document Your Contributions

A widely recommended technique for coping with a narcissistic manager is to document your contributions so you will be able to present your side of the story in case the narcissistic manager unjustly accuses you of having poor performance. The concern about false accusation of poor performance is valid because an intense narcissist will frequently devalue the ability and contributions of other workers. Also, he or she will readily blame others, including subordinates, for his or her own poor performance.

Here is an example of the need for documentation. The narcissistic manager might be accused by upper management of having failed to attain a cost-reduction target. In self-defense, the manager might reply, "I made our cost-cutting targets quite clear to all the people in my department, and they signed off on the cost-reduction goals. But Jennifer really messed up. She hired two new workers at higher-than-market-rate salaries." Jennifer would be able to defend her position if she had maintained detailed records of how the boss had ordered to hire the two new workers despite the cost-cutting drive. It was thought that the new workers would more than pay for themselves because of the operating efficiencies they would bring to the department.

Documenting your accomplishments for a narcissistic manager can also be a positive tactic, not strictly defensive. The narcissist in power is typically self-absorbed, so he or she might neglect to record the accomplishments of group members. As a result, if you can present him or her with a clear record of accomplishments, it will be to your advantage. For security purposes, it is best to have both electronic and hard-copy documentation of what you have accomplished. If your narcissistic manager tends toward paranoid thinking, it is especially important not to rely only on e-mail messages in the company computer system to keep track of what you have done. A paranoid thinker might have unwanted documentation removed from the system.

In fairness to the narcissistic manager, "What have you done for me lately?" is a question on the minds of many managers. To the extent that you can clearly document what you have accomplished recently, as well as in the past, you are therefore likely to enhance your relationship with your narcissistic manager, as well as with any other manager. You can help your manager better understand your contributions by explaining exactly what work you are doing, problems you are solving, and successes you are attaining.

Document legitimately what you have accomplished, and communicate it in a factual, matter-of-fact manner. The occasional FYI e-mail provides useful documentation, providing you do not appear to be bragging.[15] A collection agent might report to her boss, "In March, I collected an average of $310 from my block of delinquent accounts. So far, I have collected at least something from 25 out of the 31 accounts I am currently assigned. We should be getting something from three more of these delinquent accounts."

Be Willing to Accept Criticism

A key characteristic for being able to deal effectively with a narcissistic manager is to have a thick skin, or be able to accept criticism without becoming unduly upset. According to Michael Macobby, "A narcissist won't show much emotional intelligence. While he is very sensitive about his ego, he's not sensitive about yours. You've got to be willing to accept that reality if the reward is great enough. People who hung on at Microsoft got very rich."[16] (Macobby implies that Bill Gates was a high-level narcissist during the high-growth period of Microsoft. The extraordinary philanthropy of Gates and his wife Melinda in later years could be interpreted as narcissism because the generous giving has brought more world attention to Gates. An equally valid interpretation is that Gates has considerable empathy for people who need help in such areas as preventing and conquering AIDS, and in learning how to read and do math. Gates is therefore genuinely concerned about the welfare of others, not just himself.)

Another reason for being willing to accept criticism is that narcissistic managers enjoy criticizing subordinates because to criticize another person often means that the criticizer is superior in some way. To be narcissistic is to feel superior. As a result, the narcissist frequently self-aggrandizes yet criticizes others. Sometimes the criticism of others takes the form of micromanagement, such as expressing disapproval about the font chosen by a subordinate in an e-mail message.

Over-Respond to the Narcissistic Manager's Pet Peeves

Part of the way a narcissistic manager operates is to have strong preferences over small matters. These minor preferences or pet-peeves are part of the narcissist's way of being ego-centered and expressing individuality. If your narcissistic boss has a pet-peeve, cater to that demand. A territory manager knew that his boss likes orders to get processed immediately. (The boss's pet peeve is a delay in the processing of an order.) So the manager tried to process an order upon arrival. If he couldn't get to it immediately, he would send an e-mail stating that he was tied up on another project. Eight out of ten times, the boss would then do the order processing for the manager.[17] To be less manipulative, you might do an honest job of staying on top of any task that your boss deems to be extra important.

Maintain a Strong Network

A strong network helps you deal with a narcissistic manager in two major ways. First, you may need power contacts to help you find another position inside or outside the organization in case working with the narcissistic manager becomes intolerable. Also, the narcissistic manager might try to fire you for invalid reasons. Second, you may need effective network members for emotional support with respect to your dealing with the peculiarities of your manager. As part of emotional support, network members can listen to your concerns and offer advice.

In addition to making contacts, networking involves gaining the trust and confidence of influential people. Before you can network with influential people, you must identify who those power players are. You might make observations of your own, such as listening for whose names are mentioned frequently by people in the company. Asking the opinions of others about which people influence decision making can be illuminating. Sometimes a person without a fancy job title might be a highly influential person. An example is that an administrative assistant might heavily influence the decisions of his or her boss.

Networking also takes place with people inside and outside the organization who are not your managers. Developing contacts with influential people is likely to pay big career dividends in addition to helping you deal with a narcissistic manager. A standard procedure is to create a card or computer file of the people in your network and update it frequently. To keep your network effective, it is necessary to contact people on your list periodically. Developing a network of influential people requires alertness and planning. You have to identify influential people and then think of a sensible reason to contact them. Here are a few possibilities:

- Send an e-mail message to a high-ranking manager, offering a money-saving or revenue-producing suggestion. A related tactic is to inform the person of something of significance you did that might lie directly in his or her area of interest. Social networking sites such as Facebook, LinkedIn, and Twitter can be used for networking with influential people.

An influential person who joins such a site is usually open to making new contacts. (You may find, however, that many influential people are not willing to become your "friend," but you will often at least be able to send them a message.)

- Do a standout job as a member of a task force or committee that includes a high-ranking official.
- Take the initiative to develop a friendship with an influential person who is a member of your athletic club, YMCA, YWCA, or place of worship.

Networking is so often used – and abused – that suggestions and guidelines for networking etiquette have emerged. A starting point is to be clear, concise, and specific when making requests of networking contacts. Explain, for example, that you want to become an industry specialist and would like to acquire specific information. Be frank about the amount of time you would want from the network member, such as 15 minutes per month of e-mail and telephone contact.

In developing your network it is essential not to display highly narcissistic tendencies of your own. After making contact with a potential network member, explain the benefit this person is likely to derive from his or her association with you. Provide a *benefit statement* for interacting with you and helping you with your career.[18] Indicate specifically how this person might benefit from you being in his or her network. (If a person is in your network, you are also in that person's network.) If the potential network member is more powerful than you, it is still possible to think of what benefit you might be able to provide. Two examples follow:

- "I would like to contact you a few times a year about career concerns. In return, I would be happy to help you identify some groups on Twitter that might be worthwhile for our company to contact."
- "In return for my receiving career advice from you from time to time, I would be happy to collect information for you about how people in my area perceive one of your products. I have lots of useful contacts in my community."

Avoid being a pest. Many influential people are bombarded with requests to be part of someone's network, so ask for a modest amount of time and assistance. Good networking etiquette is to request a collaborative relationship in which you give as much as you get. The benefit statement just mentioned will place you in a collaborative relationship with the influential person. You will then be in a better position to rely on network members to help you deal with a narcissistic manager, including finding a new position.

GUIDELINES FOR APPLICATION AND PRACTICE

1. Much of this chapter contains guidelines for application and practice for
    dealing with a narcissistic manager. The checklist presented in Exhibit 8.2
    serves as a reminder of the many suggestions already presented for dealing
    constructively with a narcissistic boss.

Exhibit 8.2   Suggestions for dealing with a narcissistic manager

Number	Suggestion
1.	Outwardly display admiration toward the "grandiose: psychodynamic" manager.
2.	Show admiration and avoid criticism of the "grandiose: learned" manager.
3.	Avoid direct suggestions to the control freak type of manager.
4.	Avoid provoking the antisocial type of manager.
5.	Make good use of your emotional intelligence.
6.	Emotional intelligence can be learned to a degree, much like musical talent or numerical ability can be developed.
7.	To develop the personal competence aspect of emotional intelligence, do as follows: (a) pay attention to your emotional reactions to situations; (b) enhance your understanding of why you react as you do; (c) interpret upsetting situations in alternative ways; and (d) find constructive ways to deal with emotional stress.
8.	To develop the social competence aspect of emotional intelligence, do as follows: (a) pay attention to the emotions and behaviors of others; (b) understand the behavior of others through reflection and discussions with people you trust; (c) think of various ways to deal with situations; and (d) observe the effects of your own actions.
9.	Avoid threatening behavior, particularly if she or she appears to have fragile self-esteem.
10.	Realistically assess your relationship, such as understanding his or her major weakness. Also do not compete for attention with him or her.
11.	It is important not to become readily upset because you object to his or her decision or behavior.
12.	A useful perspective on maintaining professionalism when being upset is that most reporting relationships are only temporary.
13.	The most direct approach to building an effective relationship is to flatter that person sensibly and credibly. Also, listen to the manager attentively, which is a form of flattery.
14.	A general-purpose way of dealing with a problem manager is to gently and tactfully confront the problem, then look for a solution.
15.	A widely recommended technique for coping with a narcissistic manager is to document your contributions, so that you will be able to present your side of the story in case you are unjustly accused of being a poor performer.
16.	Be able to accept criticism without becoming unduly upset.
17.	If he or she has a pet peeve, cater to that demand.
18.	A strong network helps by assisting you find a new position if needed, and also serves as a source of emotional support and advice.

2. A realistic starting point in improving your emotional intelligence is to
    work with one of its four components at a time, such as the empathy aspect
    of social awareness. A complex behavior pattern or trait such as emotional
    intelligence takes considerable time to improve, but the time will most
    likely be a good investment. Follow these steps:

    a. Begin by obtaining as much feedback as you can from people who
        know you. Ask them if they think you understand their emotional reac-
        tions and how well they think you understand them. It is helpful to ask
        someone from another culture or someone who has a severe disability
        how well you communicate with him or her. (A higher level of empathy
        is required to communicate well with somebody much different from
        you.) If you work with customers, ask them how well you appear to
        understand their position.
    b. If you find any area of deficiency, work on that deficiency steadily.
        For example, perhaps you are not perceived as taking the time to
        understand a point of view quite different from your own. Attempt to
        understand other points of view. Suppose you believe strongly that
        only people with lots of money can be happy. Speak to a person with a
        different opinion and listen carefully until you understand that person's
        perspective.
    c. At a minimum of a few weeks later, obtain more feedback about your
        ability to empathize. If you are making progress, continue to practice.
    d. Prepare a document about your skill development. Describe the steps
        you took to enhance your empathy, the progress you made, and how
        people react differently to you now. For example, you might find that
        people talk more openly and freely with you now that you are more
        empathetic.
    e. Repeat these steps for another facet of emotional intelligence. As a
        result you will have developed another valuable interpersonal skill.

SUMMARY

When your immediate manager is narcissistic, developing a positive relationship
with him or her is all the more challenging. Four types of narcissistic managers
are (a) grandiose: psychodynamic, (b) grandiose: learned, (c) control freak, and
(d) antisocial. Different survival tactics have been recommended for each one,
such as displaying admiration for the grandiose: psychodynamic.

Emotional intelligence is particularly helpful in dealing with a narcissistic
manager because the situation is so emotionally charged. A person with high

emotional intelligence would be able to engage in such behaviors as sizing up people, pleasing others, influencing them, and not taking narcissistic behaviors by others personally. Four key factors included in emotional intelligence are as follows: self-awareness; self-management; social awareness; and relationship management.

Given that emotional intelligence is composed of different components, to acquire and develop emotional intelligence would usually require working on one component at a time. Personal competence (self-awareness and self-management), and social competence (social awareness and relationship management) are developed in slightly different ways.

Most of the strategies for coping with a narcissistic manager require good emotional intelligence. For example, you need to be able to size up a person's feelings to understand how to compliment him or her effectively.

One of the most effective tools for early recognition of dysfunctional narcissism is the 360-degree feedback, a formal evaluation method using input from many people who work with the manager. Many 360-degree surveys give the manager an opportunity for self-rating, as well as receiving self-ratings from others.

Eight strategies for coping with a narcissistic manager described in this chapter are as follows: (1) assess the relationship realistically; (2) maintain your professionalism; (3) flatter the narcissistic manager; (4) confront the problem gently and tactfully; (5) document your accomplishments; (6) be willing to accept criticism; (7) over-respond to the manager's pet peeves; and (8) maintain a strong network.

CASE HISTORY OF A WORKPLACE NARCISSIST

The following case history is about an executive and media personality who is adored by millions, yet poked fun at by many others. She is also one of the best-known women in the US.

Martha Stewart, the Mega Personal Brand and Demanding Boss

In her prime, Martha Stewart was labeled, "the world's No. 1 living mega-brand" by *Fortune* magazine. Martha Stewart's ascent to fame can be traced to her book *Entertaining*, published in 1982. As a result, she developed a reputation as an expert on home decorating and elegant weddings, as well as cooking and gardening. Martha Stewart has often been described as a perfectionist in her cooking, gardening, and entertaining. She places heavy demands on herself and her staff.

Early in her career Stewart was a highly successful model, and then a successful stockbroker. Later, Stewart leveraged her small catering business into an empire that included books, a magazine, and a syndicated television show, *Martha Stewart Living.* Her company, Martha Stewart Living Omnimedia was first listed on the New York Stock Exchange in 1999. At its peak the company had an annual sales volume of $200 million built around the themes of domesticity, style, and elegance. Her name was eventually used as a brand name for a variety of household products at Kmart and Sears.

Perceptions by Stewart and of Stewart

When asked about Donald Trump, another celebrity with a powerful personal brand, Stewart replied that she and he are not close friends but that they have a cordial relationship. Stewart commented, "I always like people who are themselves. Donald is himself. You see it on TV. He's the same person on TV that you know in person – the same guy. He's not an actor. He's not a fake. And his hair is really horrible. When I get close to him, I just want to get the scissors. But he is a nice guy, and his wife is really nice. All his other wives were really nice, too."

In 2005, Stewart changed her title at Living OmniMedia to founder, and Susan Lyne was appointed as CEO. In reflecting on whether she would like to be CEO again, Stewart said, "I am very happy with my current status. I am doing the same work I have always done. I'm working hard to develop the business with Susan. She is a very competent CEO. I consider myself the visionary still. I have lots of visions, and I want to help develop those visions intro real, substantial businesses."

In 2004, Stewart was convicted of conspiracy and obstruction of justice in an insider stock trading case, and was sentenced to five months in prison. She said that the time in prison was the least bad part of the three years surrounding her sentencing. Stewart claimed that the prison environment was pleasant, and that she used her time productively. Before prison she was surrounded by the press.

Stewart said that one day she was visiting a Kmart just to check out the display of her products. "One woman was buying a sheet and her husband said. 'You can't buy that. She was just convicted.' And he threw it back on the shelf. I went over to him and I said, 'Oh, hi, I'm Martha. If you really look at the product, you will see that your wife should buy it because it's really good. It doesn't matter that I was convicted because the product is the same.' They bought it."

A former sales manager at Martha Stewart's *Body and Soul* magazine sued the company for job discrimination in 2009. The manager, Kris Paris, claimed she was pressured to return to work shortly after a severe automobile crash, and then fired. Paris was hit by an automobile while she crossed the road in May 2008. She suffered multiple fractures to her spine and left elbow, according to court records. Paris had a seven-pound metal "halo" attached to her head.

Martha Stewart is the subject of many blogs and gossip reporters. On the positive side, hundreds of people comment on how Stewart is the embodiment of the American Dream, working her way up from an attractive young model to become a remarkably successful celebrity, entrepreneur, and business executive. Jeffery Racheff, who conducts a blog about celebrities, looks at Stewart differently, with this comment: "Some people weren't meant to be on Twitter. Take Martha Stewart for example. The woman has created such an overly-doting, crafts-loving persona that anything she tweets is either hard to take seriously… or just sounds like she's off her rocker."

At one time Stewart said she preferred Twitter to Facebook because Twitter is a more direct form of communication that does not require going through some of the foolish routines on Facebook. A *Huffington Post* blogger commented, "Martha Stewart doesn't care about anyone but herself, so why should she log onto Facebook and look at pictures and accept friend requests? She just wants to get her snobby voice out to as many people as possible."

Two perspectives on *The Martha Stewart Show*
The Martha Stewart Show, similar to other shows featuring a presentation by a celebrity, includes a clapping and/or cheering audience as a prop. Internet columnist Lisa Takeuchi Cullen was curious about the audience experience for Stewart's television show. A blogger responded to Takeuchi that being a member of the audience is demanding. He says that members of the audience, many of them frail old ladies, are herded from one waiting

pen to another. The plastic chairs are uncomfortable, and Stewart and her producers are quite rude. He writes:

> After filming was completed, the stage manager told the entire audience to wait before leaving because Martha had to film a few promos. All 120 of us watched while she spoke into the camera about various upcoming shows, taking about ten minutes. After the promos were done, Martha (who didn't look up at, or acknowledge the audience at all, never mind thanking us for coming) walked off and we were allowed to begin filing out.
>
> That's when I realized that 120 people had been inconvenienced, kept ten minutes past the completion of the show that we signed up to see, so that Martha wouldn't have to wait for us to file out before she could start filming the promos. She would rather inconvenience 120 people than herself.

Andrew Ritchie, inventor of the Brompton folding bicycle, offers another perspective about appearing on the Martha Stewart television show. He said that 2010 marked the most amazing Martha moment he could have expected, by taping a segment on her show. Ritchie said, "Meeting her was extraordinary in itself, but working with her, even for that brief segment, was an amazing opportunity I will remember for the rest of my life. Her crew and the producers who put her show together were wonderful and I will always be grateful for their generosity in inviting me to be even a small part of her 2010 season."

Martha Stewart the leader

Observers remark that Stewart's high standards and perfectionism make their way into her leadership style. Stewart has been analyzed as using an autocratic leadership style. She is an extremely successful businesswoman who appears to rule with a no-nonsense attitude. She pays exceptional attention to minute details, makes very specific requests of subordinates, and is known to be quite demanding. Stewart has been able to build a successful organization with her abrupt and harsh leadership style.

During an MSNBC interview, Stewart defended her leadership style, with these words, "My whole life has been based on the pursuit of perfection and the pursuit of accuracy and good information and good inspiration. So if I am ever called difficult to work for, it's by people who really don't care about those qualities in work. But my whole life is based on those qualities."

Narcissism Analysis

Martha Stewart is without doubt a productive narcissistic leader and celebrity. The fact alone that the Martha Stewart name is so prominent in so many venues suggests that she is narcissistic. You can even purchase cans of paint and coffee percolators branded with Martha Stewart. A subtle point about being narcissistic is that perception counts, and many people including Michael Maccoby perceive her to be a narcissist. There is some evidence that Stewart treats some people with cold indifference and a lack of empathy. (Yet the incident about the injured worker could well be attributed to a manager lower in the organization, not Stewart herself.) Despite concern about how Stewart treats people, many individuals enjoy interacting with her – particularly her key subordinates and television guests.

A suggestion about working well for a productive, demanding narcissist like Martha Stewart is to demonstrate a strong work ethic and perform at your absolute best. Otherwise, you would fall out of her favor.

Source: Announcement for Maccoby, Michael (2003), *The Productive Narcissist*, New York: Broadway, April, www.randomhouse. com/features/pronar; "Martha Stewart Praises Twitter, Trashes Facebook," www.huffingtonpost.com (accessed January 2, 2011); Cullen, Lisa Takeuchi (2010), "Martha Stewart Still the Queen of Mean," *True/Slant* (http://trueslant.com/lisacullen), January 5; "Martha Stewart: Biography from Answers.com," pp. 1–32 (accessed January 1, 2011); Martha Stewart (2005), "I Consider Myself a Visionary Still," *Business Week* (www.businessweek.com), December 19; Boyle, Christina (2009), "Martha Stewart Body and Soul Magazine Sales Manager Sues, Says Bias Cost Her Job," *Daily News* (NYDailyNews.com), October 8; *Martha Moments* (http://marthamoments.blogspot.com), January 3, 2011, pp. 1–2; Racheff, Jeffrey (2010), "Martha Stewart Tweets 'I'm Not Drunk,'" *LimeLife* (www.limelife.com), September 22; "Martha Stewart and Donald Trump Are Big Fans of the Autocratic Leadership Style. Could It Be for You?" *Setting Goals 101* (www.settinggoals101. com), copyright 2009.

REFERENCES

1. Lubit, Roy (2004), "A Tyranny of Toxic Managers: Applying Emotional Intelligence to Deal with Difficult Personalities," *Ivey Business Journal*, March/April, pp. 3–4.
2. Lubit (2004), pp. 1–7.
3. Quoted in Mayer, John D. (2004), "Leading by Feel: Be Realistic," *Harvard Business Review*, **82** (1), 28.
4. Goleman, Daniel, Richard Boyatzis, and Annie McKee (2001), "Primal Leadership: The Hidden Driver of Great Performance," *Harvard Business Review*, **79** (12), 42–51.
5. Goldberg, Elkhonon (2004), "Leading by Feel: Train the Gifted," *Harvard Business Review*, **82** (1), 31.
6. Lubit (2004), pp. 6–7.
7. Vogel, Carl (2006), "A Field Guide to Narcissism" *Psychology Today*, **39** (1), 70.
8. Lubit, Roy(2002), "The Long-Term Impact of Destructively Narcissist Managers," *Academy of Management Executive*, **16** (1), 136.
9. Toegel, Ginka and Jay A. Conger (2003), "360-Degree Assessment: Time for Reinvention," *Academy of Management Learning & Education*, **2** (3), 297–311.
10. Hotchkiss, Sandy (2003), *"Why is it Always About You?" The Seven Deadly Sins of Narcissism*, New York: The Free Press, p. 155.
11. Monster Career Centre, www.monster.com (2002) "Managing Your Boss – How to Play Your Cards Right," vol. 4, p. 2.
12. Westphal, James D. and Ithai Stern (2007), "Flattery Will Get You Everywhere (Especially If You Are a Male Caucasian): How Ingratiation, Boardroom Behavior, and Demographic Minority Status Affect Additional Board Appointments at U.S. Companies," *Academy of Management Journal*, **50** (2), 267–88.
13. Goldsmith, Marshall (2003), "All of Us Are Stuck on Suck-Ups," *Fast Company*, December, p. 117.
14. Cited in Fisher, Anne (2002), "Ask Annie," *Fortune*, April 1, p. 171.
15. Sills, Judith (2008), "How to Improve Your Credit Rating," *Psychology Today*, **40** (2), 67.
16. Quoted in Weiss, Tara (2008), "The Narcissistic CEO," *Forbes.com* (www.forbes.com), June 29, 2008.
17. Anonymous (2008), "How to Live with the S.O.B.," *Business Week*, August25/September 1, pp. 48–50.
18. Hilliard, Brian and James Palmer (2003), *Networking Like a Pro*, Atlanta, GA: Agito Consulting, p. 52.

9. Dealing with the narcissistic subordinate

A narcissistic worker can create problems for a manager, such as being so self-centered that work is neglected. In the two previous chapters we have described tactics and strategies for coping with workplace narcissists when they are your coworker or superior. All of these methods might have relevance in dealing with the narcissistic behavior and attitudes of a person who reports to you as his or her manager or team leader. Yet the interpersonal dynamics change considerably when you have formal authority over a narcissist – there is an organizational expectation that he or she will obey, or at least listen to you. It might be true that organizations are more democratic than in the past and that the concept of superior–subordinate seems a little antiquated. Yet the person who writes the performance evaluation and makes recommendations about salary increases and firing still has some formal authority, even in a relatively egalitarian organization.

We approach the subject of the dealing with the narcissistic subordinate in several ways. First we look at the key behaviors of a narcissistic subordinate that might represent a challenge to the manager. We also describe the narcissistic organization, because this type of environment triggers or intensifies workers with tendencies toward behaving in narcissistic ways. Three sections of the chapter look squarely at helping the workplace narcissist overcome problems that might be interfering with productivity and morale, or at least with a smooth running of the manager's organizational unit. We place particular emphasis on coaching as a way of facilitating a worker with narcissistic tendencies to become a productive narcissist.

KEY BEHAVIORS OF THE NARCISSISTIC SUBORDINATE

All the characteristics and behaviors of workplace narcissists mentioned in the previous chapters are likely to manifest themselves when a narcissist reports to somebody else. Yet several of these characteristics are more likely to be a concern for the manager of the workplace narcissist. Here we describe a sampling of these characteristics and behaviors likely to be apparent in the role of a subordinate or group member.[1]

1. *Hypersensitivity to negative evaluation.* A manager who plays an active leadership role must often evaluate the performance of group members. Periodically scheduled performance evaluations are only part of the evaluation process. The active manager provides feedback as needed, including asking questions about why a particular action was taken or not taken. A highly narcissistic subordinate will often respond with intense negative emotion upon receiving negative feedback. A typical response by the subordinate would be, "Who are you to judge? You weren't close enough to the details to know what was going on."

   The manager who intended to provide constructive feedback now becomes embroiled in a confrontation with the narcissistic subordinate. The confrontation is time consuming, and an uncomfortable experience for many managers.

2. *Grandiosity in the form of inflated sense of self-importance, arrogance, preoccupation with status, and excessive admiration seeking.* Grandiosity of this nature results in the narcissistic subordinate being a high-maintenance employee because he or she requires above-average attention. During a team meeting one member kept banging away on the keyboard of her laptop computer. The noise became distracting to other members. When asked what she was doing, the woman replied, "Oh, I need to get this report done for a client by late this afternoon." (The woman's behavior showed several aspects of grandiosity at the same time: She thought she was important enough to engage in individual work activity during the meeting; typing instead of listening during a meeting is arrogant; and perhaps she thought she would be admired for ignoring the meeting.)

3. *Lack of concern for and devaluation of others.* Most work in organizations is accomplished by groups, including teams. Consequently, a lack of concern and devaluation of others on the part of one group member creates difficult problems for the manager. The narcissistic worker who does not care about others and devalues them will not be concerned about doing his or her fair share of work, or sharing responsibility for undesirable tasks, such as cleaning up after a flood. A major problem arises when the narcissistic worker occupies a customer-contact role and is indifferent toward the frustrations of customers. A narcissistic worker at a customer support center for a telephone company happened to laugh out loud when a customer was calling to complain about a random charge of $138 for a call she never made. The manager of the support center soon heard about

the laughing incident, and had to invest about one hour in patching the problem.

4. *A sense of entitlement often in the form of demanding special privileges or maximizing whatever benefits are available.* The narcissistic subordinate can be a high-maintenance worker in another important way. He or she wants to squeeze every possible benefit from the organization, creating some resource allocation problems for the manager. Examples are as follows. An administrative assistant complains because her computer is not yet equipped with the latest Microsoft operating system, and she demands that the situation be fixed to her satisfaction. An engineer says he must have the maximum salary increase allowable this year because he is spending some of his own money for taking a job-relevant course at a local university. A marketing assistant says she does not want to attend a year-end meeting because she has two days of personal-leave time left for the year. She contends that if she does not use the two days, they will be wasted thereby violating her employment agreement.

5. *Inability or unwillingness to see their own faults.* Narcissists are not alone in having difficulty in seeing their own faults. "The paradox about narcissism is that we all have this streak of egotism," says Mark Leary, professor of psychology at Wake Forest University. "Eighty percent of people think they're better than average."[2] The difference between the workplace narcissist and others is that he or she has even greater problems in admitting to errors or having faults. One problem this difficulty in admitting to errors or faults creates for the manager is that the office narcissist might be very reluctant to modify a practice that is creating performance problems. For example, a medical office supervisor might explain to a receptionist, "Please stop giving health advice and suggestions to patients. They are likely to interpret your suggestions as professional medical advice coming from this office. If the advice backfires we could be sued for medical malpractice." The narcissistic receptionist (or intake clerk) sees nothing wrong in giving common-sense advice to patients so she continues.

6. *Habitual lateness.* For many managers one of the most annoying behaviors of narcissists is being late for work and for meetings so frequently. Anthony Warren, a professor of entrepreneurship at the Smeal College of Business at Penn State University, contends that showing up late is an outrageous expression of arrogance.[3] The person who is habitually late in a work environment creates such problems for others as (a) keeping them waiting for the meeting to start, (b) having to cover for him or her while he or she is not on the job, (c) having to summarize what has taken place at the meeting so far, (d) being distracted as the person walks in late to the office

or meeting, and (e) creating a productivity loss assuming that the narcissist is doing productive work.

People are habitually late for many reasons, but for the narcissist being late often reflects indifference toward rules that apply to others. Off the job, the narcissist may often not stop at stop signs, thinking, "It's okay if I just slow down a little at the stop sign. I'm a careful driver and I have never hit anybody."

7. *Strong performance when working alone and given recognition and praise.* To end this list on a positive note, the manager can sometimes capitalize on the strengths of a workplace narcissist. Quite often narcissists are intelligent and creative, thereby being high performers if they are not creating problems for others. (Also, many successful leaders have an element of narcissism to their personality, as described in Chapter 5.) For the narcissistic individual contributor to perform well, the person needs more recognition for work well done than do most employees.

Based on their research and experience as managers and coaches, Ritala and Falkowski, write, "We have seen time and time again where cruel, offensive narcissists excel off the scale when they are placed in individual contributor and staff role full-time or on special segmented parts of a project. What they can produce with their skills and abilities when they do have coworker interaction and input can be incredible. They are focused and do not accept failure on their projects."[4]

ORGANIZATIONAL NARCISSISM AS A CONTRIBUTING FACTOR

Narcissism is generally regarded as an individual personality trait rather than a tendency that arises in response to a situation. The narcissist who demands attention on the job probably also demanded attention at the previous employer, at school, and on the playing field. Although the individual's personality is a dominant factor in determining the extent of his or her narcissism, the environment is at least a contributing factor. Taking the extreme case, assume that an individual attends a team-building activity. To break the ice and start the process of relationship building, each participant is required to stand up in front of the team and describe his or her five best strengths. Participants in the team-building exercise are encouraged to act a little narcissistic during the exercise.

A more comprehensive setting that can intensify tendencies toward narcissism is to work within a *narcissistic organization*, or one that is self-absorbed and suffers from delusions of success and grandiosity. An organization might attempt to protect its identity (in the sense of being known and recognized) to the extent of becoming self-obsessed, and will display intense narcissistic behaviors. Organizational theorists Dennis Duchon and Michael Burns caution that these extreme narcissistic behaviors will, in the long run, lead to decline.[5]

People working for a narcissistic organization find it comfortable to express whatever narcissistic tendencies they might possess. One example would be a store associate at Lord & Taylor, the upscale retailer, acting in a haughty manner when an customer inquired whether the store had any dresses on sale for $35 or less. Another example would be a recruiter at Google laughing in a condescending manner when asked by an applicant if you needed good software skills to apply for a job at the company.

A narcissistic organization is composed of the collective personalities of its members. The greater the percentage of managers and other workers with narcissistic tendencies, the more likely the organization will be narcissistic. Physical features and assets can also play a role in making an organization narcissistic. When a restaurant has some wine selections for $2000 per bottle, the restaurant will have a narcissistic feel. Extraordinarily luxurious company headquarters might also contribute to organizational narcissism.

Notable Characteristics of a Narcissistic Organization

As can be inferred from the examples of Lord & Taylor and Google, a narcissistic organization can often be described as one that is proud and elite. When making a judgment about whether an organization is narcissistic, it is important to separate how people in the firm actually behave versus the image that advertising and public relations specialist have created for the firm. The advertising firm, in particular, will sometimes attempt to create the image of a self-adoring organization.

One of hundreds of possible examples is the advertising for the tequila brand Silver Patrón. One of their ads states, "Eliminate re-gifting. This holiday season give the world's finest ultra-premium tequila. Made with only hand-selected 100% Weber blue agave. Simply perfect."[6] (To state that you are perfect is highly narcissistic.) If you should visit a Silver Patrón facility you will probably not find dozens of narcissistic workers and their supervisors preparing the tequila – just ordinary tequila drinking people.

In this section we focus on ten notable characteristics of a narcissistic organization.[7] The checklist presented in Exhibit 9.1 provides a sampling of a wide variety of characteristics of a narcissistic organization, with many of these characteristics to be included in the listing of attributes that follows.

Exhibit 9.1   Checklist of characteristics of a narcissistic organization
Directions: Visualize an organization you know well, such as a past or present employer,
or a company you have studied carefully and also have spoken to a few employees. Check
those characteristics you have observed.

No.	Characteristic	Observed
1.	Elaborate, luxurious company headquarters, occupying considerable space for viewing and walking rather than for conducting work directly.	
2.	Pervasive attitude that competitors have products and services of much lower quality than own company.	
3.	Organization believes that it is unique, with no serious competition.	
4.	Belief that the organization possesses knowledge and capabilities far beyond those of other organizations in its field.	
5.	Top-level management denies reality of problems facing the organization.	
6.	Organization denies negative facts about itself through spokespersons, blogs, press releases, and annual reports.	
7.	Office layouts and architecture are ornate and sumptuous, suggesting status, prestige, and vanity.	
8.	Corporate headquarters has attention-grabbing architecture, lavishly decorated offices.	
9.	Company uses private jets for executives, holds lavish parties, and sponsors professional sports teams.	
10.	Workers develop extensive jargon specific to their company.	
11.	Company has its own collective name for employees such as "Googlers," or "IBMers."	
12.	Admitting to problems is seen as weakness.	
13.	Need for security exaggerated.	
14.	Many workers use dismissive term for company outsiders, such as "non-Apple people," or "non-Microsoft folks."	
15.	Workers freely express pride in the organization.	
16.	Widely-held belief that people who work for competitors have inferior careers.	
17.	Top management believes that almost every position in the organization is occupied with a highly talented and dedicated worker.	
18.	Members of executive suite have no clue about any morale or productivity problems that might exist throughout the organization.	
19.	Company founder or founders is regarded as a genius, and perhaps a great humanitarian.	
20.	Employees are expected to be cult-like in their devotion to the organization.	

No.	Characteristic	Observed
21.	Executives surround themselves with yes-people because the executives dislike being criticized.	
22.	Executives do not take personal responsibility for mistakes, but instead make other organization members the scapegoats.	
23.	Several of the top leaders are treated with exalted status.	
24.	Questioning anything about the organization is discouraged.	
25.	Working for the organization is perceived as a privilege that should be greatly appreciated by each employee.	
26.	Total loyalty to the organization in the form of not being critical is expected of all employees.	
27.	Constructive criticism, including bringing ethical breaches to the attention of upper management, is unwelcome.	
28.	Working for the organization is regarded as a great career opportunity.	

Scoring and interpretation: The more of the above characteristics you have accurately observed in the organization you have in mind, the more likely it is narcissistic. Scores of 23 and higher suggest a narcissistic, smug organization. If you checked 5 or less items, maybe the organization you had in mind could use some self-esteem building.

Note: An organization does not truly believe or think anything, because an organization really refers to a collection of people and physical assets. As a result, a statement such as "the company believes" really refers to a collective attitude of key people, usually executives.

Source: Most of the characteristics are based on information from Duchon, Dennis and Michael Burns (2008), "Organizational Narcissism," *Organizational Dynamics,* October–December, pp. 354–63; Ritala, Jean and Gerald Falkowski (2007), *Narcissism in the Workplace*, US: Red Swan Publishing for IT Service Management Institute, pp. 29–31.

1. *An attitude of smugness and superiority is pervasive throughout a narcissistic organization.* The statements many managers and others make about the company are indicative of this self-adoration. Three examples:

   > "Almost nobody ever quits our company who we really wanted to stay."

   > "Our annual revenues are greater than the gross domestic product of the ten poorest African countries combined."

   > "We receive about 500 unsolicited résumés per day from people who would like to work for us."

2. *Delusions of success and grandiosity.* The attitude of executives and lower-ranking workers is that the company can do no wrong, including the belief that the company's products and services are world class. The

term "centers of excellence" is used frequently to describe organizational units, and the term "world-class leadership" is often used to describe the heads of these units. When the organization does experience a setback it is attributed to external forces beyond anyone's control such as an unrealistic government regulation. A narcissistic retailer will often blame "lowered consumer demand" for poor sales even when several key competitors have not experienced a decrease.

3. *A focus on protecting an identity that has taken on narcissistic qualities.* A narcissistic organization is proud, and managers work hard to protect the identity of the firm. Preserving the identity is usually a positive behavior because it strengthens the brand. Workers throughout the company refer to it with pride and a sense of elitism. The venerable investment banker Goldman Sachs represents an outstanding example. Many Goldman employees make reference to belonging to a privileged elite group, despite fines imposed on the company for ethical breaches such as not explicitly describing the risks associated with certain investments.

4. *Denial of problems.* The narcissistic organization, similar to the narcissistic individual, will often deny that problems exist, thereby not taking action to correct the problems. Working for an organization that denies problems could possibly encourage the worker to behave similarly. Involuntary turnover is a frequent area in which denial takes place. Top-management might deny that too many talented workers are joining the competition. The denial might take this form, "A major reason that a few of our most capable managers have left is because the industry recognizes how talented they are. A few of our managers are recruited away from us not because of problems here but because the managers are so good."

5. *Takes on a sense of entitlement.* An extremely narcissistic organization will often take on a sense of entitlement that is accompanied by a lack of empathy for what customers want. An organization of this type assumes that it is entitled to continued success because of its natural superiority. Many fine retailers have eventually gone out of business because management believed there would always be a market for their high-priced luxury goods despite satisfactory competitive alternatives. Several jewelry chains have a sense of entitlement. Yet, in their defense, it is part of the culture of a jewelry marketer to behave in a smug, aristocratic manner. A sales associate in a fine jewelry store almost never says to a couple visiting the store, "What do you guys want?"

6. *Extreme high self-esteem.* Organizational narcissism beyond healthy limits occurs when the organization becomes unduly proud of what it has accomplished and can accomplish. Executives at Enron Corporation bragged about how they had invented new business models and new ways of making money. During its heyday, Enron was heralded by many

management observers as highly creative and successful. However, the extreme high self-esteem and lack of concern for the welfare of others eventually created a climate favoring unethical and illegal behavior, such as hiding financial losses. To quote business writer Kurt Eichenwald in reference to Enron, "Crime was just one ingredient in a toxic stew of shocking incompetence, unjustified arrogance, compromised ethics, and utter contempt for the market's judgment. Ultimately it was Enron's tragedy to be filled with people smart enough to know how to maneuver around the rules, but not wise enough to know why the rules had been written in the first place."[8]

7. *Questioning any aspect of the organization is discouraged.* Executives in an intensely narcissistic organization do not want to hear criticism from its workers. The culture of the organization strongly dictates that part of showing loyalty to the organization is to accept whatever practices and policies exist. For example, it would be frowned upon to suggest that the company outsource manufacturing only to companies that paid fair wages, had safe working conditions, and protected the environment.

8. *Self-aggrandizing fantasies of success.* Top management at an extremely narcissistic organization will sometimes brag outlandishly about its success, and engage in rituals and entertainment to publicize its success. One multilevel (or pyramid) marketing company that sells liquid food supplements brags about its success on YouTube videos. The founder makes frequent reference to the success of its distributors and talks about the exotic locale of its annual sales meeting. The focus is on how much money everybody associated with the company is making, but you need to visit the company website to figure out what product this company is actually selling.

9. *A selfish organizational culture.* A subtle characteristic of a narcissistic organization is that the culture breeds selfishness. Selfish behavior is most likely to surface when the organization is at risk. Managers and other workers become concerned chiefly about themselves, with a disregard for the welfare of others. According to author Don Schmincke, selfishness infects cultures when you see people:[9]

   • spending more time looking good to the boss than serving customers;
   • taking credit for the ideas of other employees;
   • avoiding accountability by backstabbing or blaming others;
   • adopting entitlement attitudes;
   • engaging in silo building and turf protection. (*Silo building* is a buzz word for developing organizational units that are self-sufficient and minimize interaction with other units. A replacement buzz word for the same idea is *creating firewalls* around your organizational unit.)

Selfishness creates problems because it contributes to sacred cow projects, blaming others for mistakes, accountability avoidance, backstabbing, organizational politics, surf protection, power plays and gossiping. An additional problem noted is *grin faking*, meaning that people smile in agreement although they have no intention of truly supporting a project. Selfish behavior is a productivity drain because so much time is devoted to looking out for personal welfare rather than in helping the organization.

10. *Healthy pride.* Just as individuals with the optimum degree of narcissism can be productive, an organization that is proud without being excessively smug will often experience success. John Deere seems to qualify as a business organization that is tinged with narcissism, including a healthy pride that pervades the company. Founded in 1837, John Deere managers and employees have a right to be proud. The company is the leading manufacturer of agricultural products in the world and is also a leading supplier of construction equipment. The pervasive pride at Deere has not blocked the company from maintaining high operating efficiencies and closely monitoring the competition. At the local dealer level also, an outsider can observe the self-admiration of a person who sells and services John Deere equipment.

General Motors: A Previously Narcissistic Organization

General Motors began a wonderful comeback in 2010, to emerge again as a widely admired, successful company. In 2011, hourly workers began receiving generous year-end bonuses based on vehicle quality and sales. The combined forces of shedding debt by declaring Chapter 11 bankruptcy, mammoth loans from the federal government, less costly labor-management agreements, and a surge in consumer demand helped transform GM. Yet in decades past, particularly during the 1950s through the 1970s, GM exemplified a smug, narcissistic organization that thought its supremacy in the design and manufacture of vehicles was unshakable. The appliance division with its Frigidaire and the finance division with GMAC were also brimming with self-adoration.

According to *Fortune* writer Alex Taylor III, GM was still the Great American Company in the 1970s. In working for GM for a long period of time, its top-level managers had had become too comfortable, insular, self-adoring, and too committed to the status quo. Between the 1960s and 2010 GM was losing its relevance. Customer preferences changed, the competition became intense, and technology outside GM was advancing more rapidly than inside the company.[10] (The present author notes, however, that GM has always had pockets of substantial success such as the Cadillac division. These successes include the acceptance of the Escalade by a wide variety of people, especially the hip.)

GM often attempted to improve but it was doomed by what once made it successful: doing things the GM way. When Rick Wagoner, chairman of GM at the time, was asked why GM wasn't more like Toyota, he would say, with a tilt toward narcissism, "We're playing our own game – taking advantage of our own unique heritage and strengths." Years before that, GM executives dismissed the entry of Japanese cars into the North American market as irrelevant because such small vehicles would be rejected by American and Canadian consumers.

Contributing to GM's historical smugness was that, during the 1950s, GM sold half of the automobiles in the US, and the Chevrolet division was larger than most car companies. Most adults and children were familiar with the advertising slogan, "See the U.S.A. in your Chevrolet." The infiltration into the pop culture of the terms "Chevrolet" and "Cadillac" contributed to the self-esteem of GM people. (The term *Cadillac* still has some currency as a synonym for top of the line.)

During its heyday, conformity was expected at GM and rebellion was frowned upon. People who led a flashy lifestyle – those who were not organization men – were looked upon as a poor fit for the organization. (Expecting conformity in dress and behavior suggests organizational narcissism because heavy conformity carries the idea that "our way is the right way.")

During the 1980s, Roger Smith was the Chairman and CEO of GM. Smith was credited with being a big thinker who saw the need for the company to become less complex and faster thinking. Nevertheless, several people who worked for Smith regarded him as a petty tyrant who was demanding and intolerant of dissenting ideas – strongly suggestive of narcissism.

For a long period of time, GM was in a perpetual state of turnaround. The company often promised that it had finally understood how to make cars that consumers really wanted to buy and the cars would be arriving at dealers soon. One critic called it the *mañana* company. Despite the self-puffery, the GM market share continued to dwindle.

A few years ago, Taylor thought that the insular, self-absorbed culture of GM would make it difficult for the company to return to glory, even with a federal government bailout. Yet, to its credit, GM has recaptured much of its past glory. Perhaps the hard times, such as having lost $72 billion in one four-year period, declaring bankruptcy, and accepting a giant government loan, has helped soften the organizational narcissism.

Returning to the point of the description of organizational narcissism at GM, a person working in an environment of this nature could readily be triggered into narcissism. This would be particularly true if he or she had underlying tendencies toward narcissism.

RELATIONSHIP-FOCUSED COPING TACTICS AND STRATEGIES

The emphasis of a relationship-focused coping strategy in dealing with a narcissistic subordinate is on the person's attitudes and behavior rather than on the task he or she is performing. Relationship-focused tactics and strategies make considerable sense because most of the challenges in dealing with a narcissistic subordinate stem from his or her personality rather than the task. Here we look at several approaches to dealing with the behavior of a subordinate with accentuated narcissistic tendencies.[11]

1. *Help overcome hypersensitivity to evaluation and potential negative feed-back or criticism.* In dealing with this core behavior of the narcissist, it is important to tread lightly yet still be explicit about what behaviors require change to meet company standards. It may be helpful to explain to the narcissist that you want to discuss a potential area for improvement, rather than focus on the negative. Suppose that you have a subordinate who is taking too much time in meetings bragging about his accomplishments and discussing his leisure activities. You might approach the problem this way during a one-on-one session: "I've noticed something you do in meetings that requires a little modification. The rest of the team and I appreciate your contribution when it is problem-focused. Yet when you drift into tangents about yourself and your outside interests, it does not appear that you are contributing to the meeting."
2. *Discuss the exaggerated sense of entitlement.* Narcissistic group members will often feel that they should be exempt from difficult or dull tasks, and therefore may seek to avoid doing their share of grunt work. At the same time, the narcissist will attempt to extract every possible advantage from the organization, such as maximizing sick days and time off for personal reasons. It will therefore be necessary to remind narcissistic subordinates frequently of the importance of shared responsibility for unpleasant tasks. It may also prove helpful to have an occasional two-minute chat about the true purpose of sick days and personal leave days – to deal with emergencies that prevent coming to work.

    Another aspect of entitlement is expecting the maximum allowable salary increases and bonuses. A narcissistic worker might feel no compunction about saying to the manager, "I've heard the top performers are getting four percent salary increases this year, and that's what I want." The narcissist has to be gently informed that the manager, not the employee, decides who will receive the maximum salary increase or bonus. It can also help the narcissist to be informed that salary increases and bonuses are based on merit, not the worker's preferences for a specific increase.

3. *Coach about the limited empathy for the plight of others.* The limited empathy of narcissists manifests itself in many ways. Within a work group a consistent way in which limited empathy expresses itself is not appreciating the work demands placed on others, with the administrative assistant or office assistant often being the brunt of limited understanding. The narcissist will unhesitatingly make a demand on an overburdened assistant at close to quitting time, such as, "I need that spreadsheet analysis we did last year on exports to Europe. I have no idea where to find it. Can you get it for me right now?" Another example of a narcissistic demand on the office assistant would be suddenly to change a lunch order, after the take-out lunch has already been submitted. The assistant, as well as the restaurant, has to change direction quickly just to suit the preferences of one workplace narcissist.

    A coaching-style approach to these types of narcissistic demands is to collect a couple of examples to discuss as feedback about the problem. In recognition of the sensitivity to feedback, a non-threatening lead-in might be: "I know that you are intensely goal-oriented but it appears that you can be a little too demanding on the office assistant."

4. *Decrease the confusion of boundaries between the boss and subordinates.* Nina Brown notes that narcissistic behavior can become disruptive when clear boundaries are not established between the manager and subordinates.[12] The problem is that the narcissist will often capitalize on the situation when the boss does not establish appropriate boundaries. An especially effective action for setting appropriate boundaries is for the manager or team leader to separate professional activities from personal and social activities.

    When participating in a business social activity such as a dinner, picnic, or gathering at the boss's residence, the boss should make it clear by his or her actions that the occasion is business-related, not strictly social. Physically touching subordinates or making sexually suggestive comments are boundary-crossers that make it difficult to criticize a subordinate for narcissistic behavior back at the work setting. A narcissist who discussed personal life in depth with the boss during a company-sponsored dinner might easily make this comment when criticized at the office: "Come on now. You are not going to pull rank on a personal buddy are you?"

    Appropriate boundaries can also be maintained by not playing favorites. It can be demoralizing to the group when the manager appears to favor one or two people in the work group. The destructive narcissist will go out of his or her way to become a favorite of the boss through such means as bringing him or her small gifts, sending him or her holiday cards (both hard copy and electronic), and showering the boss with smiles and warm greetings. The narcissist who is successful in becoming the office pet will often take advantage of the situation by making unreasonable demands on the boss, such as expecting a maximum allowable salary increase or extra vacation time.

Brown also suggests that another way of maintaining appropriate boundaries is for the manager not to ask for favors from subordinates, especially personal favors. An example of a personal favor would be asking a group member to help resolve some problems in setting up a smart phone used mostly for non-work. When asked to do a personal favor, destructive narcissists will assume that they are being singled out as superior to others, are perceived by the boss to be unique and special, and entitled to special treatment and consideration.[13]

5. *Make an appropriate referral for frequent disruptive behavior.* The gravest problem for the manager attempting to deal with a narcissistic subordinate is when the subordinate's behavior is disruptive and annoying to the work group, perhaps creating morale and productivity problems. Disruptive narcissistic behavior might include the following:

- frequently interrupting meetings with joke telling and tangential comments;
- consuming an inordinate share of office supplies or travel budget;
- sending far too many e-mails, instant messages, or social network messages to coworkers, thereby taking up too much of their time;
- accepting and making cell phone calls while engaging in joint problem solving with a coworker or manager;
- checking messages and apps on his or her smart phone while engaging in joint problem solving with a coworker or manager; and
- frequently calling in sick when extra work is required of the group, including working on weekends or holidays

Assuming that the manager has already discussed these problems with the office narcissist and not enough change has resulted, the next step might be referral for help. Most large organizations have an employee assistance program, and most medium-sized organizations have access to an outside assistance program. The pitch to the self-absorbed employee should be that he or she is creating so many disruptions in the work group that counseling about these problems is warranted. The manager then states that he or she is making a referral to the human resources department, who can arrange for the counseling.

If the combination of warnings by the manager and counseling from an employee assistance program does not work, the next step in dealing with the disruptive behavior would be employee discipline. The last step in discipline, of course, is firing. However, being a workplace narcissist is not grounds for dismissal. Only when narcissism leads to substandard performance can it be a legitimate cause for firing.

TASK-FOCUSED COPING TACTICS AND STRATEGIES

Certain tactics and strategies for dealing with a strongly narcissistic subordinate focus more on the task being performed than on the relationship between the manager and the subordinate or the latter's personal characteristics. Effectiveness in dealing with a narcissistic subordinate is likely to increase if the manager uses a combination of relationship-focused and task-focused tactics and strategies.

1. *Provide accurate performance evaluations.* A major problem with most workplace narcissists is that they have inflated perceptions of their own performance. Often they perceive themselves to be the outstanding performer in the group. A manager who gives the narcissist an inflated performance evaluation (or appraisal) just to placate him or her is strengthening the narcissist's tendency to claim superior performance. Telling a narcissist that he or she is only an average, or below average, performer can trigger conflict. The employee is likely to rebel against being labeled anything less than a superior performer. Perhaps part of a manager's job is to manage interpersonal conflict, yet many managers feel uncomfortable dealing with the anger of another person.

    To minimize conflict during a performance evaluation, the manager can follow the recommended procedure of giving the narcissist feedback from time to time between the formal evaluations. Of course, if the manager perceives the narcissistic worker to be a superior performer, the performance evaluation session will be conflict free. The performance feedback delivered between performance evaluation sessions can often be quite brief, with a quick objective statement of any problem. For example, assume that a narcissistic holds the position of *social media director*. The purpose of the job is to bring in more customers and sales, using social media. If positive results are not forthcoming, the narcissist might be told during a planning meeting, "I like what you are posting on Facebook and Twitter, but so far I don't see any increase in sales volume. When do you think we will get some results?" (Observe that the narcissist is given a mild compliment yet also receives some feedback about disappointing results.)

2. *Use positive reinforcement and mild punishments.* The most well-established fact about human behavior is referred to as the *law of effect*: Behavior that is rewarded tends to be repeated, whereas behavior that is

punished tends not to be repeated. The word *tends* is critical because, with respect to human behavior, nothing works 100 percent of the time. Positive reinforcements and mild punishments can help the workplace narcissist develop a more realistic perception of his or her own performance, and at the same time help him or her perform well. When the narcissist performs a task well, he or she should be recognized and complimented. If the efforts of the social media director result in a sudden surge in customer orders, the director might be sent a congratulatory note or in-person compliment. In this way legitimate accomplishment will be recognized. Mild punishment can take the form of negative feedback, as in the example for point 1 above. Other forms of mild punishment include not authorizing a bonus or being moved to a less desirable cubicle until performance improves.

3. *Document problems.* A standard technique for dealing with any performance problem is careful documentation of what the worker is doing wrong. It is well known that firing for poor performance without documentation can lead to a lawsuit against the company. Documentation is required if the narcissistic worker is performing poorly. Such behaviors as being haughty and arrogant do not themselves constitute substandard performance. Yet, if the haughtiness and arrogance leads to problems in customer relations, such behavior does create performance problems. Three other examples of substandard performance linked to narcissism are as follows:

- During a meeting with a key customer, Ted talked so much that the customer had considerable difficulty in explaining what changes in product features he needed to be fully satisfied with our machine.
- Marsha (a supervisor) continues to ask personal favors of her direct reports to the extent that three of them have made formal complaints to the human resources department. Marsha asked one employee to style her hair, another to help her remove a tree stump, and another to drive her to the automobile repair shop.
- Gerry has refused several times to come to work on Saturday mornings to help with a huge workload surge although all of his coworkers did show up to deal with the emergency. The first time Gerry said his back hurt; the second time he said his dog was poisoned and had to be taken to the vet; the third time Gerry said that his wife was ill and needed him home.

For dealing with a narcissist who is performing poorly, Ritala and Falkowski recommend having a signed work plan for improvement, including dates for attaining improvement goals. Furthermore, each offensive, unprofessional behavior should be documented along with a plan for coaching with respect to performance improvement. Written documentation is important, including electronic and printed messages. Hard-copy records are still necessary because electronic records can mysteriously disappear from a server. (Some destructive narcissists might be computer hackers at the same time!) According to the dictates of progressive discipline, if certain agreed-upon improvements are not forthcoming, the substandard performance can be terminated.[14]

THE ROLE OF COACHING

Coaching is a humane and constructive approach to dealing with narcissists who are performing poorly or who are simply difficult employees. Both relationship-oriented and task-oriented approaches to dealing with narcissists include an element of coaching. Managers have varied aptitudes for coaching. One way to acquire coaching skill is to study basic principles and suggestions, and then practice them. Another is to attend a training program for coaching that involves modeling (learning by imitation) and role playing.

Here we examine a number of suggestions for coaching, and link each suggestion specifically to dealing with a narcissistic subordinate who is creating problems. If implemented with skill, the suggestions will improve the chances that coaching will lead to improved performance of individuals and groups.

1. *Communicate clear expectations to the narcissist.* For people to perform well and to continue to learn and grow, they need a clear perception of what is expected of them. The expectations of a position become the standards by which performance will be judged, thus serving as a base point for coaching. An expectation to a narcissist is that the person is supposed to treat others in the group, as well as customers, with respect. Another expectation might be that the narcissist will be a good team player, including such behaviors as taking his or her turn in being inconvenienced, such as collecting data for a warehouse inventory.
2. *Build relationships.* Effective coaches build personal relationships with team members and work to improve their interpersonal skills.[15] Establishing rapport with group members, including any workplace narcissist, facilitates entering into a coaching relationship with them. The suggestions that follow about active listening and giving emotional support are part of relationship building. Showing empathy is another important part of relationship building. Although some narcissists may be short on showing empathy toward others, they much appreciate it when it is directed toward them.
3. *Give feedback on areas that require specific improvement.* As already mentioned, feedback is a major tactic for dealing effectively with workplace

narcissists. To coach a narcissist toward overcoming a performance or behavior problem, the manager pinpoints what specific behavior, attitude, or skills require improvement. An effective coach might say: "At yesterday's meeting I heard you insulting engineers who did not graduate from the top 25 engineering schools in our country. That kind of trash talk hurts teamwork. Also your accusations are unwarranted because some of our top-performing engineers are graduates of schools outside this country."

Another important factor in giving specific feedback is to avoid generalities and exaggerations such as, "You are too insulting," or "You are the most self-centered mechanical engineer I have ever known." To give good feedback, the manager has to observe performance and behavior directly and frequently, such as the example in question of the engineer who insulted the other engineers based on the engineering school they attended.

To make the feedback process less intimidating, it is helpful feedback to ask permission before you start coaching, indicate your purposes, and explain your positive intentions: for example, "Jack, do you have a few minutes for me to share my thoughts with you?" (permission); "I'd like to talk to you about the presentation you just made to the venture capitalists" (purpose); "I liked your creativity, yet I have some ideas you might use in your next presentation" (positive intentions).[16]

Feedback is also likely to be less intimidating when the coach explains which behaviors should decrease and which should increase. This approach is a variation of combining compliments with criticism to avoid insulting the person being coached. For example, you might say, "Tanya, I need you to cooperate more with the other members of the group in sharing data."

4. *Listen actively*. Listening is an essential ingredient in any coaching session. A narcissist will appreciate being listened to even more than most workers. An active listener tries to grasp both facts and feelings. Observing the narcissist's nonverbal communication is another part of active listening. The manager must also be patient and not poised for a rebuttal of any difference of opinion between him or her and the subordinate with a performance or behavior problem. Beginning each coaching session with a question helps set the stage for active listening. The question will also spark the employee's thinking and frame the discussion: for example, "How might you collect more input from other team members when you work on social media postings?"

Part of being a good listener is encouraging the person being coached to talk about his or her performance. Asking open-ended questions facilitates a flow of conversation: for example, ask, "How did you feel about the way you handled conflict with the marketing group yesterday?" A close-ended question covering the same issue would be, "Do you think you could have done a better job of handling conflict with the marketing group yesterday?"

5. *Help remove obstacles.* The problems facing workplace narcissists are usually of their own doing. Yet it is also reasonable to assume that the worker with narcissistic tendencies is facing other problems that trigger narcissistic behavior. Faced with pressure, most people will exhibit weaknesses. To perform at anywhere near top capacity, individuals may need help in removing obstacles, such as a maze of rules and regulations, and rigid budgeting. An important role for the manager of an organizational unit is thus to be a "barrier buster." As a starter in the coaching conversation, it is helpful to ask about any external impediments to getting the job done the narcissist might be facing. (Of course, you have to be aware of the narcissist's tendency to blame others for problems.)

   A manager is often in a better position than a group member to gain approval from a higher-level manager, find money from another budget line, expedite a purchase order, or authorize hiring a temporary worker to provide assistance. Yet, if the coach is too quick to remove obstacles for the group member, the latter may not develop enough self-reliance.

6. *Give emotional support.* By being helpful and constructive, the manager provides much-needed emotional support to the group member who is not performing at his or her best. A coaching session should not be an interrogation. An effective way of giving emotional support is to use positive rather than negative motivators. For example, the manager might say, "I liked some things you did yesterday, and I have a few suggestions that might bring you closer to peak performance."

   Displaying empathy is an effective way to give emotional support. Indicate with words that you understand the challenge the group member faces with a statement such as, "I understand that working with a reduced staff has placed you under heavy time pressures. As a result you might get irritated more readily." The genuine concern you show will help establish the rapport useful in working out the problem together.

7. *Reflect content or meaning.* An effective way of reflecting meaning is to rephrase and summarize concisely what the group member is saying. The narcissist might say, "The reason I've fallen so far behind is that our company has turned into a bureaucratic nightmare. We're being hit right and left with forms to fill out for customer satisfaction. I have fifty email messages that I haven't read yet." You might respond, "You're falling so far behind because you have so many forms and messages that require attention." The group member might then respond with something like, "That's exactly what I mean. I'm glad you understand my problem."

(Notice that the leader is also giving the group member an opportunity to express the feelings behind his or her problem.)

8. *Give some gentle advice and guidance.* Too much advice giving interferes with two-way communication, yet some advice can elevate performance. The manager should assist the group member with negative narcissistic behavior in answering the question "What can I do about this problem?" Advice in the form of a question or suppositional statement is often effective. One example is, "Could the root of your problem be not listening enough to customers?" A direct statement, such as "The root of your problem is obviously insufficient listening," often makes people resentful and defensive. By responding to a question, the person being coached is likely to feel more involved in making improvements.

   Part of giving gentle guidance for improvement is to use the word *could* instead of *should*. To say, "You should do this," implies that the person is currently doing something wrong, which can trigger defensiveness. Saying, "You could do this," leaves the person with a choice: accept or reject your input and weigh the consequences.[17] (You *could* accept this advice to become a better coach!)

9. *Allow for modeling of desired performance and behavior.* An effective coaching technique is to show the group member by example what constitutes the desired behavior. Assume that a narcissistic customer service representative has been making angry rebuttals to customers who criticize a product or service. The manager has received complaints that the service rep often blames a customer's poor technical skills as the real cause of the problems. In coaching her, the manager might demonstrate how to accept criticism gracefully.[18] The manager will probably have the opportunity to model how to accept criticism because the customer service representative is likely to criticize the manager for having criticized her.

10. *Gain a commitment to change.* Unless the manager receives a commitment from the subordinate to carry through with the proposed solution to a problem, the team member may not attain higher performance or soften his or her narcissistic behavior. An experienced manager develops an intuitive sense for when employees are serious about performance or behavior improvement. Two clues that commitment to change is lacking are (1) over-agreeing about the need for change and (2) agreeing to change without display of emotion.

11. *Applaud good results.* Effective coaches on the playing field and in the workplace are cheerleaders. They give encouragement and positive rein-forcement by applauding good results. Some effective coaches shout in joy when an individual or team achieves outstanding results; others clap their hands in applause. A narcissistic worker might be applauded for having

listened to others in a meeting and not monopolized the discussion. He or she will undoubtedly appreciate the applause.

GUIDELINES FOR APPLICATION AND PRACTICE

1. Most of the ideas already presented in this chapter constitute guidelines for application and practice because they focus on constructive ways of dealing with a workplace narcissist. A persistent theme throughout the chapter is that coaching is particularly useful for the purposes of helping a narcissistic worker whose performance and behavior is substandard or unacceptable.
2. At times coaching alone will not bring about the necessary changes to help the narcissistic worker overcome significant performance and behavior problems. In such circumstances, coaching will have to be embedded in *progressive discipline*, a step-by-step application of corrective discipline.

    Progressive discipline alerts the employee that a performance problem exists, such as not properly documenting claims on an expense report. (The narcissistic employee might think that he or she is beyond adhering to standard procedures.) The manager confronts and then coaches the poor performer about the performance problem. If the employee's performance does not improve, the employee is informed in writing that improvements must be made. The written warning contains more specific information than the oral warning. Some of this specific information might be documentation of the problem. The written notice often includes a clear statement of what will happen if performance does not improve. The "or else" could be a disciplinary layoff or suspension. If the notice is ignored and the disciplinary action does not lead to improvement, the employee may be discharged.
3. Progressive discipline, an old concept, continues to be widely used for two key reasons. First, it provides the documentation necessary to avoid legal liability for firing poorly performing employees. Second, many labor-management agreements require progressive discipline because of the inherent fairness of the step-by-step procedure. Employees are not harshly punished for first offenses that fall outside the realm of summary discipline.

SUMMARY

All the characteristics and behaviors of workplace narcissists mentioned in the previous chapters are likely to manifest themselves when a narcissist reports to somebody else. Yet several of these characteristics are more likely to manifest themselves, as follows: (1) hypersensitivity to negative evaluation; (2) grandiosity in the form of inflated sense of self-importance, arrogance, preoccupation with status, and excessive admiration seeking; (3) lack of concern for and devaluation of others; (4) a sense of entitlement often in the form of demanding special privileges or maximizing whatever benefits are available; (5) inability or unwillingness to see their own faults; (6) habitual lateness; and (7) strong performance when working alone and given recognition and praise.

Although the individual's personality is a dominant factor in determining the extent of his or her narcissism, the environment is at least a contributing factor. A comprehensive setting that can intensify tendencies toward narcissism is to work within a narcissistic organization, or one that is self-absorbed and suffers from delusions of success and grandiosity. People working in a narcissistic organization find it comfortable to express whatever narcissistic tendencies they might possess. A narcissistic organization is composed of the collective personalities of its members. The greater the percentage of managers and other workers with narcissistic tendencies, the more likely the organization will be narcissistic.

A narcissistic organization can often be described as one that is proud and elite. The advertising about a firm and reality are not always the same. The checklist presented in Exhibit 9.1 provides a sampling of a wide variety of char-acteristics of a narcissistic organization. Notable characteristics of a narcissistic organization include the following: (1) delusions of success and grandiosity; (2) a focus on protecting an identity that has taken on narcissistic qualities; (3) denial of problems; (4) taking on a sense of entitlement; (5) extreme high self-esteem; (6) questioning any aspect of the organization is discouraged; (7) self-aggrandizing fantasies of success; (8) a selfish organization culture; and (9) healthy pride.

General Motors (GM) is again a widely-admired, successful company. Yet in decades past, particularly during the 1950s through the 1970s, GM exemplified a smug, narcissistic organization that thought its supremacy in the design and manufacture of vehicles was unshakable. According to automotive and busi-ness writer, Alex Taylor III, some of these attitudes contributed to the decline of GM up through 2010.

Several relationship-focused tactics and strategies have been developed to deal with a narcissistic subordinate, as follows: (1) help overcome hypersensi-tivity to evaluation and potential feedback or criticism; (2) explain the problems with an exaggerated sense of entitlement; (3) coach about the limited empathy for the plight of others; (4) decrease the confusion of boundaries between the boss and subordinates; and (5) make an appropriate referral for frequent disrup-tive behavior.

Task-focused tactics and strategies for coping with a workplace narcissist include the following: (1) provide accurate performance evaluations; (2) use positive reinforcements and mild punishments; and (3) document problems created by the narcissism.

Coaching is a humane and constructive approach for dealing with narcissists who are performing poorly or who are simply difficult employees. The coaching suggestions presented here are as follows: (1) communicate clear expectations to the narcissist; (2) build relationships; (3) give feedback on areas that require improvement; (4) listen actively; (5) help remove obstacles; (6) give emotional support; (7) reflect content or meaning; (8) give some gentle advice and guidance; (9) allow for modeling of desired performance and behavior; (10) gain a commitment to change; and (11) applaud good results.

CASE HISTORY OF A NARCISSIST

The following case history is about a self-adoring sales representative along with his manager's frustrations about some of his narcissistic behaviors and episodes.

Basil, the Self-Adoring Sales Rep

Courtney is the director of marketing for the western region of Benefit Advantage Inc., a company that provides outsourcing services for several aspects of the human resource function. Among the services provided by Benefit Advantage are payroll processing, medical claims processing, wage and salary administration, and diversity training. The vast majority of the company's clients are small and medium-sized firms. Benefit Advantage has enjoyed strong growth in recent years. A major contributing factor has been an effort by small and medium-sized companies to reduce costs by outsourcing part or all of their human resource function.

Courtney began her employment for Benefit Advantage as a sales representative, responsible for generating new business as well as expanding the services provided to existing clients. She had been placed on a management track upon entering the company. The management track is a category of workers who, based on their formal qualifications and personal characteristics, appear to have potential for occupying a high-level management position in the future. Aside from several years of industrial sales experience, Courtney had already earned an MBA from San Diego State University before she joined Benefit Advantage.

Courtney manages a few key accounts herself, and also assists her sales staff in closing deals on complex accounts. Most of Courtney's work activities, however, concentrate on coaching and training the sales representatives on her staff. She also recruits and selects new sales representatives as needed. Courtney, as well as company executives, heavily emphasizes the coaching aspects of a manager's job. Part of the company culture is to work with employees who have a performance or behavior problem, rather than quickly firing and replacing them.

Courtney contends that the biggest challenge she faces these days in terms of working with staff members is sales representative Basil. He is attaining results just slightly under quota in terms of developing new business and expanding services with existing accounts. Courtney feels that Basil could easily meet and perhaps exceed quota, if he were less preoccupied with himself. Courtney made these comments about Basil's self-preoccupation:

> "I like Basil, but not nearly as much as he likes himself. Just yesterday, we met for coffee to discuss the progress he was making on a few of his accounts. Basil spent the first five minutes telling me about what a glorious weekend he and a few friends spent on the beach. You should have seen the outfit Basil was wearing to our coffee meeting. He looked as if his job were selling Rolls Royce cars at a Rodeo Drive dealership. Even his cologne was a little on the strong side.
>
> "After trying a couple of times, I was able to get Basil to tell me how he was doing in landing a potential decent-size account he had been working on for at least six months. Basil then described in detail about how he felt being on the prospect's premises, and how he felt about being made to wait outside the CEO's office for fifteen minutes. Basil then went on about how good he would feel if this account would add to his commissions.
>
> "Not once did I hear Basil tell me anything about the CEO being pursued, and the type of potential there was in the account. Basil didn't say anything about what specific needs the client has, and how Benefit Advantage could meet those needs. At that point I was wondering if Basil had forgotten the basis of selling. I mean he said zilch about satisfying customer needs.
>
> "To finish our little meeting, I asked Basil to give me a few details about the product line of the prospective customer. He then said he hadn't paid too much attention but that he thinks the company makes something boring like pumps for factories and mines."

About two months after the coffee-break discussion about sales activities, Courtney held a combined performance evaluation and coaching session with Basil. She began by asking Basil how well he thought he was performing. Basil answered, "I'm doing pretty well considering the dull type of customers I have. Most of them don't understand how to make effective use of a professional problem-solver like me. I think they are a throwback to a 50-year-old version of a salesman. They want me to tell bawdy jokes and take them to lunch at a fancy restaurant."

Courtney responded that other sales representatives at Benefit Advantage were not experiencing the same problem. Next, she informed Basil that he would be receiving a performance rating of average for the entire year because he was just about making quota. Basil said that the major reason his performance was average is that his territory contained so much dead wood. If he had more dynamic clients, he would perform much better.

Courtney then asked Basil what plans he had for improving his sales performance for the upcoming year. Basil said immediately, "I am a totally professional sales consultant. If more of my dull-witted clients could understand my value, I would sell beyond quota. My plans are to educate my clients a little more about making better use of my professional sales skills. I know that they like me personally."

"I like your pride, Basil," said Courtney. "Yet I think I can offer you a little advice. You need to pay more attention to what your clients are thinking. At the same time, you might tone down your self-importance. Reach out more to people. I think that you should work extra hard at becoming a good listener. I know you can do it because you are a bright guy."

"Really, Courtney? Are you in a position to judge me?" said Basil with an irritated tone and a frown. "Are you my boss? Or are you a shrink?"

Narcissism Analysis

Basil shows many indicators of being a workplace narcissist. He blames his mistakes on others in an almost contemptuous manner, in such terms as calling them dull witted and dead wood. Basil does not listen carefully to others and is under-observant for a sales consultant. For example, he was not particularly familiar with the product line of his biggest prospect. Another narcissistic tendency is that Basil does not think he needs any improvement. Coaching Basil will not be easy for Courtney because Basil appears to be resisting her initial attempts at coaching.

REFERENCES

1. Bergman, Jacqueline Z., James W. Esterman and Joseph P. Daly (2010), "Narcissism in Management Education," *Academy of Management Learning & Education*, **9** (1), 119–20.
2. Vogel, Carl (2006), "A Field Guide to Narcissism" *Psychology Today*, January/February, p.74.
3. Cited in Sandberg, Jared (2007), "I'm Not Really Late, I'm Just Indulging in Magical Thinking," *The Wall Street Journal*, November 13, p. B1.
4. Ritala, Jean and Gerald Falkowski (2007), *Narcissism in the Workplace*, US: Red Swan Publishing for IT Service Management Institute, p. 45.
5. Duchon, Dennis and Michael Burns (2008), "Organizational Narcissism," *Organizational Dynamics,* **37** (4), 354–63.
6. Advertisement appearing in *Bloomberg Business Week*, December 20, 2010–January 2, 2011, p. 13 (www.patrongift.com).
7. Many of the ideas in this list are from Duchon and Burns (2008), pp. 354–63; Ritala and Falkowski (2007), pp. 29–31.
8. Eichenwald, Kurt (2005), *Conspiracy of Fools: A True Story*, New York: Broadway Books, as quoted in Duchon and Burns (2008), pp. 357–8.
9. Schmincke, Don (2009), "Climb Higher," *HR Magazine*, **54** (6), p. 122.
10. The information about GM is based mostly on Taylor, Alex III (2008), "GM and Me," *Fortune*, December 8, pp. 92–100.
11. Some of the information in this list is an extension of Bergman *et al.* (2010), pp. 125–8.
12. Brown, Nina (2002), *Working with the Self-Absorbed*, Oakland, CA: New Harbinger, pp. 116–18.
13. Brown (2002), p. 118.
14. Ritala and Falkowski (2007), p. 48.
15. "Coaching – One Solution to a Tight Training Budget," *HRfocus,* August 2002, p. 7.
16. "Request Permission to Coach," *Manager's Edge,* June 2003, p. 5.
17. "Fast Tips for Savvy Managers," *Executive Strategies,* April 1998, p. 1.
18. Bergman *et al.* (2010), p. 128.

10. Social media, mobile phones, email, and narcissism

Computer-mediated approaches to communication create substantial opportunities to express narcissistic tendencies. Literally millions of people share details of their life with anyone who will read their messages, such as the tweet, "I had a nice warm shower this morning." In years past few people would post such a message by writing a note and affixing it to the door of their home. Thousands of people march through airports and malls sharing their personal conversations in a loud voice, enabled by a smart phone and a microphone attached to their ear. In the past, people who behaved in this manner were perceived to be mentally ill.

In this chapter we describe opinion and research about how the social media, mobile phones, email and instant messaging are forces for encouraging narcissism in the workplace. For many people the narcissism encouraged by these devices can result in such dysfunctional consequences as being rejected as a job candidate or job loss.

As a starting point in the discussion of communication technology and the expression of narcissism, you are invited to take the checklist presented in Exhibit 10.1. It will help you think about your standing on the expression of narcissism electronically.

SOCIAL MEDIA AND THE EXPRESSIONS OF NARCISSISM

You have probably heard more times than you want about how social media, particularly Facebook, has changed our lives. How did people live without consulting Facebook every hour to see if a friend has a new post? What did supervisors do before they had to check to see if workers were accessing social media instead of working? Supposedly the phenomenal growth of social networking websites is fueled primarily by the healthy human need to affiliate with others and stay close to friends whenever the urge arises.

Exhibit 10.1   The electronic expression of narcissism checklist

Indicate whether each of the following statements is mostly true or mostly false as it applies to you (or would apply to you if you were in the situation indicated by the statement). Even if your reaction to a particular statement is "duh," remember that all the statements reflect incidents of real behavior.

No.	Statement	Mostly true	Mostly false
1.	I become upset if I send a coworker an instant message (IM) and I do not receive an answer back within three minutes.		
2.	I can't get through a meal with other people or alone without sending an email, texting or talking on the phone.		
3.	I text or email while driving even when I have a passenger.		
4.	I sleep with my phone near me even when I am not sleeping alone.		
5.	While working in a group, I regularly check my email and text messages.		
6.	I post more than a dozen photos of me on social networking sites.		
7.	I frequently post on social networking sites what type of meal I recently ate.		
8.	I let all my "friends" or "followers" on my social networking sites know if I am not feeling well, such as having a headache or stomach virus.		
9.	When I receive a compliment from a coworker, outside friend, or family member I sometimes post it on my Facebook wall.		
10.	I check to see if I have any posts on my social networking sites at least once every 30 minutes, even during work.		
11.	For me, social networking sites are a useful place to post nasty things about people whom I do not like.		
12.	If I were giving a presentation at a business banquet, I would keep my personal digital assistant in my hand.		
13.	I often eat while talking on the phone.		
14.	I see no problem in sending and receiving text messages while attending a funeral.		
15.	When I leave a phone message on a landline, I never indicate my phone number because I assume that everybody has caller I.D.		
16.	I often walk through a shopping mall or other public place talking loudly on my cell phone or smart phone, using a microphone next to my ear.		
17.	While standing at the counter ordering food at a fast-food restaurant, I often talk on my phone.		
18.	When in a setting such as a medical office that has a sign forbidding the use of cell phones, I usually ignore the sign.		

No.	Statement	*Mostly true*	*Mostly false*
19.	If I were irritated by a company policy or something the CEO said, I would post my gripe on a company website, or a public website.		
20.	If I received an above-average performance review, I would post it on a social networking website or my own blog.		
21.	I post photos of myself as a child on my social networking sites or my personal blog.		
22.	Even when I am employed full-time, I keep my job résumé posted on one or more job boards.		
23.	My email address reads like a screen name such as, KillerGuy007@gmail.com, or FabPrincess1@Yahoo.com.		
24.	My smart phone has a beautiful custom casing such as ostrich leather or crystals.		
25.	If I am engaged in conversation with someone I find boring, I see no problem in taking out my iPad (or similar product).		

Scoring and interpretation:
Give yourself one point (+1) for each statement you indicated was *Mostly True* about yourself.

15 or higher: You use digital devices in a strongly narcissistic manner that most likely annoys people with traditional views of etiquette.

6–14: The amount of narcissism you display with the use of your digital devices is about average by contemporary standards. Most communication technology fans would perceive your behavior to be acceptable.

0–5: You have below-average tendencies toward narcissism in your use of digital devices. Most etiquette specialists would regard your digital behavior as acceptable, yet you still might be committing the occasional etiquette blunder.

Source: Items 2, 3, and 4 are based on Bernstein, Elizabeth (2011), "Your Blackberry or Your Wife," *The Wall Street Journal*, January 11, p. D1.

Marketing consultant, writer, and producer Val Brown has a more penetrating analysis of the real driver of the phenomenal growth of these sites: basic human narcissism.[1] Brown reasons that the social media do satisfy a need for communication and interaction, but these sites have also allowed our narcissism to be unleashed. The person who craves attention is having his or her moment in the sun. As one worker wrote to another by email, "You must have seen all those great things my family wrote about me for Father's Day. The great comments are posted on my FB wall." (The narcissist who wrote the email assumes that all his contacts would be reading his "wall" on Facebook regularly.) With posts on social media sites, narcissists can believe that people are reading all their comments, and that the same readers are impressed by their intelligence and humor.

Brown continues that the social media allow us all to be published, to have a presence, to show our accomplishments, and to applaud ourselves. For many people, it is easier to be candid online than in the physical world. The narcissist in the lumber department of a Home Depot in South Dakota can tell the CEO how to run the company by posting a tweet. In this way the lumber specialist doesn't risk being rejected by the CEO – unless Home Depot management does not take kindly to public criticism by store associates.

A legitimate work-related reason for the explosive growth in the use of social media has been the high unemployment rate in recent years. It is much easier to reach out to potential contacts via a computer or mobile device than attempting to visit these people for face-to-face interaction. Yet Brown sees Facebook as continuing to grow because there are new narcissists being born every day, taking their first wobbly steps into self-disclosure before blossoming into full-blown self-obsession.

According to Twenge and Campbell, social networking websites reinforce narcissism in an endless loop. Narcissists have more contacts ("friends") on these sites, and narcissistic behavior and images are rewarded with more comments and posts by other people. As a result social networking users are more likely to be connected to people who are more narcissistic than average.[2]

An important tie-in of social networking to workplace behavior is that the display of narcissism and self-promotion encouraged by social networking websites can result in an unprofessional image that can damage a reputation as an employee or job candidate. Observing that other adults holding professional positions post revealing or simply goofy photos of themselves on Facebook, or making inappropriate comments, a worker might be tempted to imitate such behavior. The brief moment of narcissistic self-expression results in a tainted reputation.

Our approach to social media and the expression of narcissism focuses on academic research about the subject, as well as dealing with the potential problem of businesspersons posting negative comments.

Academic Research about the Link between Social Media and Narcissism

The easy opportunity for people to express their narcissistic tendencies on social media has caught the attention of academic researchers. The research sheds some light on a complex issue of cause and effect. Do narcissists seek out social networking websites to express their narcissism? Or does the presence of these sites triggers people into expressing narcissism? The issue is similar to whether people with a propensity toward gambling seek out casinos, or does the presence of casinos foster gambling?

Here we look at two studies of the links between social media and the expression of narcissism. Although the studies were conducted with college students, they appear relevant for the workplace because college students do not change their personality and preferences substantially upon holding a full-time job. Also, a substantial number of college students work at least 20 hours per week.

Generation Y and Generation Me

Narcissism researcher Jean Twenge collaborated on a national poll with Youth Pulse of 1068 college students. Students were surveyed about their social media usage, generation attitudes, and whether or not websites such as Twitter and Facebook were used for self-promotion. Another issue explored was whether attention-seeking is helpful for success. A major survey question was, "How much do you agree or disagree with this statement: 'People in my generation use social networking sites (e.g. Facebook, Twitter, MySpace) for self-promotion, narcissism, and attention-seeking?'" The responses were as follows:

Response	Percent
Disagree Strongly (1)	3.47
Disagree Somewhat (2)	12.21
Neither Disagree or Agree (3)	27.32
Agree Somewhat (4)	36.62
Agree Strongly (5)	20.38
Total	100.00
Average value	3.58

A straightforward interpretation of these responses to the preceding question is that the students surveyed were midway between neutrality and agreeing somewhat that their generation uses social networking sites for self-promotion, narcissism, and attention seeking. A more revealing finding of the survey was that 39.27 percent of respondents agreed that "being self-promoting, narcissistic, overconfident, and attention seeking is helpful for succeeding in a competitive world." For these people, narcissism and related personality traits are success factors, thereby providing support for the concept of the productive narcissist.

An interpretation of the results of the study by Twenge focuses on the narcissism displayed: "College students have clearly noticed the more self-centered traits of their peers. It is fascinating how honest they are about diagnosing their generation's downsides. And students are right about the influence of social networking sites. Research has shown that narcissistic people thrive on sites like Facebook, where self-centered people have more friends and post more attractive pictures of themselves."[3]

How narcissism is manifested on a social networking website[4]

Narcissism researchers Laura E. Buffardi and W. Keith Campbell dove directly into the issue of how people express their narcissism on Facebook. Social networking websites such as Facebook present individuals with the opportunities to engage in activities such as (a) posting self-relevant information (e.g. self-descriptions and photos), (b) linking to other members, and (c) interacting with other members. The key research questions explored in the study were as follows: Is the presence of narcissism associated with overall activity in a web community? Is narcissism obvious in the content of a web page and, if so, how? Can the extent of narcissism of a page owner be estimated from the content of the web page?

The researchers speculated that narcissism might operate in a social networking website in several ways. First, narcissists function well in shallow relationships. Social networking websites are built on superficial relationships, such as a celebrity having one million *friends* or *followers*. Some of the relationships on a social networking website might be with true friends, but most of the relationships are with people who have never met in person or even talked on the telephone. Second, social networking websites are highly controlled environments. Web page owners control their self-presentation. Individuals can present attractive photos of their self or even use a photo of somebody else. They can also write self-descriptions that are distorted in a positive direction.

The participants in the study were 129 undergraduate Facebook page owners, 100 of whom were female. The raters of the pages were 128 undergraduates, 86 of whom were female. Participants and raters ranged in age from 18 to 26 years. The participants completed the Narcissistic Personality Inventory, and provided demographic information about who they were. Four objective criteria were taken from the Facebook pages: (a) number of friends; (b) number of wall posts; (c) number of groups; and (d) number of lines of text in the About Me section.

Facebook pages were saved for the purposes of the experiment. Five research assistants coded the pages in terms of the extent to which they were self-promoting, such as the content of the About Me section, and the main profile photo.

The analysis of results found good support for the research questions of the study. Higher scores on the NPI were related to a greater number of interactions on Facebook. This meant that people with stronger narcissistic tendencies use the social networking site more extensively. The narcissistic tendencies of page owners were positively related to the measure of self-promoting information posted. Narcissistic tendencies were also positively associated with self-promoting quotes and entertaining quotes found on the pages.

Narcissism scores were related to the main photo attractiveness, the main photo self-promotion rating, and the main photo sexiness rating. Participants with higher NPI scores tended to be perceived as more narcissistic based on their Facebook page. Higher narcissistic impression ratings (by the raters) were positively related to higher quantities of social interaction on Facebook, and also to more information posted about the self. A few of the key implications reached by the authors of this complicated study are summarized next.

First, the expression of narcissism on social networking websites appears to be similar to its expression in other social contexts. This includes the observations that narcissism is related to a higher number of social relationships, self-promotion, and self-presentation. Second, unacquainted raters are able to judge web page owners' narcissism with reasonable accuracy. Third, viewers use web page content to form impressions of the web page owner's level of narcissism. Fourth, the network of individuals on social networking sites will contain a relatively high percentage of narcissistic individuals.

Narcissistic Content in Work-Related Social Media Messages

Narcissistic content is abundant in personal life messages left on social media sites such as Twitter, Facebook, and MySpace. Users of these sites are almost encouraged to post small details about their personal life to their friends and followers. A quick glance at any of these sites reveals personal-life comment such as the following:

"My Cheerios were delicious this morning. I added raspberries."

"Great workout today."

"My upper body strength is better than ever."

"I might have a stomach virus."

"Had sex with a stranger for the first time last night. I hope I didn't pick up an STS. LOL."

"I have decided that green is my best color."

"Look on my wall to see how much my family loves me."

"Oops, I found a few strands of grey hair this morning."

"I just ran a mile in less than 10 minutes for the first time."

"I'm lucky to be me."

Although work-related messages posted on the social media are not typically as blatantly narcissistic as some of the above messages, many workers fall into the trap of appearing self-absorbed in their postings. The workers might post their messages on a company-specific social media website or the messages might be posted on public websites such as Facebook and Twitter. A few examples follow:

"Got up this morning hating to go to work."

"I just received an outstanding performance evaluation. I'm proud."

"I think the company is headed in the wrong direction, I can help put us on track."

"Lucky me. My colleagues love me."

"The word is out that I'm promotion material."

"I'm now the go-to guy in the department."

"My boss isn't happy today, so she's making life tough for me."

"I deserve a bigger raise than I got."

"The company is beginning to appreciate me a little bit more."

"With all my Twitter followers, the company is lucky to have me."

"Oh happy day, my boss is on a business trip."

A few of the above narcissistically toned messages hint at a social media trap for many workers. They post complaints about their boss or employer and, as a result, irritate the boss or employer. A historically important case of this nature took place in 2010. An emergency medical technician in Connecticut was fired after she posted disparaging remarks about her boss on Facebook. The National Labor Relations Board came to the woman's rescue. The Board ruled that American Medical Response of Connecticut, Inc., illegally fired Dawn-Marie Souza from her job as an emergency medical technician after she criticized her supervisor on her personal Facebook page. Souza also traded Facebook messages about the negative comments with other employees.

"It's the same as talking at the water cooler," said Lafe Solomon, the acting general counsel for the NLRB. "The point is that employees have protection under the law to talk to each other about conditions at work." For a long time, federal labor law has protected employees against retaliation for talking to coworkers on their own time about their jobs and working conditions, including critical remarks about the manager.

NLRB officials contended that the ambulance company has an unlawful policy that prohibits employees from making disparaging comments about supervisors and depicting the company "in any way" over the Internet without permission. "This is the first complaint we've issued over comments on Facebook, but I have no doubt that we'll be seeing more," Solomon said. "We have to develop policies as we go in this fast-changing environment."

The trouble for Souza started when she was asked by her supervisor to prepare an investigative report when a customer complained about her work. Souza explained that her union denied her the representation she needed to combat the complaint. Later that day, Souza accessed Facebook from her home computer and wrote: "Looks like I'm getting some time off. Love how the company allows a 17 to be a supervisor."

A "17" is the code the company uses to designate a psychiatric patient. Souza also used two expletives to refer to her supervisor. Several coworkers responded in a supportive way to Souza's critical comments.

An attorney representing the company, John Barr, explained that the true reason Souza was fired was because of two separate complaints about her "rude and discourteous service" within a 10-day period. (Such behavior reflects a degree of narcissism.) Barr stated that Souza would have been fired whether or not the Facebook comments were posted. He said that American Medical Response understands that employees have a right to talk about wages and working conditions. Nevertheless, he said that the company stands by its policy against employees discussing the company on the Internet, including social media websites.

"If you're going to make disgusting, slanderous statements about coworkers, that is something our policy does not allow," Barr said.

Jonathan Kreisberg, director of the NLRB office in Hartford, Connecticut, said that the company's policy is overly broad. He did acknowledge, however, that the law protecting worker speech has limits, such as not allowing disruptive behavior in the workplace or engaging in conduct that threatens other workers. According to Kreisberg, Souza's postings on Facebook did not cross a legal line into disruptive or threatening behavior.

"Here she was on her own time, on her own computer and on her own Facebook page, making these comments," Kreisberg said. He also pointed out that if employees are upset about their supervisor and assemble on their own time to express their concerns, criticize him, and make derogatory comments about him, they are within their rights.[5]

The NLRB complaint could set a precedent for employers to keep in mind as more workers use social networking sites to share details about their job. The NLRB ruled finally that American Medical Response of Connecticut maintained and enforced overly broad rules in its employee handbook with respect to blogging, postings on the Internet, and communications between and among employees. At the same time, workers who enjoy posting self-centered complaints about the boss should recognize that, despite legal protection, an employer is likely to respond negatively to these complaints. Although Souza reached a private settlement with her employer, she most likely hurt rather than enhanced her reputation with the company.

Avoiding the Bitter Twitter and Other Posting Errors

A phenomenon has been observed in which social networks do business owners and managers more harm than good because of strongly negative postings, referred to as a *bitter twitter*. The reference to *twitter* is for the ease of posting quick, thoughtless posts on Twitter.com. A careful observation of these *bitter twitters* suggests a strong element of narcissism in many of the vitriolic comments. Narcissism also enters into strongly negative posts because it requires an element of self-centeredness to think that other people want to read your negative commentary.

A notable mistake businesspeople often make is to post a comment on a social networking website while in a wrong frame of mind. Public relations specialist Cas Purdy, of Guidance Software in Pasadena, has developed a rule of thumb that he widely recommends: "Don't twitter while you're bitter."[6]

Several other posting errors to avoid, along with their positive counterparts, are presented in Exhibit 10.2. Each error has an element of self-centeredness or self-absorption.

THE NARCISSISTIC USE OF MOBILE PHONES

Mobile phones, including cell phones and smart phones, are an indispensable business tool when used properly. Yet, when used inappropriately in a workplace setting, mobile phones can distract or offend work associates, according to Paul Siddle, principal of the Executive Protocol Group in Naples, Florida.[7] The inappropriate use of mobile phones usually has a strong narcissism component because the person using the phone is more concerned about his or her convenience than being courteous toward others. A widely used expression that hints of narcissism is "Excuse me, I must take this call." Unless the call is a true emergency, the person does not have to take the call while interacting with the work associates present.

A key point here is that not every person who uses a mobile phone rudely in the work place has strong narcissistic tendencies. Mobile phone technology triggers into action any underlying narcissistic tendencies. The availability of

Exhibit 10.2   Social networking posting errors made frequently by businesspeople

Error to avoid	Positive counterpart
Writing a political rant because a politician said something with which you strongly disagree. The rant suggests that you dislike the political affiliation of the person who made the comment.	Engage friends and followers in a rational political discussion relevant to your industry, such as discussing how immigration policy might affect employment in the construction industry.
Present a hard sell of your company's products or services, such as explaining how you will beat the price of any competitor.	Post interesting opinions, photos, and links about your industry that will interest friends and followers. For example, a travel agency might post photos of the animals of Antarctica, and explain how these animals gather food in such cold temperatures.
Mix personal announcements, such as a birthday party for a child or grandchild, with marketing messages.	Create two accounts: one for personal friends, and one for business contacts.
Impulsively air grievances and disputes with customers, partners, competitors, and the tax authorities on the website.	Recognize that angry messages may place you in an unfavorable light even if your side of the story is valid. If you do not want to be perceived as an angry person, do not make your conflicts with others public.
Ignore negative comments made by friends and followers because you think the people who made the comments are stupid, and that you are beyond criticism.	React to negative posts by stating you would like an opportunity to discuss the problem privately. If the gripe appears to be valid, indicate how you are going to rectify the problem. For example, "We have found the faulty component, and we have fixed the problem."

Source: The idea for this table, as well as part of the content, is adapted from Chickowski, Ericka (2010), "Beware the Bitter Twitter," *Entrepreneur*, September, p. 48.

the phone makes a display of narcissism almost irresistible. Many instances have been reported of people accepting or receiving phone calls, or sending and receiving text messages during a funeral or while a CEO is giving a speech.

A list follows of negative mobile phone behavior that usually reflects a strong element of narcissism in the sense of being more concerned about one's own needs than respecting the needs of others.[8] In this sense narcissism is equated with intense etiquette breaches.

1. *Accepting a call during a work conversation.* You communicate the fact that your coworker or other work associate is less important than the caller when

you allow a call to interrupt your conversation. Some people interpret making a call as even more insensitive than receiving a call, but both behaviors are dismissive of the importance of the work associate with whom you are interacting. Customers are likely to be irritated even more so than coworkers if you interrupt your conversation to accept or make a phone call. CEOs who use their cell phones while talking to other workers are likely to be perceived as power abusers, and therefore arrogant. In short, by accepting a cell phone call in the presence of others you diminish the status of the person who is physically present, suggesting a narcissistic lack of empathy.

2. *Wearing a cell phone earpiece in the presence of a coworker when not on the phone.* Wearing an earpiece while interacting with a coworker suggests that you do not intend to remain fully engaged in your conversation. Also, when wearing a phone earpiece, the person in your physical presence is never sure if you are listening to another call at the same time. Building rapport with a work associate includes making him or her feel important. The fact that you appear to be ready to connect to the outside world trivializes that person and inflates your own importance.

3. *Making frequent personal calls on your phone in earshot of coworkers.* A major complaint of people who work in cubicles is that someone in an adjoining cubicle spends much of the day making calls loudly on a mobile phone. The same practice would be possible on a landline phone, but many people perceive using their cell phone for personal calls as more justified than using the office phone. Loud, personal calls made throughout the day suggest a lack of consideration for others, as well as a low work ethic and an unwillingness to contribute a fair share of work.

4. *Talking loudly and shouting on the phone.* Whether in one-on-one interactions or in the middle of a group of work associates, talking loudly and shouting on the cell phone or smart phone is widely disliked. Particularly annoying for many people is the compulsion many cell phone shouters have to repeatedly say, "Okay" in a particularly loud voice. Talking so loudly on the cell phone suggests insensitivity to the feelings of others as well as being egocentric.

5. *Eating while making a phone call.* Eating with the mouth open in a restaurant is a major violation of etiquette. Equally annoying and disgusting to many receivers of these messages is the sender eating while talking. Although the practice of eating while talking on the phone is widespread, its vulgarity for many people is not diminished, and will not be tolerated by many customers. On display is the negative narcissistic behavior of insensitivity to others.

6. *Constant handling or looking at the smart phone or cell phone even when not in use.* Many workers have become so dependent on their cell phones and personal digital assistants that they handle them during conversations,

as well as keeping the phone in constant view. Workers have also been observed placing their cell phones on their lips while speaking with others. One manager frequently polishes his chrome covered smart phone while talking to subordinates.

The physical attachments just mentioned all suggest the negative trait of being so dependent on a physical device that it interferes with concentrating on others, thereby displaying narcissism. The constant physical or visual contact with the cell phone also has the negative impact of making the worker appear immature. An explanation offered for the physical attachment so many people have to their cell phones is that the phones have become "electronic pets." A technology reporter observed, "You constantly see people taking their little pets out and stroking the scroll wheel, coddling them, basically petting them."[9]

7. *Driving a work associate while under the influence of a cell phone, including text messaging.* The narcissism displayed here is that the physical welfare of the passenger is not important because of the desire of the driver to indulge in a personal convenience. A study published in a British medical journal reported that talking on the cell phone while driving quadruples the risk of being in an accident. Using a hands-free device does little to reduce the risk of an accident.[10] Many work associates will accept driving while using a cell phone, including sending text messages, as typical and appropriate behaviour, yet others will interpret your behavior as a propensity to engage in senseless risks.

8. *Spending much of the work day on a mobile device for purposes unrelated to the job.* Perhaps the ultimate narcissistic use of mobile devices in the workplace is when a worker believes that he or she has the right to devote most of the workday to the personal use of a mobile phone. To this worker, self-importance is so strong that doing his or her fair share of work is less important. One worker who was confronted by her supervisor about spending so much time talking on her smart phone and observing websites responded, "It's my phone, so I can do what I want with it."

9. *Accepting and sending messages from rest rooms.* A widely reported form of mobile phone rudeness is sending and receiving cell phone calls from public rest rooms. Many receivers of these calls who hear the water running from the faucets or toilets flushing will be appalled and disgusted. The restroom cell phone user therefore is perceived as insensitive and lacking in social graces – both quite negative interpersonal skills that are tinged with self-absorption.

10. *Engaging in mobile phone activity during a job interview.* Whether the problem is insensitivity, poor emotional intelligence, or narcissism, many job applicants are disqualifying themselves by using their cell phone during a job interview. A survey of hiring managers indicated that responding

to a cell or text message ranks as job candidates' most common mistake during a job interview. Seventy-one percent of managers surveyed named such phone behavior as the top blunder, according to a report released by CareerBuilder.com. Another problem related to narcissism is that 66 percent of managers cited arrogance by the interviewee as a common mistake made by job applicants.[11]

Location-Based Mobile Phone Application

Another popular way of informing people of your importance is to let them know via mobile phone where you are at the moment, particularly if you are entering a restaurant or plan to do so. A basic part of the process is that participants log onto the location-based social networking site and check-in via smart phone to let contacts who also use the website know where they are. GPS-enabled mobile technology has enabled users to broadcast their location for a number of years. However, broadcasting your location to others when you plan to enter such places as a restaurant or shopping mall became popular starting in 2009. Foursquare is the leading company in this application of informing others of the location of your physical presence at the moment. Rival networks including Twitter and Yelp also have location-based tools.

Foursquare adds a game-like twist to broadcasting one's location. Users earn badges by "checking in" at bars, restaurants, stores and office buildings by tapping a button on the app as they arrive at the destination. A user is able to earn a "mayor" icon from an establishment if he or she has checked in more than anyone else during the 60 previous days. Coveting the title of "mayor" for having visited a location the most frequently might be interpreted as a narcissistic craving.

The founders of Foursquare point out that the ultimate goal of geocentric sites is not focused on pinpointing your location. Rather, it is to offer guidance on what experiences you should look for or avoid at the location. Foursquare accumulates and distributes consumer input for users at each location, such as "The place is spotless," or "The bread is often stale."[12]

Narcissism enters into the use of the location-based mobile phone application in two primary ways. First, notifying anyone via a mobile phone that you are checking into a restaurant or other physical location inflates your self-importance. With Twitter and Facebook it is also possible to tell people where you are physically while sending them a message. For example, "I am at 44th and Broadway right now, about to cross the street." Second, broadcasting to acquaintances where you are physically at the moment sends the message that what you are doing at the moment should be quite important to others.

Revealing your physical location is a small example of how narcissistic tendencies can have unintended negative consequences. A hacker with criminal intent might be happy to know that you will be spending four hours at a retail store this afternoon, suggesting that your home might be ripe for a burglary.

EMAIL AND THE EXPRESSION OF NARCISSISM

Email, including instant messaging, offers ample opportunity for the expression of narcissism in the workplace. The self-absorbed person can readily find an opportunity to display more concern about the self than the recipient of the electronic message. A sampling of narcissistically-tinged behavior related to email and instant messaging follows:

- Establishing an address that focuses on personal attributes such as Coolpurchasinggal@yahoo.com, or Marketingstud29@gmail.com. (Below we present empirical research about narcissism revealed in email addresses.)
- Establishing an email address that contains a political statement, conveying the impression that you think all your addressees are interested in your opinion. Two examples: Ihaterepublicans@hotmail.com, and Climatewarminguntrue@gmail.com.
- Sending attachments such as lengthy videos that are not essential to the message and may take five minutes to open.
- Sending an email with an attachment, yet nothing written on the screen. The blank email suggests that the sender does not think the receiver merits an explanation.
- Passing along to work associates lengthy files with attachments unrelated to a specific work purpose, such as PowerPoint presentations of subways in Moscow or embarrassing photos of people engaged in sports.
- Commenting about one's health or feeling as if writing a tweet.
- Sending instant messages without a real work purpose just to take a break from concentrating on work. Two examples, "What kind of bonus do you think we will get this year?" and "Traffic could be heavy later today."

Company policy would usually prohibit the first two email expressions of narcissism because the company dictates the address, such as: AnneCalabrese@ CompanyName.com. Linking back to the first point made above, three researchers from the Department of Psychology at the University of Leipzig investigated the extent to which personality can be inferred from email addresses. Mitja D. Back, Stefan C. Schmukle, and Boris Egloff used the email addresses of 599 young adults to investigate how well a variety of personal traits, including narcissism, revealed the personality traits of the owners of these addresses.[13] Our concern here is with narcissism, but the other traits investigated were the standard Big Five traits (or factors) of neuroticism (low emotional stability), openness to experience, agreeableness, conscientiousness, and extraversion.

The study examined whether first impressions based solely on knowledge of an email address show some degree of consensus and accuracy. To accomplish this purpose, the researchers analyzed email addresses as a medium for personality expressions and impressions. Three independent sources of data were collected: (1) Personality scores of the holders of the email addresses. These scores were regarded as the accuracy criteria because they reflect an objective measure of personality. (2) Visible features of email addresses, or cues. These cues included such features as whether or not Yahoo was part of the address, and whether the address holder includes an own name or a fantasy name. (3) Lay personality judgments based on email addresses (observer ratings). To measure narcissism, raters responded to the question, "Regards himself or herself as something special."

Analysis of the data showed that consensus, or agreement among raters, was significant for all the personality dimensions, yet strongest for the ratings of extraversion, followed by conscientiousness and narcissism. Accuracy scores about personality traits were positive and significant for all the traits except extraversion. Narcissism was judged with average accuracy. The analysis of cues contained many results. Of concern here is that self-enhancing aspects and the salaciousness of email addresses influenced impressions of narcissism. Narcissistic persons had more self-enhancing email addresses.

According to the three researchers, the study demonstrated that personality judgments based solely on email addresses were widely shared by observers. Consensual personality stereotypes, including those about narcissism, therefore exist about email addresses. It was demonstrated that these consensual e-perceptions are reasonably accurate. The key conclusion for our purposes is that email addresses can influence the impression we make on other people, including the extent to which we appear to be narcissistic. It is certainly not surprising that a worker would be perceived as narcissistic whose email address was "Ninjatechsupport123@mail.com."

GUIDELINES FOR APPLICATION AND PRACTICE

1. Social networking sites provide an easy opportunity to display narcissism, often of an immature nature. Narcissistic displays, such as presenting oneself semi-nude on a Facebook photo, might be acceptable for many aspects of personal life. However, such exhibitionism can jeopardize some professional opportunities, including receiving a job offer or a promotion. Narcissistic rants, such as a long complaint about being mistreated by a past or present employer, can also damage a person's professional reputation.

2. Social networking sites can also serve as a legitimate vehicle for displaying a healthy degree of narcissism, such as light bragging about one's accomplishments or family. However, to avoid appearing overly narcissistic it is helpful to make favorable comments about coworkers, and perhaps present useful information that is not widely known.

3. Mobile phones are a natural opportunity for expressing narcissism in the form of rudeness and lack of consideration for others. Practicing appropriate mobile phone etiquette, such as not using the phone while conversing with a work associate, is highly recommended to soften a narcissistic impact. Yet the corporate culture helps decide what constitutes rude behavior. For example, multitasking might be acceptable in a given company, legitimizing the use of mobile phones for conversations or texting during a meeting.

4. For professional purposes, with few exceptions, a personal email address should contain a person's name or a close derivative of the name rather than a name that points to one's personal qualities, such as "Dynamiteguy." An exception is that, for some types of small business owners, an email address pointing to the nature of the person's work can be helpful. For example, the owner of a sausage shop might have an electronic address containing the component, "Sausagegal."

5. Be cautious about dismissing narcissism as a factor with only light consequences with respect to computer utilization. An online survey was conducted with 308 people, including a personality test of narcissism, and self-reports of counterproductive computer use. One of the findings was that people with narcissistic tendencies were more likely to use computers counterproductively.[14] Counterproductive uses include hacking or purposely overloading servers to the point that a website might shut down. The results of this study suggest that it could prove helpful to caution workers observed to be highly narcissistic against misusing computers.

SUMMARY

Social media satisfy a need for communication and interaction, but these social networking sites have allowed for narcissism to be unleashed. Social media allow us all to be published, to have a presence, to show our accomplishments, and to applaud ourselves. Social networking sites reinforce narcissism in an endless loop. Narcissists have more contacts on these sites, and narcissistic behavior and images are rewarded with more comments and posts by others. The display of narcissism and self-promotion encouraged by social networking websites can result in an unprofessional image that can damage the reputation of an employee or job candidate.

In one study about social media and the expression of narcissism, college students were surveyed about the social media usage, generation attitudes, and whether or not social media websites were used for self-promotion. The students surveyed were midway between neutrality and agreeing somewhat that their generation uses social networking sites for self-promotion, narcissism, and attention seeking. About 39 percent of respondents agreed that "being self-promoting, narcissistic, overconfident, and attention seeking is helpful for succeeding in a competitive world."

Another study explored how narcissism is expressed on Facebook by a sample of college students. Higher scores on the Narcissistic Personality Inventory were related to a greater number of Facebook interactions. The narcissistic tendencies of page owners were positively related to the measure of self-promoting information posted. Narcissistic tendencies were also positively associated with self-promoting quotes and entertaining quotes found on the pages. Participants with higher NPI scores tended to be perceived as more narcissistic based on their Facebook page. Two of the implications drawn from the study were (1) the expression of narcissism on social networking websites appears to be similar to its expression in other social contexts, and (2) the network of individuals on social networking sites will contain a relatively high percentage of narcissistic individuals.

Many workers fall into the trap of appearing self-absorbed on their work-related social media messages. The workers might post their messages on a company website or on a public website. A social media trap for some workers is to post complaints about their boss or employer, leading to possible discipline. However, a National Labor Relations Board ruling suggests workers have the freedom to post disparaging comments about their employers on websites. A phenomenon has been observed in which social networks do business owners and managers more harm than good because of strongly negative postings, referred to as *bitter twitters*.

The inappropriate use of mobile phones usually has a strong narcissism component because the person using the phone is more concerned about his or her convenience than being courteous toward others. A widely used expression that hints of narcissism is "Excuse me, I must take this call." Mobile phone technology triggers into action any underlying narcissistic tendencies, even among people who are not usually narcissistic.

Negative mobile phone behavior that usually reflects a strong element of narcissism includes the following: (1) accepting a call during a work conversation; (2) wearing a cell phone earpiece in the presence of a coworker when not on the phone; (3) making frequent personal calls on your phone in earshot of coworkers; (4) talking loudly and shouting on the phone; (5) eating while making a phone call; (6) constant handling or looking at the smart phone or cell phone even when not in use; (7) driving a work associate while under the influence of a cell phone or text messaging; (8) spending much of the work day on a mobile device for purposes unrelated to the job; (9) accepting and sending messages from rest rooms; and (10) engaging in mobile phone activity during a job interview.

Another popular way of informing people of your importance is to let them know via mobile phone where you are at the moment, particularly in relation to a restaurant visit. Narcissism enters into the use of the location-based phone application in two primary ways. First, notifying anyone via a mobile phone that you are checking into a particular location inflates one's self-importance. Second, broadcasting to acquaintances where you are physically at the moment implies that what you are doing at the moment should be quite important to others.

Email, including instant messaging, offers ample opportunity for the expression of narcissism in the workplace. Two examples would be (a) sending an email with an attachment but nothing written in the message, and (b) sending instant messages without a real work purpose just to take a break from concentrating on work.

A study demonstrated that personality judgments based solely on email addresses were widely shared by observers. Consensual personality stereotypes, including those related to narcissism, therefore exist around email addresses. A conclusion from the study was that email addresses can influence the impression we make on people, including the extent of narcissism.

CASE HISTORY OF A WORKPLACE NARCISSIST

The following case history presents a diary-like listing of many of the blogs, Twitter posts, and Facebook posts of a moderately successful motivational speaker.

Darryl Hunter, Motivational Speaker

Darryl Hunter, age 43, earns a living as a motivational speaker primarily to business groups, including trade organizations. The majority of the audiences he addresses are sales organizations in a variety of businesses. Darryl has a bachelor's degree in business communications, and began his career as a sales representative for advertising space in magazines. Five years later he joined an advertising agency as an account representative.

A few years later he became a sales trainer in the training and development division of a consulting firm. Part of Darryl's work involved giving motivational talks to sales representatives. After five years of good job performance, Darryl decided to go into business for himself as a motivational speaker. The network of contacts he developed during his years in the consulting business enabled Darryl to have enough speaking assignments to get started as a self-employed motivational speaker.

Darryl is a proud individual who was well liked by many of his work associates, yet regarded as conceited by others. Even before Darryl entered self-employment, he took quickly to the social media as a way of expressing his ideas to the public. After becoming a motivational speaker, Darryl used the social networking sites as a way of staying in touch with clients and potential clients. A listing of some of these postings follows:

- I turned 43 today. Holy cats, I'm half way to being 86.
- One of the reasons I have reached so many of my goals so far is that I have laser-like focus on what I need to accomplish each day.
- I had French toast and strawberries for breakfast and it make me feel happy.
- I'm a traditional thinker. I believe that if I start each day "with a smile on my face and a shine on my shoes," I will be successful that day.
- I was voted the most likely to succeed in my high-school yearbook. That was a turning point in my life.
- Last night I boosted the self-confidence of ten people in the audience. I couldn't be happier for having touched the lives of these people.
- After my talk, a woman came up to shake my hand. She said she just wanted to touch a great person like me.
- Have ten talks scheduled ahead. Must be doing something right.
- My website is getting a humongous number of visits this week. Thanks guys!
- I wore a $1500 suit to my presentation in Philly. The compliments were overflowing.
- It sure is inspirational to be inspiring others.
- I feel really motivated today. LOL.

- It's snowing a lot. I hope my flight to Dallas isn't cancelled. The audience would be very disappointed.
- My talk last night was an absolute sellout. How gratifying.

As Darryl continued his many posts on his blog, Facebook, Twitter, and LinkedIn, he soon received a few comments in reaction to his posts. A few of the comments he received in response to his posts, along with his counter-posts to these comments, are presented next.

- *Reaction comment:* Darryl, you are good. I heard you last night, and I am super-motivated today.
  Counter-reaction: Thanks. I'm glad to know I'm doing my job.
- *Reaction comment:* Darryl is better than Tony Robbins [one of the world's best-known motivational speakers].
  Counter-reaction: Much appreciated. I admire your taste!!!
- *Reaction comment:* Can't Darryl Hunter find any new material? All he says is set goals and keep trying. I heard that in the second grade.
  Counter-reaction: I don't accept absurd criticism. You aren't listening carefully.
- *Reaction comment:* Darryl is a cookie cutter motivational speaker. His hair is slicked back. His smile is frozen. He keeps pacing back and forth on the stage.
  Counter-reaction: It's your problem, not mine. Try to focus on my unique contribution. You will learn something.

Narcissism Analysis

Darryl Hunter is displaying some of his narcissistic tendencies on the social media websites. Some of these tendencies are negative, whereas others are positive. On the negative side Darryl is falling into the trap of making personal comments that contribute very little information of value to others. The comments about his age and what he ate for breakfast are trivial and detract from his professional image. Several of his comments are self-congratulatory to the point of being annoying. Two such comments dealt with the sellout and the audience that would be disappointed. The fact that Darryl counter-reacts to negative posts with negativity of his own is symptomatic of a narcissist's hypersensitivity to criticism.

> Several of Darryl's posts suggest that he combines self-admiration with concern for the welfare of others. Two examples are, "I couldn't be happier for having touched the lives of these people," and "It sure is inspirational to be inspiring others."

REFERENCES

1. Brown, Val (2010), "Narcissism, Key Ingredient in Success of Social Media," www.huffingtonpost.com, November 4.
2. Twenge, Jean M. and W. Keith Campbell (2009), *The Narcissism Epidemic: Living in an Age of Entitlement*, New York: The Free Press, p. 111.
3. Quote and survey results are from Van Grove, Jennifer (2009), "Study: Social Media is For Narcissists," http://mashable.com, July 25.
4. Buffardi, Laura E. and W. Keith Campbell (2008), "Narcissism and Social Networking Web Sites," *Personality and Social Psychology Bulletin*, **34**, July, pp. 1303–13.
5. Hananel, Sam (2010), "Facebook Posting Leads to Firing, Legal Dispute," The Associated Press, November 10; Trottman, Melanie, (2011), "Facebook Firing Case Is Settled," *The Wall Street Journal*, February 8, p. B3.
6. Cited in Chickowski, Ericka (2010), "Beware the Bitter Twitter," *Entrepreneur*, September, p. 48.
7. Lee, Louise (2009), "Cell? Well… Use Your Phone for Good, Not Evil," *Business Week Small Biz*, February/March, p. 22.
8. Many of the ideas in this list are based on the following sources: Lee (2009), p. 22; Hatcher, Cathrine (2007), "11 Rules For Good Cell Phone Etiquette," http://cbs1tv.com, December 30.
9. Quoted in Rosen, Christine (2004), "Our Cell Phones, Ourselves," *The New Atlantis*, Summer 2004, p. 31
10. Novotney, Amy (2009), "Dangerous Distractions," *Monitor on Psychology*, **40** (2), 32–6.
11. Jones, Sandra M. (2011), "Being Interviewed for a Job? Don't Answer Your Cellphone," *Los Angeles Times* (www.latimes.com), January 16.
12. Brady, Diane (2010), "Social Media's New Mantra: Location, Location, Location," *Bloomberg Business Week*, May 10–16, pp. 34–6; Fletcher, Dan (2011), "Mayoral Runs," *Time*, September 8, pp. 49–50; "Be There or Be Square: The Rise of Location-Based Social Networking," *Knowledge@Wharton* (http://knowledge.wharton.penn.edu), April 14, 2010.
13. Back, Mita D., Stefan C. Schmukle, and Boris Egloff (2008), "How Extraverted is Honey. Bunny77@Hotmail.de? Inferring Personality from Email Addresses," *Journal of Research in Personality*, **42** (4), 1116–22; Levisohn, Ben (2008), "Your Email Address is Blabbing On You," *Business Week*, September 8, p. 014.
14. Gallagher, Erin Colleen (2009), "Narcissism and Forgiveness as Moderators of Organizational Justice and Workplace Counterproductive Computer Use," *ProQuest Dissertation & Theses* (http://gradworks.umicom), August.

Name index

Subject index